The
Permanent
Majority

The Permanent Majority

THE CONSERVATIVE COALITION IN THE UNITED STATES CONGRESS

Mack C. Shelley II

The University of Alabama Press

Library of Congress Cataloging in Publication Data

Shelley, Mack C., 1950–
    The permanent majority.

    Bibliography: p.
    Includes index.
    1. United States. Congress—Voting—History.
2. United States—Politics and government—1933–1945.
3. United States—Politics and government—1945–
4. Conservatism—United States—History. I. Title.
JK1051.S56 1983   328.73′0775   82-16055
ISBN 0-8173-0137-2

To my wife, Kathy,
and our daughter, Anne

Back of the 'Conservative Coalition' is Broken

(Headline in 1965 *Congressional Quarterly Almanac*, p. 1083)

'Conservative Coalition' Shows New Life

(Headline in 1966 *Congressional Quarterly Almanac*, p. 1010)

House 'Conservative Coalition' Dominates Session

(Headline in 1967 *Congressional Quarterly Almanac*, p. 107)

Conservative Coalition Shaped Major 1968 Bills

(Headline in 1968 *Congressional Quarterly Almanac*, p. 819)

Conservative Coalition Remains Potent in Congress

(Headline in 1969 *Congressional Quarterly Almanac*, p. 1052)

Conservative Coalition Loses Strength

(Headline in 1978 *Congressional Quarterly Almanac*, p. 34-C)

Conservative Alliance Voting Jumps in '79

(Headline in 1979 *Congressional Quarterly Almanac*, p. 34-C)

Conservative Alliance Votes Less Often, More Effectively

(Headline in 1980 *Congressional Quarterly Almanac*, p. 34-C)

Conservatives Hit New High in Showdown Vote Victories

(Headline in *Congressional Quarterly Weekly Report*, January 9, 1982, p. 50)

Contents

Tables and Figures

Preface

In the aftermath of the 1980 national elections, discussions within the media and among academic political scientists and historians concentrated on the immediate or future prospects of a new era in American politics. ''The New Deal is dead. The country is now and for the foreseeable future probably will be governed by a conservative majority on economic and social issues.'' This only slightly over-simplified statement summarizes the tenor of the prognosticators' conclusions about the polity of late twentieth-century America. This book was stimulated partly by the events of 1980 and was written as the first aftershocks of that election rumbled through the halls of Congress and throughout the nation at large. But there is a broader scope and a longer history to the Reagan counter-revolution that can be properly understood only by a detailed study of the half-century since the first stirrings of a traditionalist reaction against the specters of social equality, government activism, and economic leveling that were at least suggested to those of contrary persuasions by the New Deal and its progeny: the Fair Deal, the New Frontier, and the Great Society.

This book presents the story of congressional conservatism since the early 1930s from an empirical perspective, balancing verbal narrative with what I think is a judicious use of applied statistical methods. The intended audience includes students of political science and history, particularly those interested in political parties, ideology, Congress, and the presidency, as well as those in the journalistic profession, and, of course, those who practice the art of politics or hope to do so in the future. I believe this book will have appeal, too, to practitioners of the art of applied statistics, especially those who have some grounding in time-series techniques. Indeed, the proper blending of statistical methods and political realities is the chief motivation for the existence of this volume, which to my knowledge is one of the first large-scale efforts in the political science literature to apply selected methods of time-series analysis to appropriate historical data. No sophisticated knowledge of statistical methodology is requisite to follow the basic story that is told here, but glimpses of other, more detailed and perhaps more revealing perspectives on these realities should be available to anyone with minimal background in the relevant statistical applications.

For those of us fortunate enough to gain our perspectives from standing on the shoulders of giants, acknowledging the contributions of others is the least that can be done to repay debts of intellectual or data-gathering and analytical assis-tance. I would like to thank two intellectual mentors in particular—Barbara Hinckley at the University of Wisconsin, who made the study of congressional coalitions an exciting field of research, and Richard Li, who introduced me to the mechanics of time-series methods and their applicability to the social sciences. I am grateful as well to Jack Dennis, Leon Epstein, and Virginia Sapiro of the Department of Political Science and Dean Wichern of the School of Business of the University of Wisconsin for their support and constructive critical comments on an earlier version of this research.

Because portions of this work were undertaken at three different academic institutions, special thanks for help in data gathering and analysis go to a number of people: Al Schubert, John Wong, and Alice Robbin of the Data and Program Library Service/Data and Computation Center of the University of Wisconsin, Fred Davis and Jeff Wilson of the Computation Center at Mississippi State University, and Clair Maple and Jim Hoekstra of the Computation Center at Iowa State University. Thanks, too, to the staff of the Inter-University Consortium for Political and Social Research for making available their invaluable data tapes and codebooks for congressional roll calls and to Congressional Quarterly for its data and analysis of voting in Congress. I also wish to thank the Graduate School of the University of Wisconsin for making available a dissertation research grant which long ago made the beginnings of this research possible. The staffs of the libraries of the University of Wisconsin, Mississippi State University, and Iowa State University also deserve thanks for their assistance, as do the staffs of the Library of Congress and of the Fairfax County (Virginia) and Dane County (Wisconsin) public library systems.

I am also deeply in debt to Malcolm MacDonald, Director of The University of Alabama Press, who stood by this project and encouraged its completion, to Trudie Calvert for her expert copyediting work, and to the staff of The University of Alabama Press, as well as to several anonymous reviewers of earlier drafts of the manuscript whom I sincerely thank for saving me from any number of egregious errors of commission and omission.

Last, and most important, special thanks are due to my supportive and forbearing wife, Kathy, and to the newest addition to the family, Anne, who has been wondering if daddy was ever going to be finished typing on that big pile of papers. The author customarily claims credit for any remaining errors, and this I do cheerfully, just as I accept responsibility for failing to thank anyone for whom credit is due.

The
Permanent
Majority

1

Why the Conservative Coalition?
Recent Events and Larger Perspectives

By the early 1980s, it had become a commonplace of studies of American government to talk about a "conservative coalition" of southern Democrats and Republicans as a major force in shaping national public policy. The advent of the Reagan administration in January 1981 was almost immediately marked by a resurgence of interest in the policy impact of joint Republican control of the White House and of the United States Senate, together with the very open cooperation between the new administration and conservative, mostly southern, Democrats in a House that was still under at least nominal Democratic control. Interest in the phenomenon of conservatism on the march was heightened by the election of several "New Right" Republican senators replacing established Senate liberals and creating a Republican Senate majority for the first time in three decades.

This introductory chapter begins with a "current events" discussion of the consequences of the 1980 elections, focusing on the potential for conservative rule in Washington. The bulk of the chapter then briefly summarizes what has been known or surmised about the conservative coalition and endeavors to put the southern Democrat–Republican alliance of convenience in conceptual and historical perspective.

The 1980 Elections: A New Beginning?

The 1980 national elections marked a potentially important milestone in the history of American politics.[1] Ronald Reagan, a professed conservative California Republican, was propelled into the White House as the nation's fortieth president, at least partly on the strength of a perceived rightward tilt of public opinion. Reagan won an absolute majority (51 percent) of the national popular vote, as against 41 percent for incumbent Democratic President Jimmy Carter, and accumulated an overwhelming electoral vote majority of 489 from forty-four states, compared to 49 electoral votes from six states and the District of Columbia for Carter.[2]

The presidential result in 1980 represented a possibly momentous historical development that threatened to undo the programs of the New Deal and the Great Society. However, the Reagan Republican triumph at the top was not by itself unusual in light of recent presidential election outcomes. Republicans had been elected to the presidency more often—by a margin of five to four—than their Democratic opponents since the first post–World War II presidential election of 1948. From 1948 to 1980, control of the White House was divided exactly evenly (sixteen years apiece) between the two parties. Two Republican presidents (Dwight Eisenhower and Richard Nixon) were elected to two consecutive full terms since World War II, a feat not accomplished by any Democrat since Franklin Roosevelt, who was elected four times from 1932 to 1944.

Jimmy Carter was denied reelection by a greater popular vote margin in 1980 than all but two other presidents since the Civil War—William Howard Taft in 1912 and Herbert Hoover in 1932—and became the first unsuccessful Democratic incumbent since Grover Cleveland in 1888.[3] Reagan's success cut deeply into traditional Democratic bases of support, notably among Jews, rural whites, and blue-collar workers. He swept every geographical region of the country, limiting Carter to just one state each in the South (Georgia), the Midwest (Minnesota), and the West (Hawaii). Only in the urban, industrialized East was the contest close.

Republican presidential victories, even overwhelming ones, are not so rare as to make the election of Ronald Reagan a political event of epochal proportions. The outcome of the congressional elections of 1980, on the other hand, was more interesting and potentially far more consequential in terms of who controls the policy-making machinery of the federal government. The House and Senate elections represented a sharp departure from long-established patterns of legislative party control and are likely to be far more consequential both in the short and in the long run for the policy decisions made by the national government.

Two important and interrelated consequences emerged from the congressional elections of 1980. The first and more obvious partisan consequence was a Republican resurgence to the extent of net gains of thirty-three seats in the House of Representatives and twelve seats in the Senate. The Senate results enabled Republicans to gain majority control of that chamber for the first time since the Eighty-third Congress of 1953–54. The second consequence in Congress of the 1980 elections, this time with a less obvious or at least a less precisely calculable scope, is a philosophical and programmatic shift favoring conservative policy positions. This latter effect is for our purposes the more important one, especially insofar as it points to the cross-party nature of ideological cleavages in Congress. The lurch to the right in the Senate is clear from the outcomes of several individual races.

In the 1980 elections, a number of established incumbent Democratic liberal senators went down to defeat, including Frank Church of Idaho, Birch Bayh of Indiana, John Culver of Iowa, George McGovern of South Dakota, and Gaylord Nelson of Wisconsin. Their replacements—respectively, Steven Symms, Dan Quayle, Charles Grassley, James Abdnor, and Robert Kasten—all had established conservative credentials earlier in their political careers.[4] Other incoming conservative Republicans were John East of North Carolina (replacing Democrat Robert Morgan), Alfonse D'Amato of New York (replacing liberal Republican Jacob Javits), and Don Nickles of Oklahoma (replacing the somewhat less conservative Republican Henry Bellmon). Together with the generally moderate-to-conservative group of fifteen southern Democrats who are their at least occasional allies, the fifty-three Republicans could count in many policy decisions on a potential two-thirds majority over the embattled group of generally moderate-to-liberal northern Democrats in the Ninety-seventh Senate.

Although the Republicans did not achieve control of the House of Representatives in 1980, the party did gain thirty-three seats, for a total of 192. This was the Republican party's highest seat total in the House since 1956 and represented the party's greatest electoral resurgence in the House since the 1966 recovery from the Goldwater election debacle of two years earlier. The Ninety-seventh House also contained about eighty southern Democrats, many of whom frequently joined with Republicans on ideologically motivated public policy matters. The House therefore seemed to be controlled by a large potential conservative working majority of about three-fifths of its total membership.

Closely linked to the outcome of the national elections of 1980 was the activity of several political action groups espousing conservative political and social causes, notably the National Conservative Political Action Committee (NCPAC), headed by Terry Dolan. Their effect was felt most dramatically in the Senate defeats of prominent liberals who were made to look out of step with their traditionally more conservative constituencies. Negative ''smear'' campaigns and more traditional advertising efforts against established liberals and in behalf of challenging conservative candidates were successful in several states, and more such efforts were promised for later elections, both by liberal and by established conservative groups.

Within the federal government, a dramatic attempt to restructure public policy priorities was undertaken by the new administration. With the conspicuous support of conservative Democrats in Congress, the Reagan administration embarked on a campaign to destroy or scale down the social programs of a half-century of Democratic rule and to promote in their stead conservative countermeasures of greater support for the military, more power to state and local governments, and restrictive policies regarding abortion, equal opportunity/ affirmative action, busing, the environment, and myriad other issues.

If the cooperation between Democratic conservatives in Congress and the new Republican administration was highly visible, it was not unknown and not new in modern American politics. The major theme of this book is that cross-party cooperation among conservatives, especially as evidenced in agreement between Republicans and southern Democrats in Congress on roll call votes involving important public policy issues, has become a vitally important factor in the functioning of American government. It is probably not much of an overstatement to argue that for the foreseeable future this bipartisan conservative coalition represents the single dominant force on the national political scene.

Through a Glass Darkly: Perspectives on the Conservative Coalition

Students of the legislative process have often reflected upon the lack of cohesive or "responsible" party voting in the United States Congress. It is frequently argued that the structure of congressional policy decisions has been slanted in a "conservative" direction owing to the inability of "progressive" legislators and of "liberal" presidents to overcome the institutional barriers within American politics that frustrate the enactment of forward-looking legislation. This set of institutional barriers is usually said to include such factors within Congress as the overrepresentation of rural and small town areas, the seniority system, and the disproportionate power on congressional committees of unenlightened southern Democratic chairmen and members. Recently, the attention of analysts of political behavior within Congress has turned to a study of the patterns of behavior characterizing long-term, enduring policy alliances of like-minded political actors. One important example of such a policy-motivated congressional alliance is the roll call voting agreement between Republicans and southern Democrats, commonly referred to as the conservative coalition. Bipartisan coalitions are the essence of decision making in Congress because both parties are internally divided and normally must look for defectors from the opposition to get major programs adopted.

This book presents an empirically based political and historical analysis of the emergence, the evolution, and the likely future impact of this so-called conservative coalition in the United States Congress. The voting alliance of Republicans and southern Democrats has been a recognized force in national policy making at least since the New Deal era of the 1930s. A central argument of this book is that the GOP–Dixie Democrat confluence of policy interests has become one of the most important factors determining policy decisions made by Congress.

Statistical techniques, notably time-series analysis and correlational analysis, are used here to investigate some important issues regarding the behavior of Congress generally and the activity of the conservative coalition in particular which were raised in earlier studies and usually addressed there by more impressionistic methods.[5] These statistical techniques are used to study the "hard" information contained in the recorded votes of Congress. This roll call data base permits a precise analysis of the historical patterns of the appearance, success, stability, cohesiveness, and policy impact of this cross-party voting alliance. Other forms of information besides that contained in roll call records are used to flesh out the story of the conservative coalition. Demographic constituency records, committee membership rosters, and historical accounts also provide a foundation for the analysis that follows.

A recurring concern of Congress watchers has been the state of disarray commonly said to characterize the decision-making structures in Congress, which are assumed to be based primarily on partisanship or on shared ideas about the proper direction in which public policy should move. Many authors have offered explanations for the frequently bemoaned lack of cohesion within American legislative parties.[6] These explanations have included the divisiveness caused by regionalism, the diffusion and weakness of legislative party leadership, socioeconomic or demographic differences in the composition of individual Senate and House constituencies, the decentralized nature of the process by which members of Congress are elected, the shifting and temporary nature of legislative policy coalitions, the overriding drive for individual legislators to achieve reelection, the generally nonideological nature of the American party system, and the profusion of issue-specific and short-term legislative alliances.

What is commonly missing in these assessments of why legislative parties are not strong is an examination of persisting congressional coalitions that cut across party lines. This vitally important component must be included in any complete analysis of the processes and structures of policy formation within Congress. The existence of what has been since the early 1930s a more or less permanent bipartisan conservative coalition should be seen as a key force behind decisions made in Congress, in the absence of "responsible" legislative parties capable of articulating and implementing a coherent program of specific policy objectives.[7] A focus on the concept of the bipartisan congressional policy coalition provides a useful analytical perspective for explaining and understanding the outcomes of legislative activity. We may thereby go beyond "naive" explanations that presume that legislative parties represent the only significant enduring coalition of members sharing key policy interests within the United States Congress. The concept of a cross-party policy coalition also provides a more flexible framework for comprehending why public policy assumes specific forms, as well as for predicting the outcomes of policy-making activity in Congress.

As a working definition, this legislative "policy coalition" may be thought of as the joining together, either formally under a party label or informally at the time of the emergence of key motivating issues, of legislators who frequently reflect their policy agreement by acting in concert on a wide range of specific decisions. The most obvious and most easily observed form that this agreement takes is on officially recorded roll call votes or teller votes, although unrecorded floor votes and concerted activity on committees and behind the legislative scenes also count toward the definition of a policy coalition. As distinct from a voting bloc, such as the "farm bloc," a policy coalition should be durable both across a wide range of issues and over time. In this study, the conservative coalition is treated as an important manifestation of such an enduring cross-party policy coalition.

In the perspective of this book, congressional behavior is deemed to be in some large measure the product of conscious policy decisions brought about through processes operating within legislative groups. A legislative coalition, and especially a coalition that is normally very successful, may be treated as a subgroup of a larger body that regularly makes decisions for the larger aggregate of members.[8] Here, the larger group of interest is the United States Congress, and the conservative policy alliance of Republicans and southern Democrats is the smaller decision-making body frequently determining decisions of the entire body.

In light of theories of how political coalitions behave, the most intriguing question about the conservative coalition must be: how and why has it survived so long? This is a particularly important question when we consider the absence of any institutionalized patterns of leadership and the lack of formal interactions such as strategy sessions among supporters of that coalition. Indeed, liberals in the House of Representatives have a far more elaborate institutionalized pattern of interaction, primarily through the Democratic Study Group, which has been in existence since 1959, than do conservatives.[9]

It is helpful to treat the formation of the conservative coalition and its persistence over time as the consequence of what William Gamson calls the "joint use of resources to determine the outcome of a mixed motive situation involving more than two units."[10] The motivations, the policy outcomes, and the resource base of the conservative coalition are analyzed in this study. In particular, with regard to a coalition's resources, the meaningfulness of William Riker's "minimum winning coalition" proposition will be considered. This proposition holds that political coalitions are most likely to be barely large enough to win, in order to maximize each winning member's share of the payoffs, or rewards, from that victory.[11] In examining this fundamental point in the study of political coalitions, it is necessary to keep in mind that the formation and/or the persistence of a legislative coalition cannot be treated as a cost-free process filled only with payoffs and victories.[12] Such a perspective ignores the expenditure of power and influence, and possibly of friendship, that is necessary for legislators to gain desired ends through the workings of the coalition-formation process. It also ignores the effects of that process on the shape of policy outputs.

A coalition of minimum size is not necessarily one that costs its participants the least, and winning marginally is not always preferable to winning unanimously or by a vote total beyond a bare majority. These points will be important for understanding the dynamics of behavior of the conservative coalition.

This book focuses on the conservative coalition as a dynamic, historical phenomenon. The policy coalition that brings together conservatives of both parties is treated here as the product of a repetitive political game played among members of three congressional voting blocs. The most frequent members of the conservative coalition are those participating repetitively in roll calls in search of a set of policy outputs with which they are in general agreement.

One way to address the dynamic nature of the conservative coalition is to introduce a learning component into a model of its behavior. Members alter their present and future behavior in accordance with the feedback they have received from past successes and failures. Behavior also varies as the coalition's adherents find their resource base shrinking or expanding according to congressional election results, shifting party control of the White House, changing relationships between Congress and the bureaucracy, changing public perceptions of the salience of specific issues, and other institutional or constituency constraints that must be considered in assessing the strength and stability of the coalition.

Traditional coalition theory models generally vary only the resources of the players and attempt to hold all other relevant factors constant. This tendency is particularly apparent in the work of William Riker, William Gamson, and Michael Leiserson,[13] for example, who see the object of the game as being able to acquire the largest share of the payoffs that accrue from victory. As a general rule, it seems that the size principle, which flows directly from this emphasis upon the distribution of coalition resources and coalition payoffs, will tend to produce rather simple and inflexible predictions of the behavior of either potential or actual coalition partners. Real-life behavior can be explained with this approach only if it includes increasingly complex assumptions that destroy both the elegance of the minimum size principle and the parsimony of a model that relies on initial resource distribution as its sole explanatory variable.

Some form of minimum-distance component is necessary to produce a meaningful and useful dynamic theory of coalition behavior in Congress. Actors in the legislative setting would be expected to form coalitions most frequently with potential partners who possess similar issue preferences or comparable ideological positions. This consideration is self-evidently an important element for any meaningful analysis of the behavior of the conservative coalition, particularly in light of the different partisan, regional, and constituency influences that affect southern Democrats, Republicans, and northern Democrats in Congress.

This perspective on the minimum-distance principle gives rise to the notion of a "minimum ideological distance coalition," in which coalitions are expected to form among blocs that are closest together in terms of their "policy distance," that is, policy agreement. This outlook is preferred here over the more traditional focus of Riker's payoff–maximizing size principle. The concept of the minimum ideological distance coalition has been developed by several authors.[14]

This view has been expressed very nicely by Scott Flanagan, who argues for a coalition theory incorporating "(1) emphasis on the distinguishing characteristics of noninterchangeability of the players due to . . . ideological or issue polarization; and (2) the frequently felt need for larger than minimal winning coalitions to effect a solution." He sees this policy-based, larger than minimum winning coalition concept as being particularly appropriate in crisis situations or for issues that are especially important to both potential partners and opponents of the coalition.[15]

A variant of this approach has been proposed by Steven Brams, who has been interested in the processes by which coalitions form and change over time. His emphasis is on the ways in which competing coalitions try to attract uncommitted potential supporters and how defections occur as legislators shift their commitments from one bloc to another. The attention paid to defections in Brams's work provides a critical element of flexibility in the study of political coalitions.[16]

More help for the discovery of useful models of how political, and especially legislative, coalitions operate has been provided by Richard Niemi and Herbert Weisberg. Their perspective is to think of legislators making decisions about issues that come before them by choosing an action that represents only one of a set of preferences from which they could have made a selection. Using what they call a probabilistic approach to coalition behavior, Niemi and Weisberg argue that we could expect congressmen to select actions randomly from their preference set and that any departure from that random pattern provides important information about legislators' nonrandom biases toward particular coalitions or toward consistently held policy views.[17] This probabilistic model has been applied to empirical studies of the United States Congress, notably by David H. Koehler. Although he argues that minimum winning coalitions will generally form, in line with Riker's basic proposition, Koehler develops the very important principle that the legislative process is a continuous activity and not a sequence of separate, discrete events.[18] This point is crucial for the study of many different political coalitions because it provides a more realistic assessment of why coalition activity can be stable over time, rather than being sporadic and disjointed.

Emphasis on nonrandom agreement among legislators persisting over time is vitally important for understanding how and why the United States Congress makes decisions about matters of public policy. This is a point that has generally led students of the legislative process to concentrate on partisan or constituency traits as the "glue" that has held together otherwise highly disparate lawmakers. The recent emergence into political prominence of the conservative policy alliance of southern Democratic and Republican members of Congress requires a shift in the thrust of longstanding research into patterns of legislative decision making. The conservative coalition, as will be detailed in the chapters that follow, has been a potent force in shaping national policy on many issues. We can understand how that coalition has operated if we emphasize the study of political coalitions as enduring, imperfectly cohesive policy alliances that attempt to influence but also are influenced by external forces such as constituency opinion, a president's program, or pressure from party leaders.

There does not yet exist a substantial scholarly literature focusing on the conservative coalition per se. Within the context of mainstream writings on Congress, however, there is a great deal of impressionistic discussion of the significance of the conservative coalition, usually within the broader framework of attempts to analyze the structure of the congressional system and the nature of that system's outputs. Most of the general congressional literature provides only a limited understanding of the significance of the conservative coalition and its development over time. Nevertheless, this literature provides several useful points of departure for the more detailed analysis of the coalition undertaken here. I will touch only briefly on the scope of this discussion.

Stephen K. Bailey, for example, discusses the conservative coalition as a barrier to progress toward equal rights. Bailey characterizes the coalition of southern Democrats and Republicans as an ''inverted coalition,'' which is to say that the party that organizes congressional power (he means the Democratic party) cannot deliver that power when it is needed to make national policy. The result is that the national platform of the Democratic party cannot be readily enacted into law because that party is often unable to translate its partisan numerical superiority in Congress into voting majorities on substantive policy issues.[19]

This argument is similar to the distinction drawn by Charles O. Jones between procedural (that is, partisan) majorities, which form to organize the House or Senate in order to do the business of that chamber with a party-based organization, and substantive majorities, which form in order to pass specific legislation and which possess a relatively stable membership on any given issue but may include widely different memberships for different issue areas. Substantive coalitions, as Jones sees them, are formed of shifting majorities.[20] This perspective on legislative behavior suggests that the conservative coalition may be usefully treated as a substantive majority transcending partisan divisions that otherwise would place the Democratic party consistently (as long as it elects a congressional majority) in a position to legislate its programs contrary to the wishes of congressional conservatives. Unlike Jones's emphasis on the shifting, issue-specific nature of episodic substantive coalitions, the conservative coalition here is seen as a broad policy coalition with interests transcending a narrow range of fleeting issues.

Daniel Berman argues that the presence of the conservative coalition as a regularly occurring phenomenon within Congress provides an element of operational unity to the two congressional voting blocs—southern Democrats and Republicans—who have in common the general policy goal of eliminating or limiting positive federal government legislation on a wide range of social and economic issues. The two factions cooperate along the two broad issue dimensions of civil rights and economic regulation to ensure the death of progressive legislation in both areas.[21]

George Blair infers the existence of a "liberal coalition," on grounds that such a coalition must exist to explain the lower success rate of the conservative coalition in recent years. By definition, as increasing numbers of Republicans and southern Democrats desert the conservative coalition, support must automatically grow for the liberal coalition, if these two coalitions are assumed to emerge on a roll call vote in mutual conflict over policy alternatives.[22]

Charles Clapp similarly posits the existence of two large, somewhat loosely organized blocs, the conservative coalition and a liberal Democratic bloc, the latter of which manifests a formal organization in the House Democratic Study Group. The conservative coalition in this context may be treated as an informal alliance of Republicans and southern Democrats lacking any clearly institutionalized locus of authority. To Clapp, the conservative alliance is not necessarily permanent; however, he regards the power of an alternative liberal coalition as limited because the doctrinal emphasis of congressional liberalism on civil rights issues limits its appeal to southern legislators and because congressional liberals in both parties are generally poorly organized.[23]

James MacGregor Burns argues that the chief cause of the frequently bemoaned ineffectiveness of liberal policies is the bipartisan coalition of Democratic and Republican congressional parties (by which he really means congressional conservatives in both parties), which combine to thwart liberal presidential programs.[24] Of course, Burns has in mind Democratic presidents when he refers to Congress thwarting progressive executive-initiated measures, and one would expect the conservative coalition generally to work in support of Republican presidents during the terms of Eisenhower, Nixon, Gerald Ford, or Reagan.

Joseph S. Clark, former Democratic senator from Pennsylvania, argues that political lag remains triumphant in the national legislature, owing to the presence of a dominant congressional bloc determined to maintain the status quo regarding economic and property rights and to hold the line on any extension of civil rights. In Clark's terminology, "the Establishment" is essentially synonymous with the conservative coalition, at least at the level of conservative senior senators and committee and party leaders. Clark associates the conservative coalition with the philosophical position of states' rights and emphasizes, in a fashion similar to Burns, the role of the conservative coalition as a blocking alliance designed to thwart liberal programmatic intentions.[25]

In Clark's assessment, the chief consequence of the dominance of the conservative coalition within the Senate is the effective emasculation of the Democratic party platform and the elimination of any realistic prospect of the emergence of a responsible party system.[26] Clark finds that ideological and philosophical ties to national and even state party platforms are almost irrelevant and that election to Congress is merely a by-product, rather than an end product, of the party process, as a consequence of the existence of a large number of safe seats in both chambers and Congress's frequent insulation from national political currents. This notion is amplified by Morris Fiorina, who suggests that the conservative coalition unifies safe Democratic districts, particularly those that are rural, agrarian, and southern, with safe Republican districts, which are predominantly rural, agrarian, and midwestern and were separated at the congressional level only by historical accidents.[27]

William Keefe and Morris Ogul point out that on a few issues southern Democrats regularly vote with the liberal coalition, whereas some northern Democrats usually act in agreement with the conservative coalition. They note that although much of the evidence regarding the existence, function, and power of the conservative coalition is circumstantial, the cooperation of Republicans and southern Democrats has progressed from furtive courtship to virtual wedlock, with these two blocs fused on approximately the same issues that split southern from northern Democrats.[28]

George Galloway traces the emergence of the conservative coalition in the House to the period between 1910 and World War II, when the party caucus disintegrated, party discipline declined, and party government within Congress was replaced by loosely formed coalitions of disparate voting blocs with unstable leadership. He argues for a broadly based interpretation of the development of the conservative coalition as a consequence of "the growing diversity of interests in a pluralistic society, the emergence of deeply divisive political issues such as civil rights, isolationism vs. internationalism, and the extent of the 'welfare state,' the force of localism in American politics, and the decentralized, compromise character of our national parties constructed as they are, of loose alliances of strong state and local parties."[29]

Galloway finds that the power of the conservative coalition to exercise effective control over the legislative process in the House was consolidated during the Seventy-ninth Congress (1945–46) and that the obstructionist tactics of the House Rules Committee, the focal point of conservative coalition activities for many years, were representative of the opinions of an essentially permanent majority composed of Republicans and southern Democrats. He interprets the role of the conservative coalition as a parliamentary majority transcending internal divisions that otherwise serve to splinter the legislative parties:

> Behind the nominal control of Congress by the same political party in recent decades . . . have been internal cleavages in both parties and the frequent control of the legislative process by bipartisan coalitions in both houses. Fundamental divisions between liberals and conservatives have characterized both congressional parties for many years and have produced situations in which the balance of power in both chambers has been in the hands of moderate Republican–southern Democratic coalitions that have largely dominated the national legislature during the past quarter century [Galloway was writing in 1961]. Many major measures of the

Roosevelt, Truman, and Eisenhower administrations depended for their passage upon coalition support. The relations between the House and the Senate in recent times have thus been marked by the collaboration of conservative coalitions in both chambers. Bipartisan combinations in Congress have often supported the foreign policy and moderate domestic programs of the President and offset the hazards implicit in periods of divided government.[30]

Missouri Democratic Congressman Richard Bolling suggests that, with the passing of the immediate economic emergency of the Great Depression after the 1930s, the appearance of civil rights as a national issue "dissolved the paste holding together the traditional coalition of the Democratic party"[31] and provided the critical catalytic agent necessary for the formation of what he calls the "Tory coalition."

Bolling finds that, although the Democratic national party platform receives the adherence of most northern and western Democrats, it is "balked by the conservative alliance between Democrats from the South and midwestern Republicans." He makes the important point that there is no contractual or conspiratorial basis to the conservative coalition but that it is instead simply "an understandable consequence of convictions common among southern Democrats and certain Republicans, mostly from the Midwest, in respect to domestic legislation involving civil rights, welfare, labor, education, and fiscal affairs."[32] Bolling regards the conservative coalition as based on common perceptions of the desirability of a narrow scope for federal government action, except for matters of defense and domestic subsidies favoring farmers, business, and industry.

Richard Fenno suggests that there is a generally low level of cohesion among congressional conservatives, particularly those on the Senate Finance Committee, with even broad policy goals among members of the conservative coalition a matter that is "more idiosyncratic than programmatic."[33] Furthermore, Fenno regards the coalition as fulfilling primarily a blocking function rather than actively pursuing specific legislative goals.

Aage Clausen makes the important point that the simple fact that southern Democrats and Republicans agree on a variety of policy questions does not permit the inference that members of the conservative coalition vote together through a process of prior and continuing consultations over legislative goals and strategies: "The problem is that without evidence on interpersonal communication within a legislative body it is difficult to distinguish between voting behavior that results from similar, but individual, conceptions of policy responsibilities and that resulting from coalition or bloc arrangements. . . . Republicans and southern Democrats may appear to coalesce although they are doing no more than registering individual conservative biases."[34]

Clausen also finds that the policy positions of senators and congressmen are stable over time and that moderates as well as strong liberals and strong conservatives have stable issue positions. The principle of issue consistency in fact lies at the heart of this examination of the southern Democrat–Republican coalition.

The literature discussed to this point provides certain valuable points of departure for empirical investigation of some general hypotheses derived explicitly from the theory of coalition behavior and more generally from previous studies of legislative behavior. A limited body of scholarly writing directly related to the study of the conservative coalition also exists.

Richard Li and Barbara Hinckley have applied the method of time-series analysis to the behavior of congressional coalitions, a method that is at the core of the empirical analysis in this book. They studied both the party coalition of northern and southern Democrats and the cross-party conservative coalition. Their critically important argument is that "congressional coalition players, characterized by stable membership and long tenure and facing frequent repetition of games (for example, controversial roll calls), may be expected to maintain stable coalitions over time" independent of such short-term effects as elections and specific issues. In a test of this hypothesis, they find a highly stable congressional system in which the growth of coalitions is contained and insulated from explosive growth, and they note that the conservative coalition is more stable than is the party coalition that unites the two wings of the Democratic party.[35]

Joel Margolis, in an examination of the conservative coalition in the Senate between 1933 and 1968, concludes that the coalition did not make a dramatic appearance on Senate roll call votes until the Seventy-eighth Congress (1943–44), its rate of appearance increasing steadily since that time and peaking in the Eighty-ninth Congress (1965–66). He suggests that coalition size had a greater impact on its success than on how frequently the coalition appeared. Margolis found only relatively weak correlations between constituency variables and senators' voting behavior vis-à-vis the coalition.[36]

Margolis showed that the coalition was most likely to appear on issues of taxes, economic policy, health, education, welfare, and labor. Coalition success was greatest, however, on votes related to Senate rules and national security and lowest on education, health, and welfare issues. He also found a low correlation between the coalition's power on committees and its success on the Senate floor, suggesting that the coalition's strength on specific issues was not directly related to its members' committee positions. Margolis concludes that, between the ascendancy of FDR and the end of Lyndon Johnson's administration, ideology became a more important factor than party loyalty in congressional policy making, as southern Democrats increasingly defected to the Republican position and voted less and less with nonsoutherners of their own party.

James Patterson argues that supporters of the conservative coalition became unified by their opposition to the domestic program of the New Deal, particularly the increased power of the federal government and the executive bureaucracy.

More specifically, the coalition arose from opposition to defense spending, the growing power of industrial labor unions, and most social welfare programs proposed by the Roosevelt administration.

At the beginning of the New Deal, according to Patterson's account, Congress was surprisingly liberal, sometimes even more so than was FDR. Democrats were generally united and Republicans split, the congressional leadership was loyal to the president, and the strong Roosevelt presidency was highly popular among most congressmen. Congressional conservatives of the later 1930s emphasized their concern for maintaining the legislative integrity of Congress, their disquiet over FDR's early easy successes with Congress, fear for their personal financial and occupational security, and their resentment of the president's tardy distribution of the fruits of patronage in their direction. They were sufficiently secure with their largely rural constituencies to attack Roosevelt openly on fiscal or programmatic grounds.

Patterson concludes that the early Democratic supporters of the conservative alliance, though less numerous than their Republican coalition partners, were more important in the long run to the success of the coalition owing to their control of or influence over positions of congressional power. Conservative Democrats in important leadership positions saw the New Deal as full of undesirable revolutionary implications and reacted in accordance with their own, and we presume also their constituents', philosophical lights. The Democratic opposition to the early New Deal came largely from the South, but by the mid-1930s many new Democratic members of the bipartisan opposition were nonsoutherners. The coalition's power grew in large measure because of the deeply rooted feeling among basically conservative congressmen that the New Deal had gone far enough or perhaps too far, although many such legislators had originally supported the New Deal as a conservative means to deal with a potentially revolutionary impasse in American history.

Early conservative programmatic reactions against tax legislation, the expanding power of the federal bureaucracy, and especially the 1937 Supreme Court-packing plan, were eventually overlaid by southern Democratic fears of movement by the administration on the race issue. The emergent conservative coalition received new stimulus from the public reaction against a series of massive sitdown strikes and from a desire to reduce the national budget so as to ensure federal fiscal integrity. As the initial thrust of the New Deal receded, there emerged within Congress a stronger and more united conservative opposition to the Roosevelt administration based on a desire to be independent of presidential influence and on the emerging resentment against new reform proposals when the belief spread among legislators that the worst of the national emergency had passed. The opposition at this time began to take on a more clearly sectional, partisan, and rural character. Furthermore, the 1937 furor over the administration's Court proposal had led to an irreparable decline in FDR's power, smashed the unity and resolve of the northern Democratic coalition, and aided conservatives in the 1938 elections, which, of course, in turn meant a further decline in the fortunes of progressive forces in Congress.

Patterson concludes that there is no single, well-organized, monolithic conservative coalition. He also sees sharp internal divisions within both liberal and conservative ranks and argues that Republicans rather than southern Democrats are now the mainstay of support for the conservative coalition. I share this view and will devote much effort in later chapters to detailing the nature of support for the conservative position in the House and Senate.[37]

John Manley conceptualizes the coalition of southern Democrats and Republicans as an informal, bipartisan bloc of conservatives whose leaders occasionally engage in joint discussions of strategy and lining up votes. He argues that there does not exist any clear-cut consensus within Congress on the need for or the scope of federal government activism. Hence, conflict over national policy occurs both within and between the congressional parties, thereby splitting the parties into blocs and factions that must be accommodated before Congress can make any positive decisions. Majorities are built in Congress, not elected to it, so that congressional politics must be coalition politics. An informal organization operating in subtle, frequently unobservable ways, the conservative coalition exists in the no-man's-land between the two parties as one of the cross-party coalitions which of necessity are basic elements of congressional policy making.[38]

Manley argues that simple policy agreement is the single most important element holding the conservative coalition together. The coalition has only an informal structure possessing some limited internal lines of communication and a loose form of centralized coordination by recognized conservative leaders, but this minimal organization seems to be sufficient to assure the coalition's survival. Although a somewhat more well-defined structure of conservative cooperation exists today, regular, formal caucuses of congressional conservatives from both parties similar to those held by House Democratic liberals do not yet exist.[39] As Manley notes, agreement on policy makes an elaborate organization designed to ensure strong cohesion of the coalition unnecessary.

Manley finds that the conservative coalition in both the House and the Senate was more salient in congressional policy decisions after World War II than during the 1933–45 period, in contrast to V. O. Key's conclusion based on the prewar period that reports of the magnitude of conservative coalition activity were exaggerated.[40] Manley reports that the conservative coalition has formed on many of the most important issues decided by Congress since 1933 and suggests that defections from the conservative bloc and high cohesion among liberals can and do determine the outcome on a majority of issues dealt with in Congress, even when the presence of a Republican president stimulates a high rate of Republican cohesion. Finally, Manley notes that the power of southern Democrats within the congressional Democratic party has declined steadily. He speculates that the possibility of a southern Democrat bolt en masse to the Republican party, perhaps in the fashion of John Connally or Strom Thurmond, may lead to radical changes in the organization and partisan division of Congress and eventually to a realignment among the congressional membership and leadership.

David W. Brady and Charles S. Bullock have thoroughly examined the correlates of conservative coalition appearance and success in the House of Representatives. They agree with Manley that issue agreement among conservatives is the basis for the existence and persistence of the conservative coalition. They find that coalition appearances are not related to southern Democratic control of standing committees, to the proportion of Democratic seats held by northerners, to the proportion of all seats held by Republicans, or to presidential party. They show that success of the coalition on floor votes is significantly related to both the number and the cohesiveness of northern Democrats but is unrelated to southern Democratic committee control. The central element in the success of the conservative coalition, according to Brady and Bullock's research, is electoral results in combination with northern liberal solidarity.[41]

New Wine and Old Bottles:
Building on What We Already Know

The existing literature dealing with the conservative coalition has been largely confined either to very useful efforts of data collection[42] or to temporally limited and generally nonsystematic studies of the historical origins and evolution of the coalition.[43] These specialized studies and most general congressional literature, which often deals incidentally with the conservative coalition, fall short of a full explanation of why and how the southern Democrat–Republican alliance of convenience exists and operates.

This book is designed to deal in a reasonably comprehensive fashion with a number of important features of the conservative policy coalition of Republicans and southern Democrats. Chapter 2 analyzes the overall level of activity and success of the conservative coalition over the forty-eight-year time span 1933–80. Chapter 3 examines the specific policy impact of the voting bloc of congressional conservatives on several different issue areas. In Chapter 4, attention shifts to the role of committee power and the access to that power via the seniority system in determining policy outcomes in Congress. The "external" effect on patterns of congressional conservatism of differences in the composition of House and Senate constituencies is addressed in Chapter 5. Chapter 6 attempts to untangle the complexities of party and personality underlying the process of policy interaction between Congress and the White House, with a focus on the mutual success or failure of the president and the conservative coalition. In Chapter 7, the "inside" relationship between congressional parties and the formation of the cross-party southern Democrat–Republican coalition is assessed, in light of the decomposition of the Democratic party in Congress into distinctive wings of liberal northern members and conservative-to-moderate southerners. Chapter 8 assesses the impact of voting strength of the conservative and moderate-to-liberal blocs on the success of the conservative coalition, using both "potential" and "operational" definitions of coalition supporters in considering the effect of defections from expected voting tendencies among Republicans and among southern and northern Democrats. Finally, Chapter 9 presents some points of departure for future analysis of congressional decision-making processes and calls attention to potentially important recent developments that bear on the future of the conservative coalition.

Throughout the discussion of these topics, a common organizing methodology is employed when practical owing to the availability of sufficient data. This is the technique of time-series analysis, a method by which we may discover the historical patterns that have given rise to an observed set of longitudinal data and through which reasonable forecasts of the future values of that set of observations may be usefully made.

The basic theme of this book is that the conservative coalition has become an increasingly important determinant of the outcomes of legislative decision making, as measured by roll call votes taken on the floor of the House and Senate. I also argue that it is incorrect to regard the southern Democrat–Republican alliance as a rigidly structured, strongly cohesive, or issue-specific policy coalition. Instead, I will demonstrate that the conservative coalition is better thought of as a loosely structured alliance of programmatic convenience that is highly cohesive only intermittently and that forms frequently but with sharply varying levels of success on a wide range of issues including, but not limited to, southern Democrats' civil rights concerns and Republicans' traditional opposition to "big government."

The concrete findings of this research are directed toward answering a range of related questions. How frequently in this time span has the conservative coalition appeared, and how has its rate of appearance changed over time? How successful has the conservative coalition been on those roll call votes on which it has appeared, and how has this success rate varied with time? How many supporters of the conservative coalition are there in either chamber of Congress? What trends in the voting strength of the conservative coalition are evident over time? How does the potential strength of the coalition affect its frequency of appearance and its rate of success? To what extent may the conservative coalition be treated as a minimum winning coalition, in consonance with the "size principle" of traditional coalition theory? To what extent does the conservative coalition act as a blocking coalition interested chiefly in preventing the adoption of progressive legislation? With what degree of cohesiveness does the conservative coalition form in either chamber, and how does the structure of cohesion among southern Democrats, Republicans, and northern Democrats vary over time? How stable are levels of support for the conservative coalition within each of the three voting blocs? What is the relevance of seniority and of committee power for the success of the southern Democrat–Republican alliance? What trends in party voting and in roll call splits between northern and southern Democrats are evident over the last few decades, and to what extent have those voting patterns become associated with the appearance of the conservative coalition? Does the success of the coalition vary with different issue dimensions? What is the effect upon the appearance and success of the conservative coalition of the position taken by a president, and to what extent is the coalition affected by the partisan division of control between the White House and Congress? Does the coalition have a marked impact on a president's programmatic success? How may patterns of support for the conservative coalition be explained as a function of statewide and congressional district constituency traits?

In sum, by the analysis employed here, I mean to suggest a set of new perspectives on the activity of the conservative coalition in the United States Congress. By implication, the results of this study also may be applied to future studies of political coalition activity, of the American party system, and of policy-making structures and processes within the national legislature.

Is the Conservative Coalition Really "Conservative"?

An important understanding of the nature of the southern Democrat–Republican policy coalition phenomenon is provided in Table 1–1. Is the conservative coalition in fact correctly named, as an ideologically "conservative"[44] alliance that over time evinces a consistently rightward programmatic thrust? The tabulated values represent the product-moment correlations between levels of support among individual members of Congress for the position taken by the conserva-

Table 1–1

Correlation of Conservative Coalition
Support with ADA and ACA Scores

	House			Senate	
Year	CC,ADA	CC,ACA		CC,ADA	CC,ACA
1980	− .91	.88		− .82	.86
1979	− .93	.91		− .91	.88
1978	− .86	.94		− .89	.92
1977	− .91	.94		− .92	.89
1976	− .88	.93		− .88	.90
1975	− .94	.96		− .94	.94
1974	− .88	.91		− .93	.95
1973	− .93	.93		− .91	.90

tive coalition and two commonly employed measures of ideological purity. These measures are compiled by two ideologically polar opposite groups—the liberal Americans for Democratic Action (ADA) and the conservative Americans for Constitutional Action (ACA). Despite some differences in the way that individual members' scores are calculated,[45] each of the two indexes is intended to measure the programmatic purity of the members of Congress. In general, higher scores on the ACA ratings and lower ADA scores are consonant with a more "conservative" perspective on public policy.

Two important conclusions may be derived from Table 1–1. First, the associations between members' level of support for the conservative coalition and each of the two interest group measures of ideology are in the proper directions and are large enough in magnitude to sustain the conclusion that the conservative coalition is in fact a programmatically "conservative" policy alliance. Higher ADA scores of liberalism are associated with lower scores of conservative coalition support, while higher levels of support for the coalition correlate with higher scores on the ACA index. These relationships are very strong in every instance and hold to about the same degree in both chambers.

This leads to the second important conclusion, which is the persistence of these very strong correlations over time. From session to session, even as the membership of the House and Senate has changed through retirements, resignations, election defeats, or deaths, there is a consistently strong relationship among these measures of programmatic tendencies. Support for the roll call position of the conservative coalition is always highly correlated with low scores of liberalism and high scores of conservatism. Whatever your preferred definition of ideology, the evidence is very strong that the formation of the conservative coalition on formal roll call votes does represent in some meaningful sense an ideologically motivated alliance among a large number of the members of Congress.

Ideology and the origins of intraparty splits are not the normal stuff of legislative debate. Conservatism and its role in the division of Democratic ranks did, however, receive direct attention during Senate debate on the Alaska statehood bill on June 30, 1958. Richard Russell, a Georgia Democrat and a leading figure among conservative Democrats from the South, presented the following analysis of the principles of southern-flavored conservatism:

> Senators from the so-called Southern states are seldom unanimous on any issue. There was a time when we were unanimously opposed to so-called civil rights legislation, but that condition does not obtain today. Seldom is a vote taken in which Senators from the Southern States vote together. . . .
>
>   It so happens that a slightly higher percentage of Senators from the Southern States are traditional in their political outlook. It might be more appropriate to say that a slightly higher percentage of Southern Senators are more politically fundamental in their approach to issues that come before the Senate. As a general rule

a majority of us do not favor change merely for the sake of change. We are generally opposed to the excessive spending of public funds. We try to be very cautious in considering legislation which might lead the country down the road to state socialism.

I know that in some quarters it would be highly preferable for a man to be charged with some devious political manipulation than to be subjected to the reprehensible charge that he is a conservative in politics. That has become a label bearing great odium—that a man is a political conservative.

However, I must say that, in the sense that I am opposed to change for the mere sake of change, and that I do not favor embarking upon legislative adventures without due calculation as to the effect they would have upon the future of the country, I gladly plead guilty to being a conservative. I will wear that label without any shame, despite the attitude of so many persons who are afraid to be caught in company with one who might admit that he is a political conservative.[46]

Some Basic Definitions

Certain specific ideas are meant to be conveyed by the terminology employed in this study of congressional behavior. The *conservative coalition* is defined here as a congressional alliance of Republicans and southern Democrats which, when it forms, acts in opposition to the policy orientations of the more liberal northern Democratic legislators. A *conservative coalition vote* is any roll call vote in the Senate or the House on which a majority of voting southern Democrats and a majority of voting Republicans oppose the stand taken by a majority of voting northern Democrats. Votes on which there is an exactly even division among voting northern Democrats, southern Democrats, or Republicans are not included as conservative coalition votes. A simple majority rule is used here, rather than a more stringent criterion of, say, 75 percent of each bloc forming along the required lines, in order to encompass as wide a range as possible of the behavior that splits most southern Democrats from most northern Democrats and results in southern Democrats forming a cross-party alliance with Republicans in pursuit of common policy outlooks. The fact that even a simple majority of all Democrats would part ways on a recorded vote is sufficiently remarkable to require special notice.

The *South* is defined to include the states of Alabama, Arkansas, Florida, Georgia, Kentucky, Louisiana, Mississippi, North Carolina, Oklahoma, South Carolina, Tennessee, Texas, and Virginia—the Old Confederacy plus Kentucky and Oklahoma. The other thirty-seven states are grouped together as the North, or perhaps more appropriately, the "non-South." The term "northern Democrat" is used as distinct from "southern Democrat," despite the obvious geographical confusion occasioned by referring to a legislator wearing the Democratic party label from, say, Missouri or Arizona as "northern." The force of conventional usage plus the usual association of "northern Democrat" with a legislator who favors or at least does not overtly oppose the generally liberal program of the national party, however, lend some utility to maintaining this admittedly misleading and inaccurate jargon.

The designation of the conservative coalition as a *policy coalition* denotes that the Republican–southern Democratic alliance of programmatic convenience forms in a nonrandom manner in response to the compatibility of beliefs and/or constituent pressures impinging upon the roll call actions of American national legislators. Specifically, the conservative coalition is treated here as a manifestation of deeply rooted policy differences separating programmatically liberal (''progressive'') members of the House and Senate from their fellow conservative (or ''reactionary'') legislators. I have in mind something broader and more enduring than the use of the term ''policy coalition'' by, say, Richard Fenno.[47] Although the study of the conservative coalition certainly cannot capture the complete essence of policy-specific forms of ideological divisions within the United States Congress,[48] this research focus does present the opportunity for analyzing in depth the variables that influence the roll call behavior of Congress on those occasions when deep policy differences are manifested in the formation of the important cross-party policy coalition known as the conservative coalition.

Cohesion is defined here to mean the percentage of members of any one of the three congressional voting blocs relevant to a discussion of the conservative coalition—Republicans, southern Democrats, and northern Democrats—present and voting on the same roll call on the floor of the House or Senate who vote in the same direction for that single roll call. By definition, when a majority of both southern Democrats and Republicans vote ''aye'' on a bill, a majority of northern Democrats must vote ''nay'' for a conservative coalition vote to occur, and vice versa. The very definition of a conservative coalition vote requires that the minimum value of an index of cohesion for any one of the three blocs must be 50 percent $+ 1/n$, where n is the number of members of that bloc present and voting on a roll call.[49] The maximum value that such an index of cohesion may take is 100 percent, which would indicate perfect agreement regarding the direction of the vote among all members of any one of the three blocs on a given roll call. Hence, the analysis of cohesion in this research examines the variation in the index of cohesion within the limits of 50 percent $+ 1/n$ and 100 percent.

The *conservative coalition support score* for an individual congressman is defined as the percentage of conservative coalition votes on which a member of the House or Senate votes in agreement with the position of the conservative coalition. Failure to vote, even if a member announces a stand, lowers the member's score.[50]

Summary

What might we expect to learn by studying the successes and failures, the stability and cohesion, and the policy consequences of the conservative coalition in the United States Congress? To have much utility, such a study should at least provide a better understanding of changing patterns of voting behavior in Congress over a long period of time and should allow explanation of specific policy decisions in light of patterns of coalition activity within the House and Senate. Additionally, this study may be justified insofar as it sheds light on the impact of regionalism or sectionalism on the legislative policy-making process.

Furthermore, this analysis may provide a useful perspective on the relative influence of political parties and of cross-party working coalitions in Congress. An assessment of this phenomenon of bipartisan voting coalitions provides a useful framework for drawing important implications for democratic theory, both in the impact of public sentiment expressed through election outcomes on governmental policy making and in the closeness of the fit between constituent traits and the voting record of representatives and senators. More specifically, it should be possible to make some meaningful statements about impediments to the formation of a "responsible party system." The conservative coalition may be regarded simultaneously as a consequence of the lack of a responsible party system in the United States and a cause of the diffuseness of party control and the consequent lack of clear-cut differences distinguishing one major party from the other.

In addition, the empirical findings of this analysis may be of use in assessing the significance of time as a variable in the study of legislative behavior. The utility of a time dimension in the analysis of legislative decision making may be tested by the method of time-series analysis. An attempt is made here to use appropriate dynamic methodologies whose ultimate purpose is the development of predictive models of congressional behavior.

In short, this study will improve our ability to assess the importance for decision making in Congress of a cross-party coalition that is based largely on strongly held programmatic perspectives about the meaning and direction of national policy. The conservative coalition is an important and underresearched aspect of national policy making. It appears frequently. It is usually highly successful. It forms on a wide range of issues. It is intimately connected to the absence of effective national political parties. It is a fascinating and complex phenomenon worthy of careful detailed analysis. That is why this book exists.

2

Conservative Coalition Appearance and Success: A Historical Overview

The necessary beginning point of this study of the behavior of the conservative coalition is to examine the frequency with which the coalition has appeared and the rate at which it has formed successfully in Congress. The analysis covers each session of Congress during the period 1933 to 1980. These data provide more than simple background information because the patterns they reveal indicate the nature of the factors that explain the emergence and evolution over the past half-century of a regular cross-party alliance that has united conservative elements within both congressional parties and has exerted a strong influence over the formation of American public policy.

In this chapter, and indeed throughout much of this book, the relevant data are analyzed primarily through the time-series method, by means of which the underlying patterns over time of the rate of appearance and success of the conservative coalition may be directly assessed. The time-series technique also serves as a tool for analyzing the structure of growth and development of the coalition over time and, once the correct specification of the underlying statistical process has been achieved, the model may be employed to forecast future levels of coalition appearance and success. Such forecasts are limited to the years 1981 to 1984, or both sessions of the Ninety-seventh and Ninety-eighth Congresses. It is important to see these forecasts as projections, rather than as attempts to foretell the future. The past is indeed a prologue to the future, but projecting past patterns is not equivalent to oracular foresight. Legions of social scientists are employed in trying to explain why "expected" outcomes have been double-crossed by actual events. In this and subsequent chapters the technical aspects of time-series analysis are relegated to appendixes that appear at the end of the book. These appendixes are referenced at appropriate places in the textual material.

Table 2–1

Conservative Coalition Appearances
in the House, 1933–1980

Year	Number of Conservative Coalition Appearances	Appearances as Percent All Roll Calls	Appearances as Percent Nonunanimous Votes
1933	0	0.00	0.00
1934	2	2.44	2.67
1935	8	6.11	6.56
1936	0	0.00	0.00
1937	10	10.31	11.36
1938	0	0.00	0.00
1939	6	6.38	7.23
1940	16	12.03	13.56
1941	9	11.25	13.04
1942	11	15.28	20.75
1943	18	19.78	24.00
1944	17	26.15	32.69
1945	13	12.87	17.57
1946	35	26.92	34.65
1947	17	20.24	25.76
1948	17	21.52	27.42
1949	23	19.01	24.21
1950	19	12.34	15.97
1951	22	20.18	24.18
1952	20	27.78	33.90
1953	16	22.54	28.57
1954	8	10.53	16.00
1955	10	13.16	17.54
1956	7	9.59	13.21
1957	16	16.00	17.98
1958	14	15.05	20.90
1959	11	12.64	14.47
1960	19	20.43	26.03
1961	23	19.83	25.56
1962	16	12.90	18.82
1963	15	12.61	17.44
1964	12	10.62	14.46
1965	51	25.37	34.46
1966	37	19.17	31.36
1967	54	22.04	34.62
1968	51	21.89	33.55
1969	45	25.42	40.18
1970	44	16.54	27.16

Year	Number of Conservative Coalition Appearances	Appearances as Percent All Roll Calls	Appearances as Percent Nonunanimous Votes
1971	99	30.94	45.00
1972	82	24.92	39.23
1973	133	24.58	33.33
1974	102	18.99	28.98
1975	170	27.78	36.25
1976	143	21.63	32.13
1977	157	22.24	33.98
1978	164	19.66	31.54
1979	144	21.43	29.81
1980	95	15.73	23.63

Conservative Coalition Appearances in the House

Table 2–1 shows the number of times the conservative coalition formed in each session of the House of Representatives between 1933 and 1980. The table also presents the rate of coalition appearances both as a proportion of all roll call votes cast and as a proportion of all controversial (i.e., nonunanimous) roll calls. A noncontroversial roll call vote is defined here as one in which 90 percent or more of all votes are cast in one direction, either yea or nay. Figure 2–1 plots the annual relative frequency of the coalition's appearance in the House and Senate as a proportion of all nonunanimous roll call votes.

The first column of Table 2–1 shows that the number of times the conservative coalition has appeared in the House has increased very dramatically since the early 1930s. The data support the common argument that the conservative coalition appeared infrequently in the early years of the Roosevelt administrations and sharply increased its rate of appearance as the split between northern and southern Democrats deepened and as southern Democrats and Republicans grew to see the virtues of cross-party cooperation in pursuit of common programmatic goals.

The secular growth in the frequency of coalition appearances in the House is most meaningfully represented by the data in the final column of Table 2–1, which presents the incidence of coalition formation as a proportion of nonunanimous roll calls. The metric of nonunanimous roll call votes as a base for determining the rate of occurrence of the conservative coalition is preferable to an alternative base of all roll calls taken in a session because the nonunanimous criterion excludes most roll calls pertaining to quorum calls and most other "nonsubstantive" legislative actions that are reflected in the roll call record.

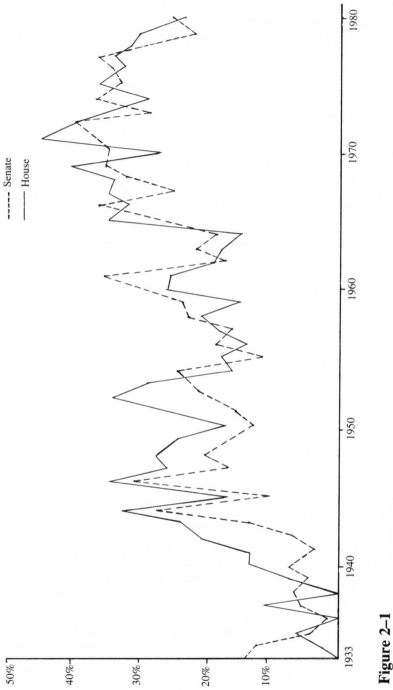

Figure 2–1

Relative Frequency of Conservative Coalition Appearances as Percent of Nonunanimous Roll Call Votes, 1933–1980

This metric indicates the presence of at least three distinct phases in the evolution of the conservative coalition in the House. The first phase, from 1933 to about 1946, includes the early very low levels of coalition appearance and its expansion throughout the first half of the 1940s. In 1946, more than one-third of all nonunanimous roll call votes in the House of Representatives were characterized by the formation of the conservative coalition. For the entire 1933–46 period, coalition appearances as a proportion of nonunanimous votes averaged about 13.1 percent with a very large variance of 125 percentage points.

The second period of coalition appearance in the House extends from about 1947 until 1964, the last session of Congress before the social welfare legislative thrust of the War on Poverty. During this time, the level of coalition appearance fluctuated about a mean of roughly 21.2 percent of nonunanimous roll calls, with a much smaller variance of 32.7 percentage points. No clear trend is evident except that the level of coalition activity declined below the level of 1944 and 1946 in every session save that of 1952.

The third phase of House coalition acitivity, extending from roughly 1965 to 1980, was a period of considerably greater stability, with levels of coalition formation varying about a mean of approximately 33.5 percent with a variance of 25 percentage points. Rates of coalition formation in the House declined markedly, however, after 1977.

For the entire period 1933–80, the data suggest relative consistency in the values of conservative coalition appearances as a proportion of nonunanimous House roll calls from one session to the next. With the methods of time-series analysis, the exact pattern of this stochastic dependence can be specified. The following section discusses the applicability of time-series methods to the kind of data that have just been encountered.

A Brief Introduction to Univariate Time Series

The time-series method provides an explicit means for dealing with coalition behavior in a dynamic context,[1] treating the activity of the conservative coalition as the outcome of a sequence of serial and interdependent games. The time-series technique is appropriate for studying coalition activity because it explicitly presumes a "fading memory" process, which can be operationalized by thinking about the formation of a legislative voting alliance as the consequence of "shocks," or strong stimuli, occasioned by a dramatic historical event or by a regular pattern of events occurring periodically over time.

In applying the method, it is assumed logically that more recent events are more consequential than those that took place farther in the past.

The time-series approach allows direct modeling of the reasonable assertion that a dramatic event or a series of regularly recurring factors may have a great impact (or "shock") whose strength dies out over time but may give rise to later related events or to a changed level of activity. The dynamic nature of the time-series method allows us to model the interconnection of historical events and the cumulative consequences of political actions, particularly actions that recur with relatively great frequency over a long period of time. It is a sophisticated modeling strategy for the study of legislative policy coalitions over time given highly realistic assumptions about coalition behavior as reflected in this technique of data analysis.[2] A very incomplete summary of time-series models is given in Appendix A.

Time-Series Analysis of House Coalition Appearances

The dominant patterns of the values in this time series are shown by an appropriate statistical model, which may be thought of as a way of representing the observed results of an underlying historical and political process. The time series of the rate of conservative coalition appearances in the House is well represented by the simple ARIMA (1,1,0), or first-order autoregressive integrated moving average, process

$$(1 + .47B)(1 - B) z_t = a_t.$$

The $(1 - B)$ term in the model means that, because this time series does not have a constant average value, we must look at the changes from year to year, or $z_t - z_{t-1}$, to understand the pattern followed by the data. The autoregressive parameter, $\phi_1 = -.47$, measures the degree of correlation among successive changes in the series of observations.

In the model, the magnitude of the autoregressive parameter suggests that this historical data set consists of a sequence of closely related year-to-year increases or decreases in the rate of conservative coalition appearances. This pattern is generally in accord with the visual assessment of the nature of the series made in the previous section. The existence of a significant first-order autoregressive parameter demonstrates that the current level of coalition appearances in the House is determined by a "memory" including the values of all preceding changes in the level of the series from one session to the next. The fact that this parameter has a negative sign means that increases in the rate of coalition formation tend to be followed by decreases or smaller increases, and vice versa. This model is nonstationary; it does not fluctuate during the entire time period around a fixed average level. The autoregressive term in the model demonstrates that the upward-trending incidence of conservative coalition appearances in the House follows a stable, nonrandom process. The most important point to be made here is that there is a pattern of stability in the rate at which the conservative coalition forms in the House of Representatives over time, and this stability is determined by events stretching far back into the past.

This model, or any other time-series model, can be used to project the likely future values that the data can be expected to take on. These projections are not meant to be prophecies. A forecast of levels of conservative coalition appearance for the years 1981 to 1984 suggests a continuation of the moderate decline in the rate of coalition formation that has been evident in the House since about 1971. Forecasted levels of appearance for each of the four years are approximately 26.6 percent in 1981, 25.2 percent in 1982, 25.8 percent in 1983, and 25.5 percent in 1984. The suggestion of a marginal decline in levels of House coalition activity and great stability in future rates of coalition formation may indicate a slight falloff in the future impact of the conservative coalition over the formulation of public policy within the House of Representatives, at least as measured by its frequency of appearance.

Conservative Coalition Appearances in the Senate

The frequency with which the conservative coalition has appeared in each session of the Senate between 1933 and 1980 is reported in Table 2–2. The column that catalogs the number of times that the coalition has formed in each Senate session shows, first, a sharp increase in the incidence of the coalition's activity since the time of FDR, and, second, a detectable stability in the frequency of coalition formation for sessions close together in time. These data provide further support for the argument that the conservative coalition emerged following, and presumably as a response to, the programs of the New Deal. If this interpretation is to be taken at face value, however, the data are curious for two important reasons.

First, the number of coalition appearances is unexpectedly high in 1933, the earliest congressional session included in this study, and this initial level of coalition activity is not again attained until ten years later. Furthermore, the number of coalition appearances in the Senate falls below the 1933 frequency as late as the 1957 session.

Second, the surge in coalition appearances in the mid-1940s occurred significantly later than the time when the programmatic consequences of the New Deal had begun to impact on the American political system. This latter fact accords less well with the original interpretation than with an alternative assessment of the emergence of the conservative coalition as a response to the pressures of internationalism, national defense, and government management of the economy occasioned by the perceived need to take action for national survival amid a world at war.

The distribution of conservative coalition appearances over time as a proportion of all nonunanimous Senate roll calls, shown in the final column of Table 2–2, suggests the presence of three distinct periods of activity, closely paralleling those shown in the House.

The first period extended from 1933 to about 1946. Initially, the coalition's appearance was relatively frequent, followed by near disappearance (1933–36),

Table 2–2

Conservative Coalition Appearances
in the Senate, 1933–1980

Year	Number of Conservative Coalition Appearances	Appearances as Percent All Roll Calls	Appearances as Percent Nonunanimous Votes
1933	13	13.27	13.98
1934	9	6.92	7.14
1935	5	3.79	4.03
1936	1	1.64	1.69
1937	5	5.38	5.88
1938	5	6.17	6.58
1939	5	4.39	4.85
1940	10	6.58	7.19
1941	3	3.06	3.45
1942	5	5.32	6.58
1943	15	12.30	13.64
1944	25	25.51	27.47
1945	10	9.26	10.10
1946	40	29.41	30.77
1947	21	15.22	16.80
1948	20	18.18	20.41
1949	35	15.49	16.36
1950	28	12.23	12.96
1951	28	14.00	15.14
1952	20	17.70	18.87
1953	18	20.00	21.95
1954	33	18.23	23.08
1955	7	8.05	11.48
1956	21	16.16	18.92
1957	12	11.21	16.00
1958	38	19.00	22.89
1959	40	18.60	23.67
1960	46	22.22	29.87
1961	65	31.86	35.33
1962	34	15.18	17.00
1963	43	18.78	21.83
1964	51	16.72	18.09
1965	61	23.64	28.11
1966	70	29.79	36.08
1967	56	17.78	24.78
1968	70	24.91	31.53
1969	69	28.16	35.20
1970	108	25.84	34.95

Year	Number of Conservative Coalition Appearances	Appearances as Percent All Roll Calls	Appearances as Percent Nonunanimous Votes
1971	120	28.37	36.70
1972	152	28.57	39.90
1973	123	20.71	28.21
1974	162	29.78	36.73
1975	166	27.57	32.81
1976	177	25.73	34.04
1977	187	29.45	35.82
1978	119	23.06	29.10
1979	91	18.31	22.03
1980	106	19.96	24.94

then a stable phase of comparatively low levels (1937–42), and finally sharp but irregular growth to a peak in 1946 at a level not again attained until fifteen years later. The relative frequency of coalition formation averaged about 10.2 percent over this time, with a variance of 71.1 percentage points.

The second period of Senate conservative coalition activity extended roughly from 1947 to 1964, encompassing the early Cold War years and the last stages of "decompression" from the effects of World War II to the last session preceding the large-scale introduction of legislation associated with the Great Society. This period was characterized by considerable volatility, with a range of levels of coalition formation between a minimum of 11.48 percent in 1955 and a maximum of 35.33 percent in 1961. Levels of coalition activity for this period varied about a mean of 20 percent, with a variance of 31.7 percentage points.

The third and final period of coalition activity, 1965–80, was for the most part highly stable, with a mean of 31.9 percent and a variance of 25.1 percentage points. Together with the findings for the House, these results suggest that in the last decade and a half the conservative coalition seems to have "matured," with relatively high and stable rates of appearance. This assessment is reinforced by the visual evidence in Figure 2–1.

Time-Series Analysis of Senate Coalition Appearances

The time series of levels of Senate conservative coalition appearances as a percent of nonunanimous votes is best represented as the first-order autoregressive integrated moving average model

$$(1 + .51B)(1 - B)z_t = a_t$$

where the autoregressive parameter is $\phi_1 = -.51$. Except for a slightly different value for the autoregressive term, this model is identical to that shown for the rate of appearance of the conservative coalition in the House. Here, as for the House model, there is a significant negative association among successive values of the differenced time series. Larger increases in the rate of coalition formation in the Senate tend to be followed by smaller increases or by decreases in coalition appearance.

The similarity of the respective models for the two chambers shows that similar histories underlie the patterns of conservative coalition appearance in both the House and the Senate. In assessing the role of the conservative coalition as a policy alliance, therefore, we are not dealing with a phenomenon peculiar to one chamber of Congress or one that behaves in a radically different fashion in either chamber.

A forecast of the relative frequency of formation of the conservative coalition in the Senate through 1984 produces results that are broadly similar to those produced for the House. The forecasts suggest steady or perhaps slightly declining levels of coalition appearance in the Senate, to approximately 23.5 percent in 1981, 24.2 percent in 1982, 23.8 percent in 1983, and 24.0 percent in 1984.

Comparing Coalition Appearances in the House and the Senate

Three major points of similarity in levels of coalition appearance in the House and the Senate stand out from the information presented in Tables 2–1 and 2–2.

First, the frequency of appearances is broadly similar in both chambers, with the coalition forming relatively infrequently in the early years under study and more often in later sessions. This is strong evidence that the southern Democrat–Republican policy alliance has "matured" over time to become a very significant factor in congressional activity.

Second, the time-series models indicate a substantial degree of stability over time in the level of coalition appearances in each chamber. Within a limited time period, there is generally little variation in the magnitude of coalition formation. In both chambers, a structure of dependency extends throughout the entire length of the time series. Furthermore, it is clear from these data that with the passage of time and events, the conservative coalition has become a persistent factor in congressional decision making. The coalition has not disappeared intermittently, as would be expected if that alliance were the consequence of substantive policy positions that are of only occasional relevance to the decision-making processes in Congress.

Third, each of the two time series may be decomposed into three phases of coalition activity covering essentially identical spans of time in the history of the House and Senate between 1933 and 1976. Perhaps the most significant point here is that the conservative coalition appeared as a major force in congressional decision making during the imposition of government social and economic controls during World War II and throughout the "decompression" from such controls in the mid-1940s.

This last finding at least partially contradicts the common assertion that the emergence of the conservative coalition as a significant element in congressional decision making is traceable to reactions against the programmatic intent of the New Deal but does not directly contradict a more limited assertion that the perceived policy thrust of the New Deal was a necessary condition for the emergence of the conservative coalition. The data demonstrate, however, that the complex set of domestic and international developments associated with World War II, and not the New Deal, was the sufficient condition for the development of the coalition into a significant and regular force in congressional policy making.

There are some minor differences in the levels of House and Senate coalition formation, with the coalition somewhat more active in the Senate. The total number of Senate coalition appearances since 1933 (2,548) greatly exceeds the total number in the House (2,001). This disparity is largely attributable to the greater incidence of roll calls in the Senate, which recorded 12,026 votes between 1933 and 1980, as against 10,170 House roll calls in the same time period. Controlling for the total number of roll calls, the rate of coalition formation in the Senate still narrowly exceeds that in the House. In the Senate, the coalition formed on 21.19 percent of all roll calls, whereas it appeared on 19.68 percent of all House roll calls.

Controlling for the incidence of "unanimous" roll calls, however, the rate of coalition formation is actually slightly greater in the House (27.56 percent) than in the Senate (25.71 percent). This reversal in the relative frequency of coalition appearances is accounted for by the much greater incidence of "noncontroversial" roll calls in the House (28.60 percent of all House roll calls) than in the Senate (17.60 percent of all Senate votes).[3]

Conservative Coalition Success in the House

Table 2–3 demonstrates that the success enjoyed by the conservative coalition in the House, measured as the number of coalition victories divided by its number of appearances in each session, has varied widely over time. Much of this variation, especially in the earlier years of the series, is a consequence of the very small number of coalition appearances for some sessions. No success rates can be computed for the 1933, 1936, and 1938 sessions of the House because there were no recorded votes on which the conservative coalition formed in those years.

Table 2–3

Conservative Coalition Success
in the House, 1933–1980

Year	Number of Conservative Coalition Victories	Number of Conservative Coalition Defeats	Victories as Percent of Appearances
1933	0	0	—
1934	2	0	100.00
1935	3	5	37.50
1936	0	0	—
1937	5	5	50.00
1938	0	0	—
1939	6	0	100.00
1940	14	2	87.50
1941	8	1	88.89
1942	10	1	90.91
1943	18	0	100.00
1944	15	2	88.24
1945	10	3	76.92
1946	32	3	91.43
1947	17	0	100.00
1948	17	0	100.00
1949	19	4	82.61
1950	16	3	84.21
1951	21	1	95.45
1952	18	2	90.00
1953	16	0	100.00
1954	8	0	100.00
1955	10	0	100.00
1956	5	2	71.43
1957	13	3	81.25
1958	9	5	64.29
1959	10	1	90.91
1960	7	12	36.84
1961	17	6	73.91
1962	7	9	43.75
1963	10	5	66.67
1964	8	4	66.67
1965	13	38	25.49
1966	12	25	32.43
1967	38	16	70.37
1968	32	19	63.75
1969	32	13	71.11
1970	31	13	70.45

Year	Number of Conservative Coalition Victories	Number of Conservative Coalition Defeats	Victories as Percent of Appearances
1971	78	21	78.79
1972	65	17	79.27
1973	89	44	72.36
1974	68	34	66.67
1975	89	81	52.35
1976	84	59	58.74
1977	94	63	59.87
1978	93	71	56.71
1979	105	39	72.92
1980	64	31	67.37

The conservative coalition has been highly successful in the House of Representatives, winning on 66.87 percent, or 1,338, of the 2,001 House roll calls on which it has appeared between 1933 and 1980. The coalition was undefeated in eight sessions. One hundred percent success, however, has not recurred since 1955, and the early undefeated sessions are based on relatively small numbers of coalition appearances. Figure 2–2 graphically plots coalition success in both houses.

The data suggest that the success of the conservative coalition in the House has declined irregularly over time and has recently stabilized in the vicinity of 50 to 70 percent success. The final column of Table 2–3 demonstrates the extraordinarily low success rate in both sessions of the "Great Society" Eighty-ninth Congress (1965–66), a finding that is discussed in detail in later chapters. The fact that the coalition did not disappear or become mired in a continuous losing rut after its disastrous showing in 1965 and 1966 or after other downturns, such as those in 1960 or 1962, lends credence to the assertion that congressional decision making is characterized by the frequent operation of relatively stable policy coalitions.

Time-Series Analysis of House Coalition Success

The historical structure of activity by the conservative coalition can be further examined by a time-series analysis of levels of coalition success in the House of Representatives. There are "holes" in the data set for the years 1933, 1936, and 1938, owing to the absence of any conservative coalition appearances for those years. Hence, the observations are not continuous from 1933 through 1980.

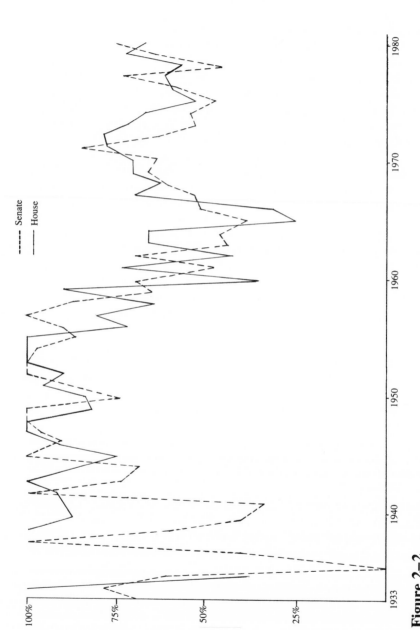

Figure 2–2
Conservative Coalition Success, 1933–1980

Consequently, the continuous set of observations from 1939 to 1980 is employed in this section.

The time series of the relative frequency of conservative coalition victories as a proportion of its total number of appearances for each session of the House between 1939 and 1980 is well-represented by the ARIMA (1,1,0) model:

$$(1 + .53B) (1 - B) z_t = a_t.$$

The negative sign of the autoregressive parameter, $\phi_1 = -.53$, shows that an increase in the rate of success enjoyed by the conservative coalition in one session was generally followed by a lesser rise or by a decrease in success in the following session. It is clear that the data are best represented by a nonstationary process, represented in the model by the $(1 - B)$ first-difference because the coalition's success rate in the House has declined sharply from its early very high levels.

A forecast of the estimated future success of the conservative coalition in the House using the above model suggests a fairly steady, although perhaps slightly increased, relative frequency of victory. The forecasted values are approximately 70 percent in 1981, 69 percent in 1982, 70 percent in 1983, and 69 percent in 1984. These results are, of course, much less an exercise in future-telling than they are a benchmark against which to compare future realities.

Conservative Coalition Success in the Senate

The pattern of success enjoyed by the conservative coalition in the Senate over time, as shown in Table 2–4, is broadly similar to the pattern in the House. The overall level of Senate coalition success is 65.15 percent, or 1,660 victories out of 2,548 appearances between 1933 and 1980. This success rate in the Senate is somewhat lower than that in the House over the same period.

As it did in the House, the conservative coalition in the Senate enjoyed complete success in eight sessions throughout the first half of the time series, a result that in many cases is a function of the very small number of coalition appearances in the earlier sessions. The success of the Senate coalition was greatest roughly from 1945 to 1957. This result reinforces the earlier finding that the conservative coalition in each chamber "matured" in the late World War II and immediate postwar years.

In recent years, the lowest level of coalition success in the Senate, 39.34 percent, occurred in 1965. This figure reflects, as do comparable results in the House, the impact of the liberal Democratic influx resulting from the 1964 general elections and from the weight of President Johnson's demands for passage of the Great Society programs.

Table 2–4

Conservative Coalition Success
in the Senate, 1933–1980

Year	Number of Conservative Coalition Victories	Number of Conservative Coalition Defeats	Victories as Percent of Appearances
1933	9	4	69.23
1934	7	2	77.78
1935	3	2	60.00
1936	0	1	0.00
1937	2	3	40.00
1938	5	0	100.00
1939	3	2	60.00
1940	4	6	40.00
1941	1	2	33.33
1942	5	0	100.00
1943	11	4	73.33
1944	17	8	68.00
1945	10	0	100.00
1946	36	4	90.00
1947	20	1	95.24
1948	20	0	100.00
1949	35	0	100.00
1950	21	7	75.00
1951	25	3	89.29
1952	20	0	100.00
1953	18	0	100.00
1954	32	1	96.97
1955	6	1	85.71
1956	19	2	90.48
1957	12	0	100.00
1958	33	5	86.84
1959	26	14	65.00
1960	32	14	69.57
1961	31	34	47.69
1962	24	10	70.59
1963	19	24	44.19
1964	24	27	47.06
1965	24	37	39.34
1966	36	34	51.43
1967	30	26	53.57
1968	56	14	80.00
1969	46	23	66.67

Year	Number of Conservative Coalition Victories	Number of Conservative Coalition Defeats	Victories as Percent of Appearances
1970	70	38	64.81
1971	103	17	85.83
1972	96	56	63.16
1973	66	57	53.66
1974	88	74	54.32
1975	80	86	48.19
1976	102	75	57.63
1977	138	49	73.80
1978	56	63	47.06
1979	59	32	64.84
1980	80	26	75.47

Time-Series Analysis of Senate Coalition Success

The time series of the relative frequency of conservative coalition victories in the Senate is summarized by the ARIMA (2,1,0) model:

$$(1 + .35B + .48B^2) (1 - B) z_t = a_t.$$

The first-order autoregressive term, $\phi_1 = -.35$, shows a strong relationship among changes in the degree of conservative coalition success from session to session, with a negative correlation between successive values. That is, larger positive changes in one session are followed by smaller or negative values, as also occurred in the House. This Senate model differs from the model for the House in that it also contains a second-order autoregressive term, $\phi_2 = -.48$. This new parameter denotes a strongly negative relationship among successive "within Congress" changes in Senate success rates. That is, the changes in coalition success from the first to the second session of the same biennial Congress are alternately negative and then positive, or large and then small.

Forecasts of future levels of Senate coalition successes using the above model produce steady and moderately high results of approximately 63 percent in 1981, 62 percent in 1982, 69 percent in 1983, and 67 percent in 1984, assuming that long-established patterns are not fundamentally disturbed. If actual results are markedly different from this set of forecasts, they at least provide a baseline for trying to explain the origin of those discrepancies.

Comparing Conservative Coalition Success
in the Senate and the House

Several major similarities, as well as some minor differences, exist in levels of conservative coalition success in the two chambers of Congress. First, the coalition clearly has been highly successful in both the House and the Senate. Over the entire period 1933 to 1980, the coalition has been slightly more successful in the House. Furthermore, there is a noticeable, though irregular, pattern of declining coalition success in both chambers over time.

In analyzing the conservative coalition's impact on public policy, it is important to note that the relative frequency of its appearance is essentially unrelated to its rate of success in both chambers. The correlation between coalition success and appearances as a percentage of nonunanimous roll calls is $-.19$ in the House and $-.03$ in the Senate. Hence, there is only a very weak tendency for the coalition to be less successful when it appears more regularly. These results suggest, however, that the conservative coalition in the House is somewhat more likely than in the Senate to form (unsuccessfully) in opposition to popular liberal legislative proposals.

Second, although coalition success in both chambers is more varied over time than is the level of coalition formation, the time-series models indicate highly stable, and rather simple, patterns of success in each chamber. The presence of stability again supports the argument that the conservative coalition should be thought of as a stable policy coalition and further demonstrates the existence of a long-term evolution of the conservative coalition in both chambers.

Third, three fairly well-defined periods of coalition success may be observed in both chambers. In the Senate, the coalition enjoyed only indifferent success between 1933 and 1941, during which time it won on 60.71 percent of its 56 appearances. Success levels from session to session varied widely in this first period. As the coalition became a more regular phenomenon in Senate decision making, its success increased. Between 1942 and 1958, the coalition success rate was a high and largely invariant 90.43 percent of the 376 appearances. In the third period, 1959 to 1980, success was varied but at generally lower levels, totaling 60.78 percent on 2,116 appearances.

Similar phases of coalition success occurred in the House, although different years are involved in each phase. The initial period of indifferent coalition success in the House covers only the years 1934, 1935, and 1937, during which time the conservative coalition managed a victory rate of only 50 percent on 20 appearances. In the second phase, 1939 to 1955, the coalition was successful on 92.78 percent of 277 appearances. The third phase, from 1956 to 1980, is characterized by widely varied but generally lower levels of success, amounting to 62.97 percent on 1,704 appearances.

This analysis suggests the following conclusions. The conservative coalition was least successful during its infancy, when it occurred infrequently and had not yet achieved a clear raison d'être. It was highly successful from the late stages of the New Deal through World War II and the early Cold War. The coalition has been only moderately successful since the reemergence of strong liberal forces in Congress in the late 1950s and the domination of the presidency by liberal Democrats from 1961 to 1968 and by a moderate Democrat from 1977 to 1980.

Conclusion

Very low levels of formation of the conservative coalition in the early years under study were followed by a gradual, irregular maturation of the coalition into a permanent, frequently occurring phenomenon in congressional roll call activity. Hence, the data suggest that it is meaningful to speak of the conservative coalition as an evolving, stable, and consequential factor in congressional behavior. This finding may be taken as at least a partial justification of this study of a clearly important component of congressional behavior.

Time-series analysis has revealed significant similar patterns of serial dependence in the two time series representing levels of appearance of the conservative coalition in each chamber. This conclusion supports the argument of this book that congressional decision making is characterized in large part by the interaction of relatively stable policy coalitions. Time-series analysis of conservative coalition success in each chamber lends further credence to the conception of congressional policy making as the product of interacting and conflictual policy coalitions. There is little here to support what might be called the "pluralist" view of congressional behavior,[4] in which the emphasis is on the formation of frequently shifting and temporary alliances of legislators, in contrast to the policy coalition interpretation of congressional policy making.

Finally, the analysis of levels of conservative coalition appearance and success has established the utility of the time-series method as a means for specifying the dynamic processes underlying historical data on congressional behavior. Further, the results given in this chapter have demonstrated that the time-series method may be used to forecast short-term future levels of this recurring congressional phenomenon.

3

The Issue of Issues

No evaluation of the significance of the conservative coalition for congressional decision making could be complete without specifying the policy thrust of the activity of that policy coalition. Although it has been shown that the coalition has become an important factor in congressional policy making, the historical data presented in the preceding chapter are reported at too aggregate a level to permit a detailed assessment of the policy relevance of the conservative coalition.

The major objective of this chapter is to combine cross-sectional and longitudinal perspectives on the issue content of the activity of the conservative coalition, as shown in the roll call record of both the House and the Senate. This chapter takes as a point of departure the five major issue dimensions underlying congressional roll call voting found by Aage Clausen in his analysis of Senate and House roll calls for the period 1953–64.[1] To this list are added two minor dimensions that incorporate votes excluded from Clausen's original typology.[2] All roll calls on which the conservative coalition formed in each chamber from 1933 to 1980 are covered in this analysis. From this data base, a number of important ideas related to the policy impact of the southern Democrat–Republican coalition will be examined.

Following Charles Jones's evaluation of the conservative coalition as one of the temporary and shifting substantive coalitions that he sees as characterizing congressional decision making,[3] we would expect that frequent occurrences and high levels of success by that coalition would be confined to a limited range of issues. Evidence of consistently high rates of conservative coalition appearance and success across a number of issue dimensions over time would support an alternative interpretation that the conservative coalition is a broad policy coalition regularly interested in a diverse mix of policies.

Several authors have foreseen the development of an increasingly liberal structure of congressional policy outputs.[4] Some see the dominance of the conservative coalition giving way to a "benign coalition" of progressives in both parties. It was established in Chapter 2, however, that the conservative coalition has not vanished but has instead formed frequently and usually very successfully. In this chapter, the decline or persistence of the conservative coalition in specific issue areas will be analyzed.

It has recently been argued that the House of Representatives has become more conservative in its policy decisions than the Senate. If this assertion is true, the conservative coalition in the House could be expected to be more successful than that in the Senate on most or all issue dimensions in more recent sessions. An examination of the historical record would also indicate what changes may have occurred over time in the relative degrees of conservatism in the two chambers across various issue areas.

Students of congressional policy making have disagreed about the relative success and interest of the conservative coalition on specific issues. Daniel Berman, for example, argues that the coalition has been most successful on civil rights votes and that it has also been successful on votes relating to education, immigration, taxation, and regulation of both business and labor.[5] In contrast, Joseph Clark asserts that the coalition is relatively unsuccessful on civil rights, though he believes that issue and congressional reform are the matters of most concern to the coalition. Clark finds that the coalition has been most successful at stopping or limiting federal spending programs.[6] Galloway asserts that the coalition emerged initially because of intra-Democratic splits on the civil rights issue and was sustained over time by the sharply divisive issues of international involvement and the extent of the "welfare state."[7] Joel Margolis has shown that in the Senate the conservative coalition was most likely to appear on the issues of taxes and economic policy, as well as health, education, welfare, and labor. He finds that the Senate coalition was most successful on rules and national security and least successful on education, health, and welfare issues.[8]

The issue content of conservative coalition appearances and success is assessed in this chapter by testing the general proposition that levels of its appearance and success differ across issue dimensions. The point is to determine the extent to which the programmatic goals of the coalition may have varied over time and to indicate the broad policy thrust of the coalition's interests.

This chapter relies on a content analysis of verbal descriptions of the policy content of individual roll call votes. Such descriptions are provided in the *Congressional Quarterly Almanac* since 1955 and, for earlier votes, by codebooks accompanying roll call data tapes made available through the Inter-University Consortium for Political and Social Research. Each roll call vote on which the conservative coalition has appeared is assigned to an issue dimension. Each of the seven issue dimensions is assessed as to the success and rate of appearance of the conservative coalition on the set of issues contained within each cluster. Comparisons of coalition success and appearance are made across the different issue dimensions and also across chambers, and the historical pattern of coalition activity within each separate dimension is examined.

The Civil Liberties Dimension

The civil liberties issue cluster includes congressional roll calls on such topics as sexual and racial equality, civil rights, abortion, and crime control. The focus is primarily upon political and judicial procedure and only secondarily upon the impact of specific policy outcomes. The conservative coalition has opposed the extension of government programs to foster school desegregation, particularly through resort to busing, opposes the adoption of legislation supporting sexual equality, favors the expansion of police power over criminal suspects, supports the death penalty, opposes gun control, and opposes steps to facilitate easier voter registration procedures.

Table 3–1 demonstrates that the conservative coalition in the House has been extremely successful on this set of roll calls, winning almost 80 percent of the times it formed on this issue dimension. The only issue dimensions on which the

Table 3–1

Conservative Coalition (CC) Votes by Issue Dimension, 1933–1980 (percent)

	House		Senate	
	CC Victory Rate	Percent All CC Votes	CC Victory Rate	Percent All CC Votes
Civil Liberties (CL)	79.5	12.2	56.9	13.5
Government Management (GM)	71.7	38.0	73.6	39.9
International Involvement (II)	57.0	23.0	66.9	18.7
Agricultural Assistance (AA)	86.2	1.4	88.9	3.2
Social Welfare (SW)	57.8	20.6	45.4	19.5
Internal (I)	72.2	2.7	69.1	2.7
Interbranch (IB)	80.5	2.0	78.8	2.6

Total House CC Votes:	2,001	Total Senate CC Votes:	2,548
Overall House CC Success:	66.8 percent	Overall Senate CC Success:	65.1 percent

Table 3–2

Success of House Conservative Coalition
across Issue Dimensions (percent), by Year

Year	CL	GM	II	AA	SW	I	IB	Total Number CC Votes
1933	–	–	–	–	–	–	–	0
1934	100	100	–	–	–	–	–	2
1935	0	0	67	–	–	100	–	8
1936	–	–	–	–	–	–	–	0
1937	100	50	0	–	50	100	–	10
1938	–	–	–	–	–	–	–	0
1939	100	100	–	–	–	–	–	6
1940	–	100	100	–	83	–	0	16
1941	100	100	–	100	50	–	–	9
1942	100	100	100	100	67	–	–	11
1943	100	100	–	100	–	–	100	18
1944	100	88	–	50	100	–	–	17
1945	100	86	–	–	50	0	–	13
1946	86	94	–	100	100	0	–	35
1947	100	100	100	–	–	–	100	17
1948	100	100	100	–	100	–	–	17
1949	100	88	–	100	50	–	–	23
1950	100	89	–	–	100	50	0	19
1951	–	100	100	67	100	100	–	22
1952	100	100	80	–	67	–	–	20
1953	100	100	–	–	100	–	–	16
1954	100	100	100	–	100	–	–	8
1955	–	100	100	–	100	–	100	10
1956	–	67	100	–	–	–	–	7
1957	–	100	0	–	82	–	–	16
1958	100	75	–	–	50	–	57	14
1959	100	–	100	–	80	–	100	11
1960	–	75	–	–	27	–	–	19
1961	100	100	0	–	73	50	–	23
1962	0	100	14	–	50	100	–	16
1963	100	100	56	–	67	–	100	15
1964	100	100	50	–	33	–	100	12
1965	50	40	0	–	15	11	50	51
1966	71	25	38	–	17	–	–	37
1967	88	83	30	100	60	100	–	54
1968	62	71	44	100	62	–	–	51
1969	88	73	65	–	75	67	50	45

Table 3–2 continued

Year	CL	GM	II	AA	SW	I	IB	Total Number CC Votes
1970	50	86	64	100	60	100	–	44
1971	89	64	90	100	60	100	100	99
1972	84	73	82	100	75	–	100	82
1973	88	72	49	–	63	100	100	133
1974	78	80	56	–	45	100	100	102
1975	62	42	74	50	36	100	100	170
1976	87	61	47	100	39	100	100	143
1977	91	56	47	100	65	78	100	157
1978	33	63	54	100	57	100	0	164
1979	85	79	53	–	76	100	–	144
1980	83	74	59	–	44	100	100	95

conservative coalition in the House has enjoyed more success are the two minor clusters of agricultural assistance and interbranch issues.

The variable but generally declining success of the House conservative coalition on civil liberties votes is shown in Table 3–2, and its annual rate of appearance on that dimension is presented in Table 3–3. The civil liberties dimension is the fourth most frequently occurring bloc of House coalition votes, after government management, international involvement, and social welfare, as Table 3–1 shows. This result suggests that the conservative coalition in the House generally has paid comparatively less attention to civil liberties issues than to economic and foreign policy concerns. A bit more than 12 percent of all House coalition votes have been concerned with this set of issues.

The annual data presented in Table 3–3 suggest that the conservative coalition in the House has been only intermittently concerned with the civil liberties dimension. In some years, particularly during the 1950s, this issue cluster was totally absent from the record of roll call appearances. The coalition's interest in this dimension was greatest in most sessions of the 1941–50 period and peaked again after 1964, when equality of blacks and later the rights of draftees, women, protesters, and criminal defendants became salient issues.

The conservative coalition in the Senate has been dramatically less successful on the civil liberties dimension than its House counterpart, winning on only about 57 percent of its appearances, as may be seen in Table 3–1. The Senate coalition was less successful only on the social welfare dimension.

Table 3–4 demonstrates both the much poorer overall record of the Senate conservative coalition on civil liberties votes relative to the coalition's success in

Table 3–3

Frequency of House Conservative Coalition Appearances across Issue Dimensions (percent), by Year

Year	CL	GM	II	AA	SW	I	IB	Total Number CC Votes
1933	–	–	–	–	–	–	–	0
1934	50	50	0	0	0	0	0	2
1935	25	25	38	0	0	12	0	8
1936	–	–	–	–	–	–	–	0
1937	10	40	20	0	20	10	0	10
1938	–	–	–	–	–	–	–	0
1939	17	83	0	0	0	0	0	6
1940	0	50	6	0	38	0	6	16
1941	33	33	0	11	22	0	0	9
1942	9	27	9	27	27	0	0	11
1943	33	50	0	11	0	0	6	18
1944	29	47	0	12	12	0	0	17
1945	15	54	8	0	15	8	0	13
1946	20	51	0	3	23	3	0	35
1947	18	71	6	0	0	0	6	17
1948	35	47	6	0	18	0	0	17
1949	9	70	0	4	17	0	0	23
1950	16	47	0	0	21	11	5	19
1951	0	59	9	14	9	9	0	22
1952	10	50	25	0	15	0	0	20
1953	6	62	0	0	31	0	0	16
1954	12	25	25	0	38	0	0	8
1955	0	60	10	0	20	0	10	10
1956	0	86	14	0	0	0	0	7
1957	0	25	6	0	69	0	0	16
1958	7	29	0	0	14	0	50	14
1959	18	0	9	0	45	0	27	11
1960	0	21	0	0	79	0	0	19
1961	4	30	9	0	48	9	0	23
1962	6	19	44	0	25	6	0	16
1963	7	7	60	0	20	0	7	15
1964	8	17	33	0	25	0	17	12
1965	20	20	14	0	25	18	4	51
1966	19	11	22	0	49	0	0	37
1967	15	22	19	6	28	11	0	54
1968	16	33	18	2	31	0	0	51
1969	18	24	38	0	9	7	4	45

Table 3–3 continued

Year	CL	GM	II	AA	SW	I	IB	Total Number CC Votes
1970	5	32	25	2	34	2	0	44
1971	22	17	30	1	25	3	1	99
1972	23	32	21	1	20	0	4	82
1973	12	35	26	0	23	2	3	133
1974	18	34	26	0	20	1	1	102
1975	8	50	25	2	13	1	1	170
1976	10	49	21	1	16	1	2	143
1977	7	32	31	1	22	6	1	157
1978	9	38	32	1	18	1	1	164
1979	9	50	26	0	12	3	0	144
1980	6	44	36	0	9	2	2	95

Table 3–4
Success of Senate Conservative Coalition across
Issue Dimensions (percent), by Year

Year	CL	GM	II	AA	SW	I	IB	Total Number CC Votes
1933	–	57	–	100	50	–	100	13
1934	–	75	–	–	100	–	–	9
1935	–	67	–	50	–	–	–	5
1936	–	0	–	–	–	–	–	1
1937	–	50	–	–	33	–	–	5
1938	100	100	–	100	100	–	–	5
1939	–	100	–	–	33	–	–	5
1940	0	50	–	–	50	–	–	10
1941	–	50	–	0	–	–	–	3
1942	–	100	–	100	–	–	–	5
1943	100	75	–	57	–	–	–	15
1944	42	100	100	100	67	–	–	25
1945	100	100	–	–	100	100	100	10
1946	67	86	100	100	100	–	–	40
1947	100	92	–	–	100	–	100	21
1948	100	100	100	100	100	100	–	20

Year	CL	GM	II	AA	SW	I	IB	Total Number CC Votes
1949	100	100	100	100	100	100	100	35
1950	100	93	14	–	100	–	100	27
1951	100	100	80	100	33	–	100	28
1952	–	100	100	–	–	100	–	20
1953	–	100	100	–	100	100	100	18
1954	100	100	75	100	100	100	100	33
1955	100	100	100	0	–	–	100	7
1956	–	100	100	100	50	–	100	21
1957	–	100	100	–	100	100	100	12
1958	60	93	100	100	50	–	100	38
1959	50	100	88	100	27	100	–	40
1960	100	67	50	100	50	–	–	46
1961	100	71	27	–	34	100	–	65
1962	100	77	33	–	80	–	–	34
1963	–	50	60	50	32	100	–	43
1964	21	78	33	100	33	67	80	51
1965	50	36	75	100	15	100	50	61
1966	90	30	75	–	44	–	0	70
1967	33	62	56	–	38	100	–	56
1968	77	90	90	100	67	33	50	70
1969	50	78	69	100	60	0	33	69
1970	95	73	62	100	43	50	50	108
1971	77	87	90	100	82	100	50	120
1972	59	67	69	–	46	100	100	152
1973	13	63	79	75	12	100	67	123
1974	43	52	77	50	38	–	100	162
1975	23	55	67	100	25	25	80	166
1976	24	64	50	100	29	33	83	177
1977	67	84	67	–	33	100	–	187
1978	31	72	27	100	44	–	–	119
1979	42	72	56	–	67	–	100	91
1980	48	82	89	100	77	0	100	106

the House and the very significant drop-off in Senate success in most recent sessions of Congress. The civil liberties dimension is the fourth most frequently occurring bloc of conservative coalition votes in the Senate, just as in the House. It appears on just over 13 percent of all Senate coalition roll calls. The coalition in both chambers seems to have been relatively much less concerned with civil

Table 3–5

Frequency of Senate Conservative Coalition Appearances across Issue Dimensions (percent), by Year

Year	CL	GM	II	AA	SW	I	IB	Total Number CC Votes
1933	0	54	0	8	15	0	23	13
1934	0	89	0	0	11	0	0	9
1935	0	60	0	40	0	0	0	5
1936	0	100	0	0	0	0	0	1
1937	0	40	0	0	60	0	0	5
1938	40	20	0	20	20	0	0	5
1939	0	40	0	0	60	0	0	5
1940	20	60	0	0	20	0	0	10
1941	0	67	0	33	0	0	0	3
1942	0	40	0	60	0	0	0	5
1943	27	27	0	47	0	0	0	15
1944	48	24	8	8	12	0	0	25
1945	10	30	0	0	30	10	20	10
1946	8	55	2	12	22	0	0	40
1947	14	62	0	0	14	0	10	21
1948	20	25	30	5	15	5	0	20
1949	3	49	9	6	9	17	9	35
1950	7	57	25	0	7	0	4	28
1951	4	61	18	4	11	0	4	28
1952	0	65	30	0	0	5	0	20
1953	0	62	17	0	6	11	6	18
1954	6	48	12	12	9	3	9	33
1955	14	43	14	14	0	0	14	7
1956	0	43	14	14	19	0	10	21
1957	0	42	8	0	17	8	25	12
1958	13	39	8	16	21	0	3	38
1959	10	20	20	5	38	8	0	40
1960	26	26	9	4	35	0	0	46
1961	12	11	23	0	49	5	0	65
1962	21	38	26	0	15	0	0	34
1963	0	9	23	5	58	5	0	43
1964	27	18	18	4	18	6	10	51
1965	10	18	20	3	44	2	3	61
1966	14	14	11	0	59	0	1	70
1967	11	23	16	0	38	12	0	56
1968	31	30	14	4	13	4	3	70
1969	9	36	23	4	22	1	4	69

Year	CL	GM	II	AA	SW	I	IB	Total Number CC Votes
1970	19	20	22	3	28	4	4	108
1971	11	19	51	1	14	1	3	120
1972	22	32	28	0	16	1	1	152
1973	12	41	27	3	13	1	2	123
1974	17	48	19	1	13	0	2	162
1975	13	39	16	5	14	10	3	166
1976	10	70	10	1	4	2	3	177
1977	5	67	10	0	16	3	0	187
1978	11	30	34	3	21	0	0	119
1979	13	58	20	0	7	0	2	91
1980	20	48	8	1	21	1	1	106

liberties matters than with matters of "big government," social welfare, and defense and foreign policy.

The longitudinal data in Table 3–5 indicate the relatively late-blooming and only intermittent interest of the Senate conservative coalition in the civil liberties dimension. The data demonstrate, however, that civil liberties has been the single most frequently appearing issue dimension in the Senate a bit more often (four times—1938, 1944, 1964, and 1968) than in the House (twice—in 1934 and 1941).

The Government Management Dimension

The government management cluster covers a wide assortment of "big government" issues pertaining to the role of the federal government in stimulating and regulating the nation's economy, specifically the regulation of labor unions, the relationship between the federal government and state and local governments, congressional control over the affairs of the District of Columbia, energy legislation, the size of the federal budget and the distribution of the federal tax burden, and pollution control. The conservative coalition consistently opposes expansion of government economic controls, stimulation of the economy through increasing the budget deficit, more equitable distribution of tax payments, and programs to make business more responsible for cleaning up or preventing pollution. The coalition is in favor of strict limitations on the rights and power of labor unions, maintaining the power of local political and economic elites against federally sponsored economic and social programs, continued congressional control over the District of Columbia, lifting of federal control over business pricing policies, and pursuing a balanced budget.

It can be seen from Table 3–1 that in the House the government management issue cluster is by far the single most frequently occurring dimension on which the conservative coalition forms. In the House, 38 percent of all coalition appearances were concerned with the government management dimension.

The dominance of the government management dimension does not fully carry over to the conservative coalition's success on this set of House roll calls. The coalition's success rate on these issues has been a bit under 72 percent, only slightly above its overall victory rate of about 67 percent and below its level of success on civil liberties, internal, interbranch, and agricultural assistance roll calls.

As is evident from Table 3–2, the success of the House conservative coalition on government management votes has varied greatly since the early 1960s, falling to extremely low levels in 1965, 1966, and 1975. Overall, the trend over time is one of declining but still generally high levels of success. The conservative coalition has not lost its influence on this dimension even after suffering severe reverses in some sessions.

Table 3–3 shows that the government management dimension in the House has been consistently on the agenda of the conservative coalition. This was the most frequently occurring single dimension during twenty-nine of the forty-five sessions in which the coalition appeared in the House. This dominance was most pronounced from the 1930s to the mid-1950s, after which time issues of economic control declined in relative importance until the Ninetieth Congress (1967–68).

The conservative coalition in the Senate has devoted an even greater proportion of its attention to the set of government management issues than has the coalition in the House. This may be seen in Table 3–1, which shows that nearly 40 percent of all Senate coalition appearances are concerned with this issue cluster. In both chambers, the frequency of occurrence of government management votes far outstrips the salience of any of the other six issue dimensions.

The coalition's success rate on government management votes in the Senate is approximately 74 percent, which is slightly higher than the rate of success enjoyed by the House coalition on this dimension and also somewhat in excess of the overall Senate success rate of 65 percent. Table 3–4 demonstrates the highly variable success of the Senate coalition on the government management dimension over time, broadly comparable to the performance in the House. The long-term decline in Senate coalition success on this issue cluster, partially offset in the Ninety-fifth and Ninety-sixth Congresses, is evident from the table. A comparison of the success of the conservative coalition on government management issues in the two chambers, as seen in Tables 3–2 and 3–4, shows that success in the Senate has recently been greater than in the House.

A glance at Table 3–5 reveals that government management is the only issue dimension to appear in all forty-eight Senate sessions covered in this study. With relatively few exceptions, primarily in sessions dominated by social welfare issues, the government management dimension has been overwhelmingly dominant among Senate coalition appearances. There is a somewhat curvilinear pattern over time in the Senate coalition's concern with this issue dimension. Government management issues were strongly in evidence from 1933 up to 1958 and again since 1972, but much less significant during most sessions of the 1959–71 period. In the late 1970s, this dimension assumed massive importance, when a large number of ideologically divisive votes were taken on energy policies, deregulation of oil and natural gas pricing, regulation of business and labor practices, and budget targets.

The International Involvement Dimension

The direction of congressional conservatives' policy positions on international involvement issues has undergone a significant transformation. Strongly isolationist before World War II, the conservative coalition subsequently adopted a stridently anticommunist and interventionist foreign policy. It strongly supports high levels of defense spending and the adoption of new weapons systems. Conservatives in Congress have generally favored restrictive immigration policies, high levels of foreign military aid and low levels of foreign economic assistance, expansion of the nation's defense establishment, and American involvement in defense-oriented international institutions. The conservative coalition has generally opposed multilateral foreign aid programs, assistance to the United Nations and other nondefense international organizations, restrictions on military actions in Indochina and elsewhere in the world, and efforts to cut new programs from the military budget.

Table 3–1 shows that international involvement is the second most frequently occurring dimension of conservative coalition votes in the House, exceeded only by the government management issue cluster. About 23 percent of House coalition appearances have been devoted to international involvement issues.

The conservative coalition in the House has been relatively unsuccessful on its international involvement votes, winning on 57 percent of the roll calls that constitute this dimension in the House. The House coalition was more successful on every one of the other six issue dimensions.

The highly variable success of the House conservative coalition over time on international involvement issues is demonstrated in Table 3–2. In general, the coalition in the House only occasionally enjoyed a high degree of success on international involvement votes in the 1960s and 1970s.

The longitudinal data in Table 3–3 show the inconsistent and relatively late interest of the House conservative coalition in the international involvement dimension. This issue cluster was totally absent from the list of coalition appearances for eleven House sessions and did not regularly appear at a substantial level until 1962, although it was the single most frequently occurring issue cluster in 1935, 1962–64, 1969, and 1971. In more recent sessions, the Indochina war, foreign assistance, and efforts to expand defense programs have dominated this set of votes.

The conservative coalition in the Senate has been somewhat less interested in the international involvement dimension than has the coalition in the House. International involvement issues, forming on a bit less than 19 percent of all Senate coalition votes, constitute the third most frequently occurring set of issues in the Senate, after government management and social welfare. The Senate conservative coalition has been substantially more successful on this dimension, winning on just under 67 percent of the times it formed on these issues. This is, however, the third lowest victory rate for the conservative coalition among the seven issue dimensions in the Senate, exceeding the level of success of only the civil liberties and social welfare dimensions.

Table 3–4 shows that the success rate of the conservative coalition in the Senate was highly variable on international involvement issues during the 1960s and 1970s. Levels of coalition success were very low in 1950, 1961–62, 1964, and 1978. Table 3–5 indicates that the frequency of appearance of the international involvement dimension in the Senate has gone through three distinct phases. The dimension was totally absent in the Senate until 1944 and appeared very rarely until 1948. The rate of occurrence varied widely between 1949 and 1960, peaking at 30 percent of all appearances in 1952. Rates of appearance were relatively high though variable since 1961. The results for 1971 are distinctive, with over one-half of all coalition roll calls devoted to international involvement issues, especially the Indochina war and new defense programs. This was also the year in which the overall rate of appearance of the conservative coalition in the House as a proportion of nonunanimous roll calls attained its highest level in history.

The Agricultural Assistance Dimension

This dimension involves a narrowly constricted set of votes relating to acreage restrictions, federal health standards for food processing and food growing, and provision of federal subsidies in the form of price supports to the farm sector. The coalition has generally favored laissez faire in the farm sector. It has, for example, opposed the direct payment of subsidies to farmers and opposed federally mandated health inspections of livestock and crops.

Table 3–1 demonstrates the relative insignificance to the conservative coalition in the House of the agricultural assistance dimension, which, as the least frequently occurring dimension in the House, appears on less than 2 percent of all

House coalition roll calls. Only a small fraction of all House votes pertaining to agricultural assistance are characterized by formation of the southern Democrat–Republican alliance.

Although the conservative coalition in the House seems to be decidedly uninterested in most agricultural assistance issues, it has enjoyed its greatest success on that set of votes, winning on over 86 percent of the roll calls on which this dimension emerged. Of course, the small base for the calculation of this success rate makes interpretation of the relative power of the coalition on this issue dimension rather tenuous.

It is shown in Table 3–2 that the House conservative coalition has been consistently very successful on agricultural assistance votes in the sixteen sessions during which the coalition formed on this dimension. This issue cluster, however, has appeared only spasmodically in the House and was a significant factor only in the 1941–44 period and again in 1951. It has never, with the possible exception of 1942, represented a dominant dimension of House conservative coalition votes.

The conservative coalition in the Senate has been somewhat more concerned with the agricultural assistance dimension than has the coalition in the House. As Table 3–1 shows, about 3 percent of all Senate coalition appearances involve agricultural assistance issues. In both chambers, this dimension is clearly a relatively insignificant source of conservative coalition activity.

The success rate of nearly 89 percent is the highest enjoyed by the coalition on all Senate issue dimensions, as in the House. From Table 3–4 it can be seen that the Senate conservative coalition has remained highly successful on this issue dimension over five decades. Sessions of low coalition success occur infrequently, and total success on the small number of agricultural assistance votes occurring in a session is the norm.

The data in Table 3–5 show that the agricultural assistance dimension in the Senate has appeared in all but seventeen of the forty-eight sessions covered in this study, a substantially greater rate of formation than in the House. This dimension dominated Senate coalition votes in 1942 and 1943, but has disappeared periodically and appeared as an important issue cluster only during the 1941–43 and 1954–56 periods.

The Social Welfare Dimension

The social welfare dimension pertains to a wide range of issues concerning the quality of human life: public housing, urban renewal, food stamps, the rights of labor unions to organize and pursue the interests of their members, educational support and educational opportunities, urban needs, mass transit, employee safety, and employment opportunities and the monetary rewards of employment. Programmatic and budgetary support for all such policies connote a liberal policy position. The conservative coalition forms in opposition to proposals to endorse the above principles or to expand either symbolic or material support for efforts in keeping with those principles.

Table 3–1 demonstrates that social welfare issues constitute the third most frequently occurring dimension of conservative coalition roll calls in the House, accounting for just over 20 percent of all coalition appearances. Only the government management and international involvement dimensions occur with greater frequency.

The conservative coalition has been successful on about 58 percent of the votes on which the social welfare dimension has appeared in the House. This is the second lowest rate of success for the House coalition on any issue cluster, exceeding only the success rate on international involvement issues. The policy significance of this finding lies in the fact that on what might be regarded as "gut" liberal issues, the liberal forces are frequently victorious and congressional conservatives are often incapable of preventing (and perhaps occasionally not willing to forestall) the adoption of social legislation that promises benefits to substantial segments of almost every congressional constituency.

It is clear from Table 3–2 that the success of the House conservative coalition on social welfare issues has been highly variable and has probably declined over time. Success on this dimension was lowest in 1960, 1964–66, and 1975–76. The longitudinal data on House coalition appearances in Table 3–3 show the dominance of the social welfare dimension in 1942, 1954, 1957, 1959–61, 1965–67, and 1970. This dimension, however, is totally absent in six sessions, most recently in 1956. The data suggest a noticeable decline since the 1960s in the salience to the House conservative coalition of social welfare issues.

In the Senate, the social welfare dimension of conservative coalition votes is the second most frequently occurring issue cluster, after government management. As is evident from Table 3–1, just under 20 percent of all Senate coalition appearances fall into the social welfare dimension, approximately equal to the relative frequency of House coalition appearances on the same cluster of issues.

Compared to the other six issue dimensions, the Senate coalition has been markedly less successful on social welfare issues, winning on only about 45 percent of the roll calls on which it has formed on these issues. This is by far the lowest success rate for the Senate coalition on any issue dimension, a result that is generally consistent with that for the House. Table 3–4 demonstrates that the success of the Senate conservative coalition on social welfare issues has varied greatly over time and has generally declined in recent years. The Ninety-fifth Congress (1979–80), however, was characterized by sharply higher rates of conservative victories on social welfare issues.

The data in Table 3–5 show that with some exceptions (in 1935–36, 1941–43, 1952, and 1955) the social welfare dimension has been a consistent component of the issue agenda of the conservative coalition in the Senate. This was the single largest issue dimension in 1937, 1939, 1945, 1959–61, 1963, 1965–67, and 1970, but declined noticeably in significance in the 1970s.

The Internal Dimension

The cluster of conservative coalition roll calls constituting the internal dimension consists of votes on the rules of each chamber, quorum calls, and votes on such "housekeeping" issues as the ages and remuneration of Capitol pages, the number of Capitol elevator operators, and the assignment of staff and allocation of funding to congressional committees. The conservative coalition supports retention of most extant congressional rules, particularly Senate Rule 22 governing extended debate, and generally opposes expanded committee staffing and financial support.

This dimension is clearly not of major importance among House conservative coalition appearances. It accounts for less than 3 percent of all coalition House votes. We can see in Table 3–1 that the internal dimension is the third least frequently occurring vote cluster in the House, exceeding only the interbranch and agricultural assistance dimensions in number of appearances.

The conservative coalition in the House has been only moderately successful on the internal dimension, winning about 72 percent of the time that it has formed on this issue cluster. The data in Table 3–2 demonstrate substantial variation over time in the level of conservative coalition success in the House on the internal dimension. The table further shows that coalition success has increased on this issue cluster since its very poor showing in 1965.

Table 3–3 shows that the internal dimension is only intermittently a visible component of House conservative coalition roll call activity. This dimension is totally missing in twenty-four sessions and has exceeded 10 percent of all coalition appearances in only five sessions.

From Table 3–1 we see that the frequency of appearance of the internal dimension on conservative coalition votes is the same in the Senate and the House. In both chambers, this dimension is relatively insignificant. The coalition in the Senate has been slightly less successful on the internal dimension than in the House, winning about 69 percent of the time this dimension has appeared on Senate coalition roll calls.

From Table 3–4 it appears that the conservative coalition in the Senate has gone through two distinct phases of success on the internal dimension. The coalition was undefeated on this issue cluster before 1964. Since 1964, the coalition's success rate has been highly variant and frequently at a level of 50 percent or below. The overall trend seems to be toward reduced success for the Senate conservative coalition on the internal dimension.

Table 3–5 demonstrates the intermittent significance of the internal dimension to the coalition in the Senate. Not surprisingly, it has generally occurred with greatest frequency during those Senate sessions in which liberals attempted to eliminate or revise the filibuster rule.

The Interbranch Dimension

The interbranch dimension of conservative coalition votes is concerned primarily with decisions on the distribution of power within the federal government. This dimension includes attempts to limit the scope of judicial review or to restrict the size of the White House staff, as well as efforts to determine the basis of representation of state legislatures, as in the "Dirksen amendment," and certain exercises of the legislative veto over actions taken or proposed by administrative agencies. The direction of conservative coalition policy positions on this dimension is largely a function of the specific intent of judicial decisions and of the explicit policy thrust of executive branch actions. The coalition favors restrictions on the scope of such actions when they have a liberal flavor in the sense of endorsing a greater scope and more openness of national government institutions and processes.

The interbranch dimension is the second least frequently occurring issue cluster in the House, accounting for only about 2 percent of all House coalition appearances, as shown in Table 3–1. The House conservative coalition has been highly successful on this dimension, winning on over 80 percent of the votes that form this issue cluster. This level of success is exceeded only by the agricultural assistance dimension of House roll calls and is substantially above the overall success rate of the House coalition. Table 3–2 shows the variable but increasing success of the conservative coalition in the House on the interbranch dimension. Since 1971 the coalition has been defeated on this set of issues only once, in 1978.

Table 3–3 demonstrates the infrequent salience of the interbranch dimension to the House coalition. This issue cluster disappears periodically and was absent in twenty-five House sessions. Interbranch votes exceeded 10 percent of annual House coalition appearances only in 1955, 1958–59, and 1964, although this issue cluster was dominant in 1958.

The conservative coalition in the Senate has been only marginally more interested in the interbranch dimension than has the House coalition. In the Senate, interbranch issues constitute the single least frequently occurring dimension of coalition roll calls, covering just over 2.5 percent of Senate coalition appearances. As Table 3–1 shows, the Senate conservative coalition has been highly successful on the interbranch dimension, winning at a greater rate (approximately 79 percent) than on any other dimension except for agricultural assistance.

Table 3–4 demonstrates that there has been a long-term decline in the success of the Senate conservative coalition on the interbranch dimension, though a recent resurgence is evident in the Ninety-fifth Congress. The data suggest that there have been two distinct periods of coalition success on this issue cluster, with the bloc of Senate conservatives going undefeated until 1964 and winning at highly variant rates afterward.

In Table 3–5 the only occasional salience of the interbranch dimension becomes clear. This set of issues constituted 10 percent or more of annual Senate coalition appearances only in 1933, 1945, 1947, 1955, 1956, 1957, and 1964. This dimension has not dominated coalition appearances in the Senate in any session. During the 1970s, interbranch issues appeared at a low and steady level.

On the Distinctiveness of Issue Dimensions

Some important evidence bearing on the separability, or distinctiveness, of the issue dimensions examined in this chapter is presented in Table 3–6. The table shows overall mean (average) levels of cohesion with which Republicans, northern Democrats, and southern Democrats have fought their policy-making battles, together with a rough distribution of cohesion scores for individual votes across several ranges of intensities. Cohesion here simply means the percentage of all members of a bloc who vote together on a roll call. The Republican and southern Democrat cohesion scores indicate the intensity with which each group supports the position taken by the conservative coalition; the northern Democrat cohesion scores measure the intensity with which that group opposes the conservative policy position.

The crucial point that emerges from Table 3–6 is that each issue dimension has a fairly distinctive average level of cohesion for the three relevant voting blocs and a distinctive distributional pattern of intensity of commitment to a policy position among Republicans (R), northern Democrats (ND), and southern Democrats (SD). In the House, for example, Republicans have been intensely cohesive on civil liberties, internal, social welfare, and government management issue roll calls, while northern Democrats have shown the greatest interest in social welfare issues and southern Democratic representatives have shown their greatest commitment to the civil liberties dimension. In the Senate, the southern Democrats' intensity on the civil liberties issue dimension and the northern Democrats' commitment to social welfare issues are evident, just as in the House, but Senate Republicans have shown most intense interest in the interbranch cluster.

We can conclude with some certainty, then, that what were treated earlier as substantively diverse issue dimensions or categories actually do show empirically different patterns of Republican, southern Democrat, and northern Democrat involvement. These are in that sense distinct issue areas.

Table 3–6

Mean Cohesion Scores by Issue Dimension (percent)

Issue Dimension	Bloc	Mean Cohesion	Distribution				
			50 + −60	60 + −70	70 + −80	80 + −90	90 + −100
			HOUSE				
Civil Liberties	R	81.6	7.0	11.1	22.5	30.3	29.1
	ND	73.4	23.8	20.5	18.4	21.7	15.6
	SD	77.8	19.7	13.9	16.4	20.1	29.9
International	R	76.5	15.4	18.0	20.3	26.8	19.5
Involvement	ND	76.0	14.3	16.9	26.0	27.9	14.9
	SD	72.4	23.6	21.2	25.1	18.8	11.3
Internal	R	81.2	3.7	16.7	18.5	31.5	29.6
	ND	76.7	20.4	18.5	16.7	18.5	25.9
	SD	71.1	37.0	11.1	24.1	13.0	14.8
Agricultural	R	77.9	13.8	20.7	17.2	20.7	27.6
Assistance	ND	72.6	20.7	27.6	17.2	17.2	17.2
	SD	76.1	24.1	6.9	27.6	17.2	24.1
Interbranch	R	80.5	14.6	4.9	24.4	29.3	26.8
	ND	80.1	9.8	17.1	14.6	29.3	29.3
	SD	75.6	19.5	24.4	17.1	12.2	26.8
Social Welfare	R	81.1	7.5	10.4	20.9	34.7	26.5
	ND	84.4	6.6	9.5	16.0	21.8	46.1
	SD	69.3	29.9	24.8	23.1	16.5	5.8
Government	R	81.5	9.4	12.0	20.0	27.7	31.0
Management	ND	77.0	14.4	17.7	22.1	26.7	19.1
	SD	70.3	27.3	23.6	24.1	16.6	8.4
			SENATE				
Civil Liberties	R	69.5	25.9	34.4	18.4	12.5	8.7
	ND	79.8	9.3	14.3	26.2	24.5	25.7
	SD	81.8	10.5	12.5	21.9	19.8	35.3
International	R	74.3	15.2	22.3	30.3	21.9	10.3
Involvement	ND	74.0	17.9	22.1	24.2	27.2	8.6
	SD	73.2	23.2	22.7	20.0	20.2	13.9
Internal	R	72.6	16.2	35.3	22.1	14.7	11.8
	ND	75.6	14.7	22.1	26.5	19.1	17.6
	SD	79.3	13.2	14.7	29.4	13.2	29.4
Agricultural	R	75.3	14.8	27.2	18.5	17.3	22.2
Assistance	ND	66.9	30.9	32.1	24.7	11.1	1.2
	SD	74.3	22.2	18.5	24.7	16.0	18.5
Interbranch	R	82.3	6.0	17.9	16.4	20.9	38.8
	ND	75.2	14.9	22.4	31.3	17.9	13.4
	SD	74.1	19.4	22.4	22.4	23.9	11.9

Issue Dimension	Bloc	Mean Cohesion	Distribution				
			50 + –60	60 + –70	70 + –80	80 + –90	90 + –100
			SENATE				
Social Welfare	R	73.4	18.1	27.4	23.3	17.7	13.5
	ND	82.5	10.9	12.3	13.3	22.7	40.8
	SD	74.0	19.1	21.9	26.6	19.3	13.1
Government	R	78.7	11.0	18.6	21.6	24.9	23.9
Management	ND	75.4	17.5	21.0	22.5	21.0	17.9
	SD	73.0	20.8	22.4	24.0	24.1	8.7

Time-Series Analysis of the Major Issue Dimensions

The data given in Table 3–1 clearly indicate that congressional conservatives show a great deal of interest in certain issues that appear on roll call votes taken in the House and Senate but tend to devote much less attention to other substantive matters. For convenience, the seldom occurring agricultural assistance, internal, and interbranch clusters may be referred to as the minor issue dimensions. The four remaining issue clusters—civil liberties, government management, international involvement, and social welfare—are considered the major dimensions of ideological cleavage in Congress.

A closer look at the historical patterns of the rate of appearance of each major dimension is important in providing useful insights into the processes that have shaped the importance of different issue dimensions and helping to project past trends into the future. The time-series method serves both these purposes. Table 3–7 is a set of forecasts resulting from reasonable time-series models for the data in Tables 3–3 and 3–5 on conservative coalition appearances on each of the four major issue dimensions in each chamber. The time-series models that produced these forecasts are presented in Appendix B.

Two salient points should be made about the results in Table 3–7. The first important finding is that each major issue dimension follows a relatively simple historical process, as may be seen from the models in the Appendix. Each model reveals a strong pattern of stability relating current values to past values. The second useful conclusion is that the forecasted values for the 1981–84 period show that, in the absence of dramatic events that may disrupt previous patterns of coalition formation on major issue dimensions, we can expect little change in the future relative import of these four issue clusters. Practically all future conservative coalition roll call votes should occur along these well-established lines. One potential future development is a decline in the relative significance of the

Table 3–7

ARIMA Model Forecasts for Major Issue Dimensions, 1981–1984

	Forecasts (Percent)			
Issue Dimension	1981	1982	1983	1984
	HOUSE			
Civil Liberties	8	7	8	7
Government Management	46	45	46	46
International Involvement	29	25	22	20
Social Welfare	17	18	17	18
	SENATE			
Civil Liberties	16	18	17	18
Government Management	45	44	43	42
International Involvement	10	12	12	13
Social Welfare	20	20	20	19

international involvement dimension in the House. Otherwise, these results by themselves do not suggest any marked changes in the focus of conservatives' interests in Congress.

Summary and Conclusions

The conservative coalition clearly concentrates on certain issues and largely ignores others. In both chambers, the conservative coalition devotes by far the greatest attention to the single dimension of government management issues, pays much less and roughly equivalent attention to social welfare, international involvement, and civil liberties issues, and virtually ignores the agricultural assistance, internal, and interbranch dimensions.

It is equally clear that the Republican–southern Democrat alliance has not been a one-issue coalition. It has formed at substantial and practically identical rates on the same four major issue dimensions in the House as in the Senate. With the major exception of the social welfare dimension in the Senate, the coalition has won substantially more than a majority of its appearances on all issue clusters in both chambers.

The longitudinal data summarized in Tables 3–2 through 3–5 also generally support what I have called the policy coalition interpretation of congressional decision making. For the most part, the conservative coalition has been consistently very successful over time on most issue dimensions, with social welfare the standout exception in both chambers.

On the whole, the interpretation of the conservative coalition as a policy coalition is sustained by these data. The coalition appears often and successfully across a broad range of issues. Because levels of coalition success remain relatively high on all issues except social welfare in both chambers, the case cannot yet be made that a "benign" liberal coalition has supplanted the conservative coalition as the chief policy-making force in Congress. Such a coalition may become dominant at some future time, but such a fundamental change in the policy processes of Congress seems highly unlikely in light of the historical pattern of conservative resurgence after periods of low success or near disappearance. The high success rate of the coalition in both chambers in the Ninety-sixth Congress, combined with the election of large numbers of new conservatives to the House and Senate in 1980, provide an important object lesson in regard to the futility of declaring the demise of cross-party conservative cooperation when liberals enjoy their temporary periods of victory.

These results show, in contrast to what might be expected from the work of Berman, Lewis A. Froman, Jr.,[9] and others, that the conservative coalition in the House is not uniformly more successful than the coalition in the Senate on all issue dimensions. The House coalition has indeed been slightly more successful overall than the Senate coalition and, specifically, has a better record on the civil liberties, social welfare, internal, and interbranch dimensions. The House coalition was less successful, however, on the government management, international involvement, and agricultural assistance issue clusters. Probably the single most important cross-chamber comparative result is that House and Senate differences are substantial on only two issue dimensions, with the conservative coalition in the House markedly more successful only on the civil liberties and social welfare issue clusters.

Sharp fluctuations have occurred over time in the appearance and success of the conservative coalition on each policy dimension. Nonetheless, the major issue areas—government management, international involvement, social welfare, and civil liberties—arise in most sessions and show considerable long-run continuity. These results, together with the analysis of the policy direction of the coalition on the different issue areas, strongly suggest that the programmatic intent of the conservative coalition has remained generally constant over time. The exception is the policy shift to interventionist internationalism after World War II, but this may be read more as a change in the definition of the conservative foreign and defense position than as a reflection of any shift in the fundamental world view of congressional conservatives.

As the 1980s began, evidence of conservative success in congressional policy making led to the formation or revitalization of ideologically opposed interest groups. More will be said about this development later, but a 1982 form letter mailed out by one such group, the National Committee for an Effective Congress, details the issue content of liberal efforts to mobilize support against the surging conservative coalition in Congress. The emphasis in the following excerpt is in the original:

In reviewing the record of the current (97th) Congress, many concerned Americans are tempted to throw up their hands in despair. After all, a coalition of New Right Republicans and conservative Democrats has already managed to . . .

. . . *Slash* essential funds for child nutrition programs, *destroy* the job opportunities for unemployed urban teenagers, *restrict* family planning counseling, *virtually eliminate* support for the arts, humanities, and scientific research.

. . . At the same time this coalition of New Right Republicans and Southern Conservative Democrats has offset nearly all of the cuts it made in domestic programs by giving the Pentagon carte blanche approval for every new weapon system and other expenditure it can rationalize. And, to add insult to injury, this Congress has created unprecedented federal budget deficits by enacting a tax give-away program filled with loop-holes and tax breaks for oil companies and other special interests.[10]

As the decade of the 1980s progresses, the agenda for policy debates promises to follow the cleavages outlined here.

4

Committees, Seniority, and the Conservative Coalition

The literature on congressional committees, especially when focused on the effects of the seniority system, is replete with discussions of the disproportionate power exercised by conservative southern Democrats and midwestern Republicans who have survived in office long enough to climb the seniority ladder to positions of authority as chairmen or ranking members of standing committees. That this conclusion is a considerable oversimplification, especially as regards southern Democrats, has been shown, however, by Barbara Hinckley and others.[1] The safeness of most congressional elections throughout the nation provides potential rewards of committee power for members elected from any region.

The important point here is the potential impact on public policy decisions of skewing the positions of committee authority in favor of Congress's more conservative members. I will concentrate in this respect on the role of southern Democrats because Republicans have had an opportunity since 1933 to act as committee chairmen in both chambers only in 1947–48, in 1953–54, and, of course, at least for 1981–84 in the Senate. Of particular importance is to assess what relationship, if any, exists between the purported dominance of the committee system by conservative interests and the rates of appearance and success of the conservative coalition on the floor of the House and Senate.

Some interesting questions must be addressed on this score. Is there a trade-off between the recent loosening of conservative control over the committees and a higher rate of appearance by the conservative coalition on the floor? Is the coalition more successful on the floor when it is supported by conservative committee chairmen, whether they are southerners or nonsoutherners?[2] Is it true, as alleged, for example, by Joseph Clark,[3] that majorities of Republicans plus

Table 4–1

Democratic Standing Committee Chairmen and Ranking Minority Members, by South and Non-South

Year	Senate			House		
	Southern Democrats	Northern Democrats	Percent Southern Democrats	Southern Democrats	Northern Democrats	Percent Southern Democrats
1933	16	17	48	27	20	57
1934	16	17	48	25	22	53
1935	16	17	48	24	23	51
1936	16	17	48	24	23	51
1937	16	17	48	23	24	49
1938	15	18	45	23	24	49
1939	16	17	48	21	27	44
1940	15	18	45	21	27	44
1941	17	16	52	19	29	40
1942	15	18	45	20	28	42
1943	17	16	52	25	23	52
1944	18	16	53	26	22	54
1945	17	15	53	25	23	52
1946	15	16	48	25	21	54
1947	7	8	47	12	8	60
1948	7	8	47	11	8	58
1949	7	9	44	11	9	55
1950	7	8	47	12	9	57
1951	8	7	53	10	9	53
1952	8	7	53	11	8	58
1953	6	6	50	11	8	58
1954	6	6	50	11	8	58
1955	8	7	53	13	6	68
1956	9	7	56	13	6	68
1957	8	7	53	12	7	63
1958	8	7	53	12	7	63
1959	10	6	63	13	7	65
1960	10	6	63	13	7	65
1961	10	6	63	12	8	60
1962	10	6	63	11	9	55
1963	10	6	63	11	9	55
1964	10	6	63	12	8	60
1965	10	6	63	13	7	65
1966	10	6	63	11	9	55
1967	10	6	63	11	9	55
1968	10	6	63	11	9	55
1969	10	6	63	9	12	43

	Senate			House		
Year	Southern Democrats	Northern Democrats	Percent Southern Democrats	Southern Democrats	Northern Democrats	Percent Southern Democrats
1970	10	6	63	9	12	43
1971	9	8	53	9	12	43
1972	9	8	53	9	12	43
1973	8	9	47	9	12	43
1974	8	9	47	9	12	43
1975	6	12	33	10	12	45
1976	6	12	33	10	12	45
1977	6	9	40	6	16	27
1978	6	9	40	6	16	27
1979	3	12	20	6	16	27
1980	3	12	20	6	16	27

conservative southern Democrats dominate the membership of many of the leading committees in Congress?

The Decline of the Southern Democrats

An important finding about the distribution of power within the congressional Democratic party[4] can be extracted from Table 4–1. The table shows the allocation of committee chairmanships between southern and northern senior Democrats from the Seventy-third to the Ninety-sixth Congresses, including ranking minority member (RMM) assignments for the two congresses (the Eightieth and Eighty-third) when Republicans were in the majority. Data for this table were compiled from appropriate issues of the *Congressional Directory*.

The central point of interest here is the dramatic decline in each chamber in the proportion of chairmanships held by the southern wing of the party. A generally even balance between southern and nonsouthern Democratic committee power existed in the Senate from the Seventy-third through the Eighty-fifth Congresses, and a similar equality held in the House for the Seventy-third through the Eighty-second Congresses. Southern ascendancy in committee leadership was most pronounced during the Eighty-sixth to Ninety-first Congresses (1959–70) in the Senate and for the Eighty-third to Eighty-ninth Congresses (1953–66) in the House. This is the classic era of committee dominance by senior southerners protected by uncompetitive elections and generally not answerable to the official party leadership.

The era of southern Democratic committee dominance was, however, relatively short-lived. By the Ninety-second Congress (1971–72) in the Senate and by the Ninetieth Congress (1967–68) in the House, the steady erosion of southern power had begun. Barely a quarter of the committee chairmanships in the House and the Senate combined were held by Democrats from Dixie at the start of the Ninety-sixth Congress in 1979. Increased electoral competitiveness in the South, the emergence of a large number of safe Democratic seats in urban northern districts, combined with deaths and a greater pace of retirement among the disproportionately southern senior Democrats in the 1970s have all contributed to the rise of northern Democrats to positions of committee power. Another important influence was the reforms of the 1970s, which, among other actions, returned to the Democratic caucus the power to select committee chairmen. One dramatic consequence of the reform movement was the unseating in 1975 of three southern chairmen—William Poage of Texas on the Agriculture Committee, F. Edward Hébert of Louisiana on the Armed Services Committee, and Wright Patman of Texas on the Banking and Currency Committee.

Democratic Committee Power and the Conservative Coalition

It is a given of studies of congressional behavior that the seniority system until recently has produced southern Democratic chairmen who have generally been out of touch with their usually more numerous nonsouthern party colleagues. To what extent does the roll call record reflect this truism, and to what extent have northern Democratic chairmen more faithfully reflected the views of their fellow congressmen from above an at least metaphoric Mason-Dixon line? [5]

This question is answered by the data in Tables 4–2 and 4–3. The tables compare, separately for the Senate and the House, the average conservative coalition support scores of southern Democratic chairmen or ranking minority members, northern Democratic committee leaders, and all southern and all northern Democratic members of the Senate and the House from 1933 to 1980. Information is also presented on the degree of conservative support among Republican chairmen and RMM's and among all Republicans.

Several fairly clear-cut conclusions can be drawn from these tabular results. First, among Democratic committee chairmen and RMM's in both chambers, southerners consistently are far more likely than northerners to be supportive of the conservative coalition. Coalition support has also been higher in the Senate than in the House among senior northern Democrats. There is no comparable cross-chamber difference among southern Democrats.

A second important point emerges from comparing committee leaders against the rank and file. Senior southern Democrats in the Senate have been somewhat more likely than all southern Democratic senators to support the cross-party

Table 4–2
Average Conservative Coalition Support (percent) among Senate
Committee Chairmen or Ranking Minority Members

Year	Southern Democratic Chairmen/ RMM	All Southern Democrats	Northern Democratic Chairmen/ RMM	All Northern Democrats	Republican Chairmen/ RMM	All Republicans
1933	56	51	33	30	55	56
1934	58	50	39	31	35	40
1935	46	45	26	30	54	53
1936	38	31	47	34	28	39
1937	49	51	45	33	71	69
1938	68	63	38	31	63	68
1939	51	45	38	30	67	65
1940	51	46	29	25	45	46
1941	51	56	13	20	33	46
1942	65	56	34	35	41	48
1943	50	54	29	26	36	51
1944	52	59	13	17	56	66
1945	44	44	15	24	64	65
1946	45	50	15	20	64	64
1947	77	60	23	15	59	83
1948	60	61	16	17	70	70
1949	62	58	25	23	59	64
1950	67	53	30	18	54	60
1951	73	64	31	24	60	66
1952	70	61	33	23	54	64
1953	87	67	24	20	63	76
1954	52	55	26	29	72	81
1955	55	57	33	25	65	69
1956	69	60	22	26	66	64
1957	67	63	27	22	71	78
1958	70	64	31	23	58	67
1959	70	63	29	20	74	72
1960	77	69	28	17	73	65
1961	72	67	21	13	71	64
1962	72	67	33	24	66	64
1963	73	61	22	17	68	65
1964	74	68	25	17	63	63
1965	61	60	23	16	68	71
1966	62	59	16	14	66	67
1967	64	62	31	19	61	60
1968	67	62	39	22	62	61
1969	66	67	25	21	70	65

Table 4–2 continued

Year	Southern Democratic Chairmen/ RMM	All Southern Democrats	Northern Democratic Chairmen/ RMM	All Northern Democrats	Republican Chairmen/ RMM	All Republicans
1970	57	59	28	16	66	57
1971	73	70	31	23	66	66
1972	66	62	23	16	65	63
1973	65	64	23	15	71	67
1974	70	68	23	17	66	61
1975	76	70	22	17	66	63
1976	74	64	25	17	65	65
1977	60	64	25	23	62	72
1978	60	62	27	21	52	61
1979	68	67	29	26	63	67
1980	57	61	20	22	63	67
Overall Mean	62.9	59.2	27.1	22.2	60.6	63.4

Table 4–3

Average Conservative Coalition Support (percent) among House Committee Chairmen or Ranking Minority Members

Year	Southern Democratic Chairmen/ RMM	All Southern Democrats	Northern Democratic Chairmen/ RMM	All Northern Democrats	Republican Chairmen/ RMM	All Republicans
1933	–	–	–	–	–	–
1934	60	66	30	30	38	41
1935	53	52	23	23	55	58
1936	–	–	–	–	–	–
1937	59	57	18	21	64	65
1938	–	–	–	–	–	–
1939	51	58	15	19	72	77
1940	48	55	20	21	67	71
1941	69	68	27	20	56	62
1942	66	60	26	24	61	63
1943	67	68	22	19	69	73
1944	64	64	20	17	67	72

Year	Southern Democratic Chairmen/ RMM	All Southern Democrats	Northern Democratic Chairmen/ RMM	All Northern Democrats	Republican Chairmen/ RMM	All Republicans
1945	61	62	22	15	62	64
1946	63	59	21	12	68	73
1947	64	72	17	20	82	81
1948	64	61	20	20	78	84
1949	65	61	8	12	72	71
1950	62	60	8	13	73	68
1951	67	67	7	11	84	74
1952	62	57	6	9	76	71
1953	64	66	20	15	84	80
1954	67	60	16	15	79	75
1955	64	67	22	18	67	69
1956	55	59	10	17	58	59
1957	67	63	17	12	67	69
1958	78	68	28	24	54	56
1959	82	82	23	16	75	82
1960	67	57	12	7	61	70
1961	60	61	16	14	70	74
1962	58	55	12	12	61	66
1963	61	58	13	11	63	67
1964	70	64	9	12	64	69
1965	63	61	6	9	71	74
1966	54	53	7	11	64	67
1967	59	65	18	13	73	74
1968	62	64	14	13	59	65
1969	61	68	33	18	65	67
1970	65	64	26	15	61	62
1971	61	63	42	22	69	70
1972	54	60	33	21	65	69
1973	59	63	27	20	75	72
1974	54	62	29	21	70	66
1975	61	63	22	20	72	75
1976	63	63	23	22	72	71
1977	58	63	20	23	72	76
1978	52	59	22	23	71	72
1979	67	64	23	26	72	78
1980	65	61	20	24	64	73
Overall Mean	62.1	62.3	19.4	17.3	67.6	69.7

alliance with Republicans, while in the House southern Democratic committee leaders are on the whole no more and no less supportive of the conservative coalition than their rank-and-file regional party colleagues. Given that a Democratic commitee chairman or RMM comes from the South, then, in the Senate the odds favor his or her being slightly more conservative than the average southern Democratic senator. In the House, the likelihood is that a southern Democratic committee leader will accurately mirror the degree of conservative sentiment among co-regional partisan colleagues.

If the seniority system, as is often alleged, produces "disloyal" wielders of Democratic committee authority, this tendency is not particularly evident when one compares the cross-party voting proclivities of southern Democratic committee chairmen or RMM's with those of all southern Democrats. But the extent to which southern Democratic committee leaders are out of step with the policy wishes of their northern colleagues is very clear from Tables 4–2 and 4–3. Conservative coalition support among southern Democratic chairmen is consistently very much higher than support levels among northern Democratic committee chiefs and is even more distant from the average level of coalition support among all northern Democrats. Whenever the northern progressive wing of the Democratic party has become dominant numerically at the expense of southerners within the party and at the expense of Republicans nationally, conservative southern committee chairmen have correspondingly become anachronistic. The sharp demise of southern committee power in the 1970s reflects for the most part the delayed effects of shifting national political trends, particularly the emergence of large numbers of safe northern liberal seats.

A third key point evident from Tables 4–2 and 4–3 relates to the effects of seniority among northern Democrats. In both chambers, but more clearly in the Senate, northern Democratic chairmen and RMM's are somewhat more supportive of the conservative coalition than are rank-and-file northern Democrats. Seniority has by and large not brought the most liberal northern Democrats to positions of committee power, but there have been periods, especially the years 1949–52 and 1964–66, when the voting records of northern Democratic committee leaders in the House have been strongly liberal.

Finally, Republican committee leaders' support for the conservative coalition is not markedly different from levels of support among southern Democratic chairmen or ranking minority members. The House data, however, suggest a greater degree of conservatism among Republican than among southern Democratic committee leaders. There is no substantial difference in average levels of conservative coalition support between Republican chairmen or RMM's and rank-and-file Republicans in either chamber. As is also true among southern Democrats, the average degree of conservatism among Republican committee leaders seems to be a fair reflection of ideological commitments among Republican legislators as a whole.

Time-Series Analysis of Conservatism among Committee Leaders

The data in Tables 4–2 and 4–3 may be usefully analyzed by time-series methods. It has been established that there are sharp differences in historical levels of conservative coalition support between southern and northern Democratic committee leaders. It was also shown that conservatism was generally greater in the House among Republican than among southern Democratic RMM's and chairmen.

The appropriate time-series models for these various data sets are presented in Appendix C. Forecasts resulting from these models are given in Table 4–4. These models demonstate several important points about the relative levels of support for the conservative coalition among senior southern Democrats, northern Democrats, and Republicans who have risen to positions of committee power. First, each time series shows that there has been no long-term change in the average degree of conservatism among any of the three groups of committee leaders. Levels of conservative coalition support in recent years among committee chairmen of RMM's are a legacy of stable patterns established in earlier decades.

Second, each univariate process is a fairly simple function of all previous observations and of the immediately preceding two or three years for Senate

Table 4–4

Time-Series Forecasts of Conservative Coalition Support among Committee Chairmen/Ranking Minority Members, 1981–1984

Chairmen/RMM Bloc	Forecasts			
	1981	1982	1983	1984
Southern Democrats—House (1939–80)	64	63	63	63
Northern Democrats—House (1939–80)	20	19	19	19
Republicans—House (1939–80)	69	67	68	68
Southern Democrats—Senate (1933–80)	60	62	62	63
Northern Democrats—Senate (1933–80)	25	27	24	26
Republicans—Senate (1933–80)	64	67	63	61

Republican and northern Democratic committee leaders. That these models are all virtually identical signifies that patterns of conservatism among the more senior members of each of the three voting blocs have been firmly established and deeply ingrained within the congressional policy-making system.

Third, the 1981–84 forecasts produced by these models are generally consistent with recent historical patterns and with the total accumulated pattern of half a century. One fairly small but potentially important departure from past patterns is a projected increase in conservative support among Senate Republican chairmen/RMM's. The forecasts also imply some very modest increase in coalition support among Senate southern Democrats. Whether such trends in fact occur in the future is, of course, speculative, but these results at the very least provide useful benchmarks for comparing the actual history of future developments with what is projected under the assumption that the past is the best way to understand the present and the future.

Conservative Committee Power and Action on the Floor

If the presence of generally conservative southern Democratic or Republican chairmen has meaning for the activity of the conservative coalition, it should be manifested in two ways. One effect of conservative committee dominance should be to block the appearance of legislation containing controversial progressive provisions that might in turn lead to the appearance of the conservative coalition on the floor. That is, we would expect to see lower rates of coalition formation on roll call votes when southern Democrats or Republicans effectively dominate the consideration of which legislation will make it out of committee and onto the floor. We would similarly anticipate higher rates of coalition formation when fewer Republicans or Dixie Democrats are in positions of authority to prevent liberal initiatives from emerging for further action beyond the committee level.

The second expected effect is that southern Democratic or Republican committee chairmen would be able to use their individual prestige and the normal conservative advantage in parliamentary arithmetic to carry the battle on the floor successfully in favor of the coalition's position. We should see greater coalition success on the floor when southern Democrats or Republicans are dominant among the ranks of committee chairmen and lower coalition success when a larger proportion of committee chairmanships are held by northern Democrats.

The first of these expected relationships is minimally true for the House ($r = -.11$), but is essentially nonexistent and in the wrong direction in the Senate ($r = .06$). This result suggests that in the House, as the coalition lost strength over time at the committee leadership level, it was forced to form somewhat more often at the floor stage of consideration to block liberal initiatives from being enacted into law. In contrast, the conservative coalition in the

Senate has found itself less pressed to fight such a rear-guard action and has instead been slightly more likely to appear when southern Democrats or Republicans were more dominant among committee chairmen.

This House-Senate difference may be provisionally interpreted to mean that the conservative coalition in the Senate has historically been a more aggressive alliance in pursuit of programmatically conservative policy goals than has been true for the coalition in the House, which at least by these measures appears to have been more defensive-minded. This conclusion, however, is highly tentative in this context, considering the relatively weak correlations upon which the interpretation rests. An alternative view would be that committee chairmen are simply more important in the House than in the Senate, owing to the greater size of the House and the consequently greater need for specialization and for accumulation of power.

The second expected relationship, between coalition success and the presence of conservative chairmen, holds up to about the same moderately weak degree in both chambers. The correlations between success of the conservative coalition and the proportion of standing committee chairmanships held by southern Democrats or Republicans are .28 in the Senate and .32 in the House. Successful formation of the conservative coalition on the floor is somewhat more likely when a larger share of committee power is exercised by nonnorthern Democratic chairmen.

The Special Case of the House Rules Committee

A focal point of practically all studies of congressional conservatism is the powerful Rules Committee, which controls the flow of legislation in the House of Representatives. The traditional argument holds that conservative opposition to Rooseveltian New Deal initiatives first coalesced in the late 1930s on the Rules Committee when southern Democrats and Republicans openly joined forces to resist the trend of administration policy, specifically in reaction to FDR's plan to "pack" the Supreme Court with liberal justices.[6] The Rules Committee version of the conservative coalition formed initially in August 1937 to vote down a special rule for floor action on what eventually became the Fair Labor Standards Act. At that time, the Rules Committee consisted of five northern Democrats, five southern Democrats, and four Republicans and was chaired by the conservative John O'Connor of New York, who was subsequently one of the few anti–New Deal Democrats successfully attacked in Roosevelt's attempted 1938 "purge."

Despite the replacement of O'Connor as Rules chairman by a strong pro–New Dealer, Adolph J. Sabath of Illinois, real power on the committee remained throughout the late 1930s and into the 1940s in the hands of the Republican–southern Democratic coalition, then under the leadership of Democrats E. E.

Cox of Georgia and Howard W. Smith of Virginia. Besides delaying action on administration measures, the Rules coalition also sponsored embarrassing investigations of government activities. In 1955, Howard Smith replaced Sabath as chairman of the committee and used his position to foster the programmatic goals of the conservative forces in the House. The committee failed to meet regularly, and Smith on occasion disappeared to his Virginia farm when it was expedient to delay clearance of bills during the final days of a session.

The election of the Kennedy administration in 1960 sparked renewed liberal efforts to break the negative power of the conservative coalition on the Rules Committee, efforts that had also been undertaken unsuccessfully in the preceding Eighty-sixth Congress. After protracted lobbying by Speaker Sam Rayburn and his colleagues in the Democratic House leadership, the committee was expanded from twelve to fifteen members, making room for two additional pro-administration Democrats together with one more Republican. The result was a slender eight-to-seven progressive majority.

The overwhelming election gains made by northern Democrats in 1964 led to further restrictions on the power of the committee during the Eighty-ninth Congress. The twenty-one-day rule was revived, the Speaker was given new power to commit a bill to conference with the Senate, and dilatory procedures were more easily circumvented. These liberal successes were short-lived, however, because Republican electoral gains in 1966 strengthened the conservative coalition on the floor. Conservatives were successful in repealing the twenty-one-day rule in 1967, at the beginning of the Ninetieth Congress, although the other rules introduced in 1965 were not changed.

Chairman Smith was defeated in a renomination primary in 1966, and William Colmer of Mississippi, the new chairman and also a strong conservative, soon found himself outvoted by the liberal working majority. With Colmer's departure from Congress in 1972, the chairmanship passed to liberal Ray Madden of Indiana. The next chairman, moderate James Delaney of New York, proved to be somewhat more cooperative with the policy goals of the southern Democrat–Republican alliance, but in 1979 the chairmanship was assumed by one of the House's leading liberals, Richard Bolling of Missouri.

Patterns of relative dominance of the House Rules Committee by either conservative or liberal interests are revealed by Table 4–5. In this table, a member of the committee is classified as being in the conservative coalition (CC) or being outside of the coalition (not CC), depending on whether or not a majority of that member's roll call stands on the floor were with the coalition's position. Members who split evenly for and against are classified as being outside the conservative coalition. Average levels of coalition support are given for each of the three groups of committee members.

The table shows an impressive degree of conservative solidarity among Republican members, with John Anderson of Illinois the only committee member of that party in the past twenty years to fail to support the coalition more than he

Table 4–5

Conservative Coalition Support on the House Rules Committee, 1933–1980

Year	Southern Democrats			Northern Democrats			Republicans			Total CC	Total Not CC
	CC	Not CC	Average CC Support (%)	CC	Not CC	Average CC Support (%)	CC	Not CC	Average CC Support (%)		
1933	–	–	–	–	–	–	–	–	–	–	–
1934	2	3	70	0	3	17	2	2	50	4	8
1935	2	3	62	0	5	32	3	1	62	5	9
1936	–	–	–	–	–	–	–	–	–	–	–
1937	4	1	68	1	4	18	3	1	75	8	6
1938	–	–	–	–	–	–	–	–	–	–	–
1939	2	3	53	1	4	30	3	1	83	6	8
1940	4	1	62	1	4	29	4	0	78	9	5
1941	3	3	56	1	3	25	3	1	67	7	7
1942	3	3	50	1	3	27	4	0	70	8	6
1943	3	3	61	0	3	2	5	0	87	8	6
1944	3	3	51	1	2	24	4	1	74	8	6
1945	3	2	62	1	2	21	4	0	71	8	4
1946	3	2	50	1	2	22	4	0	82	8	4
1947	1	2	55	0	1	6	8	0	82	9	3
1948	2	1	67	0	1	0	7	0	80	9	2
1949	4	0	82	0	3	19	4	0	78	8	3
1950	3	1	78	0	4	8	4	0	82	7	5
1951	4	0	88	0	4	2	3	1	74	7	5
1952	3	1	76	0	4	2	4	0	84	7	5
1953	3	0	83	0	1	0	8	0	80	11	1
1954	2	1	67	0	1	0	7	1	86	9	3
1955	2	2	52	0	4	8	4	0	82	6	6
1956	3	1	61	0	4	11	2	2	61	5	7
1957	3	1	67	0	4	8	3	1	77	6	6
1958	2	2	54	0	4	32	3	1	66	5	7
1959	4	0	86	0	4	2	4	0	93	8	4
1960	2	2	66	0	4	5	4	0	93	6	6
1961	2	3	51	0	5	12	5	0	86	7	8
1962	2	3	49	0	5	5	5	0	83	7	8
1963	2	3	48	0	5	9	5	0	67	7	8
1964	2	3	60	0	5	11	5	0	53	7	8
1965	2	3	44	0	5	7	5	0	91	7	8
1966	2	3	42	0	5	6	5	0	78	7	8
1967	1	3	37	0	6	8	5	0	76	6	9
1968	1	3	39	0	6	14	5	0	81	6	9
1969	3	1	48	1	5	20	5	0	74	9	6

Table 4–5 continued

Year	Southern Democrats			Northern Democrats			Republicans			Total CC	Total Not CC
	CC	Not CC	Average CC Support (%)	CC	Not CC	Average CC Support (%)	CC	Not CC	Average CC Support (%)		
1970	3	1	48	1	5	20	5	0	74	9	6
1971	2	2	51	2	4	30	5	0	73	9	6
1972	2	2	48	1	5	23	5	0	78	8	7
1973	2	2	50	0	6	24	4	1	74	6	9
1974	2	2	46	0	6	27	4	1	73	6	9
1975	2	2	39	1	6	23	5	0	80	8	8
1976	2	2	36	0	7	22	5	0	79	7	9
1977	1	2	44	1	7	20	5	0	75	7	9
1978	1	2	30	1	7	19	4	1	75	6	10
1979	2	2	36	1	6	15	4	1	76	7	9
1980	2	2	37	0	7	13	4	1	73	6	10
Overall Mean			55.8			15.1			76.4		

opposed it in any year. Liberal solidarity among the northern Democrats on the committee is no less impressive. Southern Democrats on the Rules Committee, although homogeneously conservative as late as 1959, have ever since been divided fairly evenly into conservative and liberal (or at least moderate) elements.

The historical record of average levels of CC support among Rules Committee southern Democrats indicates an overall decline in the degree of conservatism, with the exception of a sharp upturn in coalition support between 1949 and 1953. Since 1975, average conservatism scores among the committee's southern Democrats have regularly fallen below 40 percent. Northern Democrats' coalition support scores have followed roughly a curvilinear pattern, with comparatively higher levels of conservatism from 1934 to 1946 and again from 1969 to 1980 and with usually much lower levels occurring in the 1947–68 period. There is some evidence of increasing liberalism among the committee's northern Democrats since the middle 1970s.

The single most important aspect of the data in Table 4–5 is the relative numerical superiority at different times of conservative and nonconservative elements. The data suggest that conservative committee dominance had begun to crack as early as 1955, long before expansion of the committee in 1961 gave it an eight-to-seven liberal "working majority." Committee expansion has not automatically ensured a nonconservative majority. Conservative members were in numerical control for the Ninety-first and Ninety-second Congresses (1969–72), and an even eight-to-eight split characterized the first session of the Ninety-fourth Congress in 1975. The last decade, however, shows overall increased liberal strength on the Rules Committee, occasioned partly by the addition of another northern Democratic seat in the Ninety-fourth Congress and partly by the loss of a southern Democratic seat in the Ninety-fifth Congress.

"Working Majorities" on Committees: A Cross-Sectional View

A similar analysis may be done usefully in a cross-sectional context. Table 4–6 presents a rough description of the "working majorities" on each of the standing committees of the Senate in the second session of the Ninety-sixth

Table 4–6
Conservative Coalition Supporters and Nonsupporters on Senate Committees, 1980

Committee	Republicans		Southern Democrats		Northern Democrats		Total	Total
	CC	Not CC	CC	Not CC	CC	Not CC	CC	Not CC
Agriculture, Nutrition, and Forestry	8	0	5	1	1	3	14	4
Appropriations	8	3	5	2	1	9	14	14
Armed Services	7	0	4	0	2	4	13	4
Banking, Housing, and Urban Affairs	6	0	2	0	0	7	8	7
Budget	7	1	4	0	1	7	12	8
Commerce, Science, and Transportation	6	1	4	0	2	4	12	5
Energy and Natural Resources	5	2	2	1	0	8	7	11
Environment and Public Works	4	2	1	0	0	7	5	9
Finance	5	3	5	0	0	7	10	10
Foreign Relations	5	1	1	0	1	7	7	8
Governmental Affairs	5	3	4	0	0	5	9	8
Judiciary	6	1	1	0	1	8	8	9
Labor and Human Resources	4	2	0	0	0	9	4	11
Rules and Administration	3	1	1	0	2	3	6	4
Veterans Affairs	3	1	2	0	0	4	5	5

Congress in 1980, just before the Republican takeover of Senate control in 1981. The same analysis is performed for the 1980 House in Table 4–7. Members of each committee are referred to as supporters or nonsupporters of the conservative coalition, depending upon whether they voted with the coalition on a majority of the roll calls in the 1980 session on which they cast a recorded vote. The resulting patterns for 1980 are merely meant to be illustrative, not to substitute for a comprehensive historical treatment of each committee.

The most important aspect of the data in Tables 4–6 and 4–7 is the nonrandom distribution of conservative and liberal members across the standing committees. Certain committees had a clear conservative working majority. In the Senate, these heavily conservative committees as of 1980 included Agriculture, Nutrition, and Forestry; Armed Services; Budget; and Commerce, Science, and Transportation. Conservative-dominated standing committees in the House were Agriculture, Armed Services, Interior and Insular Affairs, Judiciary, Public Works and Transportation, Science and Technology, Standards of Official Conduct, Veterans Affairs, and Ways and Means. Each of these committees had at least a four-member edge in conservative supporters. Other committees had a clear liberal working majority in 1980. In the Senate, these included the Energy and Natural Resources, Environment and Public Works, and Labor and Human Resources committees. Liberal-dominated House committees in 1980 were District of Columbia, Foreign Affairs, and Rules. The other committees in both chambers had roughly even balances of liberal and conservative members.

Another useful finding from Tables 4–6 and 4–7 is the distribution of relatively conservative and relatively liberal members within each of the three blocs of southern Democrats, northern Democrats, and Republicans on each committee. Among Republicans, the dominant tendency was for each committee to contain a heavy majority of conservative coalition supporters. This was especially true for the Senate committees on Agriculture, Nutrition, and Forestry; Armed Services; and Banking, Housing, and Urban Affairs, and for the House committees on Budget, House Administration, Interior and Insular Affairs, Judiciary, Public Works and Transportation, and Ways and Means. On none of these committees was there a single Republican member who failed to vote a majority of the time with the position taken by the conservative coalition. Liberal Republicans were more in evidence on certain other committees, notably Appropriations, Finance, and Governmental Affairs in the Senate and District of Columbia and Foreign Affairs in the House.

Southern Democratic members on all committees in the 1980 Senate were uniformly conservative by the measure of coalition support versus coalition opposition, with the exception of the Agriculture, Nutrition, and Forestry, Appropriations, and Energy and Natural Resources committees. There was much greater variability among southern Democrats on House committees. Agriculture, Armed Services, House Administration, Public Works and Transportation, and Standards of Official Conduct had uniformly conservative southern Democratic members, and most others had heavy majorities of conservative southern

Table 4–7

Conservative Coalition Supporters and Nonsupporters on House Committees, 1980

Committee	Republicans CC	Not CC	Southern Democrats CC	Not CC	Northern Democrats CC	Not CC	Total CC	Total Not CC
Agriculture	13	2	12	0	2	13	27	15
Appropriations	16	2	8	4	3	20	27	26
Armed Services	14	1	12	0	5	11	31	12
Banking, Finance, and Urban Affairs	14	2	5	1	1	20	20	23
Budget	8	0	3	1	0	13	11	14
District of Columbia	3	2	1	2	0	6	4	10
Education and Labor	12	1	2	1	3	17	17	19
Foreign Affairs	9	3	4	1	2	15	15	19
Government Operations	13	1	5	3	2	15	20	19
House Administration	9	0	3	0	1	12	13	12
Interior and Insular Affairs	14	0	4	1	5	16	23	17
Interstate and Foreign Commerce	14	1	4	3	4	16	22	20
Judiciary	11	0	4	3	3	10	18	13
Merchant Marine and Fisheries	12	2	7	1	1	16	20	19
Post Office and Civil Service	8	1	0	2	2	11	10	13
Public Works and Transportation	17	0	10	0	4	16	31	16
Rules	4	1	2	2	0	7	6	10
Science and Technology	14	1	8	1	3	15	25	17
Small Business	14	1	5	2	3	16	22	19
Standards of Official Conduct	5	1	2	0	3	1	10	2
Veterans Affairs	10	1	12	0	2	7	24	8
Ways and Means	12	0	6	2	2	14	20	16

Democrats. Appropriations, District of Columbia, Government Operations, Interstate and Foreign Commerce, Judiciary, Post Office and Civil Service, and Rules had heavier concentrations of nonconservative southern Democratic members.

Northern Democrats showed in 1980 a uniform pattern on all committees in each chamber of opposition to the conservative coalition, with the exception of Standards of Official Conduct in the House. There were also fairly large proportions of conservative northern Democrats on Armed Services and Interior and Insular Affairs in the House and on Rules and Administration in the Senate.

Summary and Extensions

This chapter represents in many respects a ''first cut'' examination of the interrelationship between the committee structure and programmatic decision making in Congress. Although the basic themes addressed here have led down intellectual paths that in other forms have been already well-trod, some interesting new routes also beckon.

The seniority system, though still nearly whole, has frayed appreciably in recent years with consequences for the distribution of ideological control of committees that need further examination. Similarly, the recent fragmentation of congressional power carries potentially system-transforming ramifications for the internal policy structure of Congress. Most salient here are the rising force of subcommittees and their leaders, together with the greater independence from committee and party chieftains now enjoyed by the typical member of Congress thanks to the now radically altered state of staffing, access to information, and caucus authority that work for the benefit of junior legislators.

In addition, major historical changes in the structure of congressional committees, as occurred in 1947 in both chambers and in 1977 in the Senate, together with the constant lesser changes in committee membership, leaders, and functions, create discontinuities in an otherwise smooth time series of committees' ideological structure. The cross-sectional analysis for 1980 executed here can, with considerable difficulties of data collection and research time, be extended to a much longer and more meaningful historical span. A possible model for this endeavor is shown here for the House Rules Committee, though most committees do not have such a high degree of historical continuity.

Finally, the limited applications in this chapter of the time-series method can be readily used on other relevant historical data sets. The forecasting capabilities of time-series analysis provide a set of useful guidelines about likely conditions in the future and can guide subsequent analysis of why (as will almost certainly happen) the true future conditions differ from what has been projected.

5

Constituency Influences
on Ideological Voting

The importance of a senator's or a representative's constituents in determining his or her voting decisions is well established in the literature on legislative behavior and the nature of the representational process. It is a basic tenet of democratic theory that legislators are expected to be aware of the wishes of the people who have elevated them to high public office, to do their best to reflect in their actions the beliefs and desires of their represented populations, and to provide opportunities for them to react to the legislators' policy decisions. Legislative action is the ultimate expression of the principle of representative government.[1]

The term "representation" has many valid interpretations—virtual, Burkean trusteeship, a reflection of the sociodemographic composition of a constituency, instructed delegate, and others.[2] The substance of representation, however, as distinct from its form, lies in the making of policy decisions that are consonant with the needs and beliefs of a substantial segment of the relevant constituency's population. The represented population segment may include some or all of those citizens for whom policy issues are relevant—that is, the "attentive public."[3] Representation does not require that all constituents, or even all of a legislator's electoral supporters, have their views regularly reflected in the legislator's policy choices. Responsiveness to a variety of often cacophonous constituency views is not synonymous with, and in a sense is antithetical to, the concept of political responsibility. When responsiveness pertains to attentiveness to a wide variety of viewpoints, responsibility denotes a concern for addressing and attempting to resolve public policy problems.[4]

The focus of this study is upon the policy-specific content of congressional decision processes. As such, responsibility is of greater importance as a criterion of representation than the less readily definable concept of responsiveness. Ultimately, a member of Congress is accountable to the electorate at home, and adverse decisions made too often and publicized too damagingly by the opposition will eventually reduce a member's voter support below the minimum needed for electoral survival. The combination of credit-claiming, position-taking, and advertising reelection activities discussed by David R. Mayhew [5] may be seen as an attempt by a legislator to minimize his or her position distance from the relevant elements of his or her constituency.

The important point is that regardless of a low degree of correspondence between legislators' and constituents' immediate policy views in some issue areas,[6] and despite the low level of constituent awareness of legislators' issue stands, a conjunction of broad ideological outlooks between congressmen and their constituents can usually be inferred. At the very least, disagreement with large numbers of constituents on salient issues can prove fatal to reelection hopes, especially when electoral contests are close.

The Constituency Puzzle

Which aggregate demographic or social background characteristics of a congressman's constituents should be considered in an attempt to explain his or her voting behavior? A more fundamental question perhaps should be: Does it make any sense to use sociodemographic variables to predict policy decisions? In dealing with the second question first, we need to consider the fallacies inherent in any attempt to infer a causal connection between constituent traits and congressional vote outcomes. Such shortcomings have been well articulated, for example, by Aage Clausen.[7]

One problem is the heterogeneity of the units of analysis. Certainly, all states and virtually all congressional districts contain a substantial variety of urban and rural dwellers, blue- and white-collar workers, minority and nonminority populations, renters and owners of dwellings, wealthy and poor families, and poorly and well-educated adults. Because of this heterogeneity, it is difficult to ascribe to any single social or demographic trait a given pattern of representatives' voting behavior. Not all blue-collar workers everywhere in the nation share the same attitudes toward public policy issues. Not all poor people vote for the same party or for the same type of candidate. There is no magical reason why even nearly identical mixes of constituency factors should produce similar voting proclivities among legislators elected from such districts.

A second problem is that there are many reasons to believe that constituency factors may actually be insignificant in causally determining roll call behavior. Among these reasons are the generally low level of constituents' awareness of legislators' stands on most issues, the intricate complexity of the hundreds of separate votes that a member of Congress casts, the dominance of cue-taking behavior on ordinary routine roll calls, the persistence of large numbers of electorally safe seats so that members have substantial leeway to make at least occasional "wrong" decisions, the common lack of a single clear-cut dominant structure of constituency opinion, and the decentralized, personally based rather than party- or ideologically based nature of the electoral process. Taken together, these tenets of political science make constituencies remote from all except the most personally salient, well-known, and emotionally charged issues.

A final problem in assessing the role of constituency characteristics is more empirical and pragmatic. Exactly which traits of a state's or a district's population are likely to be meaningfully related to congressional voting decisions, and what variables have actually been measured in available data sources at the proper level of aggregation? An easily measured variable such as the number of cars per family, for example, would probably not be especially salient, whereas detailed district-by-district measures of the ideological disposition of eligible voters would be invaluable but are almost wholly unavailable for analysis. Data sources at the congressional district level have been available only since the 1960 census, were relevant initially only for the Eighty-eighth Congress (1963–64), and cover only a limited set of variables. The analyst is largely a prisoner of the available data.

Regional Differences in Coalition Support

One approach to gauging the impact of constituency characteristics on levels of support for the conservative coalition is to examine differences in average levels of support for the bipartisan coalition among members of the House and Senate in each of four major geographic areas: East, West, South, and Midwest.[8] The appropriate data are presented in Tables 5–1 and 5–2. A cursory look at the tables shows considerably lower levels of conservative coalition support among eastern Republicans than among those from the other three regions. The same is true, but to a much greater degree, among nonsouthern Democrats from each of the other three regions compared to their Dixie party brethren. The high coalition support scores among noneastern Republicans and among southern Democrats would be anticipated by the very definition of the Republican–southern Democratic alliance. A broader point with more substantive significance can also be derived from these results. Given the consistently very strong positive correlations shown in Chapter 1 between coalition support and ACA measures of conservatism and the negative correlations between ADA measures of liberalism and support for the issue stands of the conservative coalition, the findings of sharp regional differences here also suggest the importance of constituency effects on the ideological voting record of members of Congress.

At a very aggregate level, the data show that eastern Republicans are decidedly more liberal than Republicans from other regions of the country and also

Table 5–1

Average Conservative Coalition Support Scores in the Senate, by Region and Party, 1933–1980

Year	Democrats				Republicans			
	East	West	South	Midwest	East	West	South	Midwest
1933	34	30	51	25	70	44	–	44
1934	49	20	50	36	57	26	–	26
1935	24	24	45	43	52	52	–	56
1936	36	53	31	8	60	60	–	0
1937	26	30	51	42	60	80	–	75
1938	39	30	63	25	68	90	–	45
1939	25	22	45	48	69	50	–	66
1940	23	20	46	35	46	38	–	50
1941	17	22	56	21	40	58	–	48
1942	21	48	56	32	28	80	–	51
1943	27	24	54	33	47	52	47	54
1944	19	11	59	31	65	56	72	71
1945	23	20	44	38	65	64	50	68
1946	18	15	50	44	65	68	62	64
1947	20	12	60	24	78	83	93	85
1948	20	16	61	15	65	80	72	69
1949	18	30	58	16	52	70	–	72
1950	14	21	53	21	42	72	–	67
1951	21	28	64	21	59	66	–	71
1952	26	28	61	8	59	68	–	64
1953	17	24	67	14	78	82	44	70
1954	32	31	55	23	82	85	70	77
1955	24	36	57	3	68	73	–	67
1956	26	31	60	17	59	71	–	63
1957	28	22	63	18	75	84	75	78
1958	31	23	64	16	61	77	59	69
1959	22	21	63	16	69	78	65	74
1960	22	20	69	7	60	66	52	73
1961	8	17	67	12	53	68	53	78
1962	24	26	67	21	60	63	47	74
1963	14	20	61	17	50	71	64	79
1964	14	21	68	15	46	71	70	73
1965	14	20	60	14	56	80	82	76
1966	11	15	59	17	50	64	76	82
1967	14	23	62	20	45	64	56	72
1968	20	28	60	17	47	64	62	70
1969	23	29	67	11	47	73	75	70
1970	18	23	59	7	44	60	68	61
1971	28	32	70	9	59	71	77	62

	Democrats				Republicans			
Year	East	West	South	Midwest	East	West	South	Midwest
1972	15	21	62	9	53	70	71	63
1973	17	22	64	7	51	72	82	67
1974	18	21	68	12	40	64	79	67
1975	16	23	70	11	31	75	87	70
1976	20	21	64	11	40	72	83	71
1977	19	30	64	21	43	84	85	76
1978	17	29	62	18	33	72	75	63
1979	19	34	67	25	45	76	78	68
1980	15	22	61	27	47	76	81	66
Overall Mean	21.8	24.8	59.1	20.4	55.0	68.4	69.1	65.1

Table 5–2
Average Conservative Coalition Support Scores in the House, by Region and Party, 1933–1980

	Democrats				Republicans			
Year	East	West	South	Midwest	East	West	South	Midwest
1933	–	–	–	–	–	–	–	–
1934	15	28	66	41	38	27	50	49
1935	15	27	52	28	57	54	33	62
1936	–	–	–	–	–	–	–	–
1937	14	24	57	27	65	58	68	67
1938	–	–	–	–	–	–	–	–
1939	11	24	58	27	72	76	72	82
1940	14	20	55	29	67	63	56	76
1941	12	24	68	28	56	58	78	66
1942	14	32	60	36	52	61	84	71
1943	16	25	68	18	67	74	83	76
1944	12	26	64	18	67	71	74	77
1945	13	18	62	15	56	67	66	69
1946	11	13	59	15	66	71	72	78
1947	15	33	72	19	78	79	82	85
1948	22	28	61	11	81	87	83	85
1949	11	18	61	10	67	75	57	74
1950	13	13	60	13	66	64	55	71
1951	9	23	67	8	67	71	84	80
1952	7	18	57	6	62	76	68	77

Constituency Influences on Ideological Voting

Table 5–2 continued

Year	Democrats				Republicans			
	East	West	South	Midwest	East	West	South	Midwest
1953	14	29	66	9	75	82	92	82
1954	9	34	60	14	69	82	81	78
1955	18	32	67	11	61	77	61	74
1956	18	16	59	15	54	54	69	64
1957	10	8	63	16	58	71	78	76
1958	25	21	68	25	50	56	69	61
1959	11	15	82	21	68	98	97	90
1960	7	5	57	9	57	84	79	76
1961	11	13	61	17	64	72	82	83
1962	9	10	55	17	49	70	83	75
1963	7	14	58	14	52	74	84	71
1964	8	13	64	18	50	74	87	79
1965	5	12	61	12	53	78	90	80
1966	7	9	53	16	49	70	78	76
1967	11	14	65	17	58	75	88	79
1968	11	15	64	15	50	64	82	69
1969	16	19	68	21	52	65	86	69
1970	13	16	64	18	49	63	76	64
1971	21	23	63	20	61	69	84	71
1972	19	21	60	22	60	66	83	72
1973	19	20	63	21	60	71	86	73
1974	21	19	62	22	54	67	81	68
1975	19	22	63	21	59	78	87	77
1976	21	24	63	23	57	67	86	74
1977	21	23	63	25	62	79	88	77
1978	22	23	59	24	59	74	84	72
1979	25	26	64	27	65	82	87	78
1980	22	23	61	27	61	73	87	73
Overall Mean	14.3	20.3	62.3	18.8	60.0	70.4	77.3	73.9

that southern Democrats are markedly more conservative than their co-partisans from any of the other three regions. Apart from these two ideologically distinctive regional party blocs, there do not at first glance seem to be any substantial differences among the remaining regional blocs. A more precise analysis of the data, however, suggests modifications in this initial impression.

Average regional levels of roll call voting support for the southern Democrat–Republican alliance are presented in Table 5–3. These mean scores are produced by averaging the annual figures in Tables 5–1 and 5–2 for each party regional

Table 5–3

Mean Conservative Coalition Support Scores
by Party, Chamber, and Region

Chamber/Region/Party	Mean Support Score
House Southern Republicans	77
House Midwestern Republicans	74
House Western Republicans	70
Senate Southern Republicans	69
Senate Western Republicans	68
Senate Midwestern Republicans	65
House Southern Democrats	62
House Eastern Republicans	60
Senate Southern Democrats	59
Senate Eastern Republicans	55
Senate Western Democrats	25
Senate Eastern Democrats	22
Senate Midwestern Democrats	20
House Western Democrats	20
House Midwestern Democrats	19
House Eastern Democrats	14

bloc within each chamber. This involves altogether sixteen combinations of region, party, and chamber. The results in Table 5–3 show that southern Republicans in the House have been the strongest supporters of the conservative coalition over a half-century. In this sense, they may be said to constitute the single most conservative regional party bloc in Congress and may be described as "reactionary." House midwestern Republicans are not far behind in their conservatism and probably deserve the same label.

These two blocs, especially the House southern Republicans, have historically been somewhat more conservative than the three closely similar partisan regional clusters of House western Republicans, Senate southern Republicans, and Senate western Republicans. All of these blocs supported the conservative coalition on at least two-thirds of all coalition roll calls. They could be called "traditional conservatives."

Another distinctive grouping encompasses the five blocs of Senate midwestern Republicans, House southern Democrats, House eastern Republicans, Senate southern Democrats, and Senate eastern Republicans. This cluster may be termed overall as "moderate conservative." House southern Democrats are distinctive as that party's most conservative regional grouping. Senate eastern Republicans differ sharply from their other Republican colleagues in each chamber in that they support the conservative coalition only approximately one-half of the time that the coalition forms in the Senate. The label "moderate-deviationist" probably best decribes this eastern wing of the Senate Republican party.

The next cluster, Senate western Democrats, Senate eastern Democrats, Senate midwestern Democrats, House western Democrats, and House midwestern Democrats, shows very low average levels of support for the conservative coalition, though by this measure Senate Democrats from the West are by a small margin the most conservative group among their northern party colleagues. Even the Senate western Democrats, however, are much less supportive of the bipartisan coalition than are southern Democrats. The programmatic cleavage within House and Senate Democratic ranks is on the whole much sharper and more clear-cut than comparable ideological differences among Republicans. This cluster of Democratic blocs might be called the "moderate progressive" elements within that congressional party.

If there is anything approaching a regionally based radical influence in congressional policy making, it exists among the ranks of House eastern Democrats. This group has the lowest level of conservative coalition support and clearly forms a polar contrast to the reactionary House southern Republican bloc. The label "progressive-innovative" conveys the notion that House eastern Democrats constitute the elements most opposed to conservative influence in Congress and most inclined to endorse or initiate forward-looking legislation.

The salience of region becomes particularly evident when the data in Table 5–3 are considered for one party at a time in one chamber. Southern members constitute the most conservative elements in both the House and the Senate within their respective parties. The western members of each party, with the exception of House Republicans, tend to be the next most supportive of the conservative coalition in each chamber, followed by midwestern legislators. Except for Senate Democrats, easterners evidence the most liberal voting records. These findings, however, are at best only suggestive of the role of constituency influences because they do not reveal precisely why, for example, southern as compared to eastern states or congressional districts produce such sharp differences in the roll call record.

Time-Series Analysis of Regional Differences

The regional differences in conservative support can be usefully analyzed by means of the time-series method. Appropriate models for each of the sixteen party-regional groupings are presented in Appendix D. Table 5–4 presents the forecasts of expected levels of agreement with the southern Democrat–Republican alliance for the years 1981–84 that are produced by each model. These results are based on the data in Tables 5–1 and 5–2 for the time period 1933–80 for all Democratic groups and for 1939–80 for all Republican groups except the

Table 5–4

Time-Series Forecasts of Conservative Coalition
Support by Region and Party, 1981–1984

Group	Forecasts			
	1981	1982	1983	1984
House Eastern Democrats	23	22	21	22
House Western Democrats	22	22	22	22
House Southern Democrats	64	62	61	65
House Midwestern Democrats	26	26	26	26
House Eastern Republicans	62	60	61	60
House Western Republicans	71	69	71	72
House Southern Republicans (1961–80)	84	85	84	84
House Midwestern Republicans	75	71	74	72
Senate Eastern Democrats	18	16	17	16
Senate Western Democrats	29	31	28	28
Senate Southern Democrats	60	60	59	59
Senate Midwestern Democrats	21	21	21	21
Senate Eastern Republicans	50	51	53	53
Senate Western Republicans	74	69	73	67
Senate Southern Republicans (1957–80)	77	75	74	73
Senate Midwestern Republicans	61	68	65	65

southern ones. Southern Republicans in the House have a consistent record of conservative coalition support and opposition only since 1961; Senate southern Republicans' voting record has been continuous since 1957. The reason for the paucity of an earlier southern Republican roll call history is that until those dates nearly all Dixie seats were controlled by Democrats.

Two important points should be made about the time-series results in Table 5–4 and in Appendix D. First, there have been significant increases since the 1930s in the degree of conservative coalition support among House eastern Democrats, House eastern Republicans, and House midwestern Republicans. Decreasing conservatism is evident among House western Democrats, House midwestern Democrats, Senate eastern Democrats, and Senate midwestern Democrats. The other groups show no significant overall trends in either direction. There have been very distinctive patterns in the degree of conservative support offered by each of these groups over time. That is, no single summary pattern is followed by each and every party-regional segment of Congress. Each group has evolved in a more or less unique way.

The second important point regarding these time-series results is that the short-term forecasts produced by these models indicate no likely change in the relative rankings of each group in terms of their degree of conservative support. Forecasted levels of conservatism by and large do not differ very much from the values established during the 1970s within each time series, and these forecasts generally are in agreement with the relative degrees of conservatism presented in Table 5–3. These results suggest that there is little reason to expect significant departures from the recent voting patterns of these party-regional groups.

The Assessment of Constituency Effects

If there are in fact important constituency traits that help explain the ideological voting records of members of the House and Senate, this should be reflected in consistent support for the conservative coalition within individual electoral districts, regardless of which party or representative is elected by that constituency to the House or Senate. Some important presumptive evidence of this constituency-legislator connection is presented in Tables 5–5 and 5–6. These two tables present, separately for the House and for the Senate, the intercorrelations over chosen spans of time among levels of conservative coalition support for each representative district. For the House, the representative district is the congressional district, which is altered each decade in accordance with constitutional dictates of reapportionment based on equal population. For the Senate, the representative district is, of course, the state which is represented by each member. In these tables, results are presented for the 1960 census apportionment and for the 1970 apportionment. The 1960 census results are computed beginning with 1967, the first year that congressional voting records were available after reapportionment in the House had been finished in the wake of the U.S. Supreme Court's "one man, one vote" decisions in *Baker* v. *Carr* (1962) and *Wesberry* v. *Sanders* (1964), which required adjustments in congressional districts that were not completed until the convening of the Ninetieth Congress in 1967. Consequently, there are only six years of comparable data under the 1960 census, but eight years of comparable data under the 1970 census from 1973 to 1980.

The critical result from Tables 5–5 and 5–6 is that patterns of support for the conservative coalition are quite durable over time. In spite of membership turnover, including changes in party and personnel, fluctuations in support for positions taken by the southern Democrat–Republican alliance on the whole were surprisingly small. This is especially the case when we look at correlations for successive years, such as 1967–68 or 1978–79, for example. These correlations are consistently .7 or better in both chambers and are often greater than .9. Of course, the correlations are stronger between an odd-numbered year (say, 1967) and an even-numbered year (say, 1968) than from an even-numbered year to another odd-numbered year (say, 1969), because the former set of correlations

Table 5–5

Persistence of Conservative Coalition Support
over Time, 1960 and 1970 Censuses: House

	1960 Census				
Year	1968	1969	1970	1971	1972
1967	.94	.89	.86	.73	.76
1968		.89	.88	.75	.79
1969			.93	.80	.81
1970				.83	.84
1971					.94

	1970 Census					
Year	1974	1975	1976	1977	1978	1979	1980
1973	.96	.73	.73	.68	.64	.61	.61
1974		.74	.74	.69	.65	.63	.62
1975			.96	.90	.85	.78	.76
1976				.90	.86	.79	.77
1977					.96	.86	.83
1978						.83	.81
1979							.96

are within a Congress, when membership is virtually constant, and the latter correlations are between congresses, when membership changes are much greater.

The magnitude of persistence in conservative coalition support falls off with the passing of time, as would be expected. What is striking, however, is the continued presence of strong correlations among constituency-specific levels of conservative coalition support even after several years in the face of dramatic membership turnover during the 1970s and somewhat less turnover in the 1960s. Clearly, there is evidence that constituency traits are involved in determining congressional voting patterns on conservative coalition appearances. What are these traits of states or congressional districts, and precisely how do they relate to variations in members' conservatism on roll call votes?

In the subsequent analysis, each member's level of support for the conservative coalition on recorded votes is correlated with the following fairly standard sociodemographic characteristics of a legislator's state or district: percent of the population living in urban areas, percent of the population self-identified as nonwhite, median years of school completed, median family income, percent of the employed labor force engaged in white-collar occupations, and percent of housing units that are owner-occupied.[9]

Table 5–6

Persistence of Conservative Coalition Support
over Time, 1960 and 1970 Censuses: Senate

| | | 1960 Census | | | |
Year	1968	1969	1970	1971	1972
1967	.91	.79	.82	.61	.65
1968		.78	.81	.68	.66
1969			.95	.81	.79
1970				.82	.82
1971					.94

| | | | 1970 Census | | | |
Year	1974	1975	1976	1977	1978	1979	1980
1973	.93	.86	.85	.61	.60	.53	.51
1974		.91	.86	.63	.67	.61	.61
1975			.94	.74	.78	.63	.60
1976				.72	.73	.56	.52
1977					.91	.75	.73
1978						.78	.78
1979							.94

Because the most recent House district-level data available at this writing are for the results of the 1970 census, their validity as indicators of voting behavior becomes increasingly dubious by the end of the decade for which they were collected. The same problem of timeliness of measurement applies to the 1960 data, which by 1972 were at least a bit stale. One sensible solution to this problem is to choose variables that are both theoretically meaningful and durable, that is, likely to remain fairly stable over a decade. This was done for both the 1960 and the 1970 census data, after making necessary allowances to ensure comparability of data collected under the two censuses.

The search for constituency correlates of congressional conservatism begins with Table 5–7. The table shows average values of each of the six sociodemographic variables under both the 1960 and 1970 censuses for each of the four regions used earlier in this chapter. The distinctiveness of the South, both at the House congressional district level and at the state level in the Senate, is readily apparent. Characterized by less urbanization, a higher proportion of nonwhite population, lower educational attainment, and lower median family income, the southern region evidences a considerable gap from the rest of the nation. But southern distinctiveness is much less pronounced on the percent homeowners and

Table 5–7

Mean Values of Constituency Variables,
1960 and 1970, by Region

Variable	Census	Region			
		East	West	South	Midwest
		HOUSE			
Percent urban	1970	78.6	82.5	63.9	71.6
	1960	77.9	77.1	57.1	68.1
Percent nonwhite	1970	9.9	9.7	19.5	8.7
	1960	7.7	8.7	21.4	6.9
Median years	1970	11.8	12.3	11.0	11.9
of education	1960	10.6	11.7	9.5	10.6
Median family	1970	10,474.8	10,279.4	7,937.0	10,151.5
income ($)	1960	6,199.0	6,344.8	4,270.6	5,894.9
Percent	1970	59.4	59.5	65.5	68.5
homeowners	1960	58.5	61.5	62.1	67.8
Percent	1970	50.7	52.1	44.2	45.5
white collar	1960	43.3	44.8	36.3	39.4
		SENATE			
Percent urban	1970	68.5	70.8	59.6	64.4
	1960	68.2	65.0	53.8	60.4
Percent nonwhite	1970	7.1	10.8	21.0	6.3
	1960	6.0	11.0	23.1	5.1
Median years	1970	12.0	12.4	11.0	12.1
of education	1960	10.6	11.8	9.3	10.7
Median family	1970	9,953.0	9,772.2	7,621.7	9,396.4
income ($)	1960	5,841.8	6,031.3	4,111.7	5,452.0
Percent	1970	63.2	60.8	65.7	68.8
homeowners	1960	61.7	61.8	61.5	67.8
Percent	1970	48.5	49.9	43.1	44.9
white collar	1960	41.0	43.2	35.7	38.6

percent white-collar variables, on which the South is similar to the Midwest in having higher proportions of homeowners and lower proportions of white-collar workers than either the East or the West. Also, the demographic gulf separating South and non-South has generally lessened between the 1960 and 1970 census results, so that the long-term trend seems to be toward greater social homogeneity across regions.

Another obvious conclusion to be derived from Table 5–7 concerns the "greening" of America. From 1960 to 1970, the nation became more urbanized within each region, the nonwhite population became more evenly distributed, educational attainment rose, median family income grew in both real and inflated terms, and the proportion of workers engaged in white-collar occupations expanded. Except in the West, there was also an increase in the incidence of homeownership. These trends indicate that in the 1970s the voting population was more middle-class, better-informed, and racially more mixed than in the preceding decade. One question that must be answered is whether this shift in the traits of congressional constituencies has had an effect on the structure of sociodemographic correlates of policy-making decisions on ideologically motivated issues.

The information that is pivotal in the study of roll call behavior and constituency characteristics is presented in Tables 5–8 and 5–9.[10] The tables show correlations for each year of relevant data (1967 through 1972 under the 1960 census and 1973 through 1980 under the 1970 census) between each of the six sociodemographic variables and the degree of support members of the House and Senate expressed in the roll call record for the southern Democrat–Republican conservative policy alliance. Average correlations for the six years under the 1960 census and for the eight years of available data under the 1970 census are presented, along with average correlations over the entire fourteen-year period. The larger a positive correlation in the tables, the greater the extent to which higher values of that constituency variable are related to greater support for the conservative policy position. Negative correlations imply that a particular constituency trait is associated with more liberal roll call stands.

In Table 5–8 for the House of Representatives, the consistent strength of percent urban as a predictor of roll call conservatism is striking. With practically no difference in magnitude from 1967 to 1980, this has been the single strongest correlate of conservative coalition support in the House. Less urban areas produce more conservative congressmen; or, conversely, more urban areas tend to produce more liberal members of the House. Weaker, though still substantial, correlations hold between conservatism and both median family income and percent homeowners. Lower median family incomes and a higher percent of nonrenters correlate with greater congressional conservatism. Percent of the work force engaged in white-collar occupations bears a still weaker relationship to House conservatism, with conservative members more likely to come from districts with proportionately less white-collar employment. The connection between conservative voting on the floor of the House and educational attainment of constituents is weak, but the consistently negative correlations suggest that representatives' roll call conservatism increases as the educational level of their constituents decreases. The final variable, percent nonwhite, bears an inconsistent and overall very weak negative relationship to congressional conservatism; more conservative congressmen tend to represent districts with lower proportions of minority populations.

A congressional district that produces conservative members of the House is

Table 5-8

Correlations between Conservative Coalition Support and
Constituency Variables: House

CC Support in Year	Percent Urban	Percent Nonwhite	Median Years of Education	Median Family Income	Percent White Collar	Percent Home-owners
1967	−.49	−.02	−.07	−.32	−.22	.36
1968	−.48	.01	−.10	−.36	−.22	.32
1969	−.51	.04	−.16	−.39	−.27	.32
1970	−.49	.04	−.15	−.37	−.25	.32
1971	−.41	−.03	−.08	−.28	−.17	.34
1972	−.42	−.06	−.05	−.28	−.15	.35
1973	−.46	−.15	−.06	−.21	−.18	.44
1974	−.45	−.16	−.07	−.23	−.18	.43
1975	−.44	−.10	−.12	−.32	−.22	.36
1976	−.47	−.09	−.14	−.34	−.25	.37
1977	−.45	−.09	−.12	−.30	−.22	.36
1978	−.41	−.06	−.12	−.29	−.21	.34
1979	−.44	−.13	−.08	−.29	−.22	.40
1980	−.44	−.13	−.09	−.29	−.24	.41
Mean Correlations						
1967–1980	−.45	−.07	−.10	−.30	−.21	.37
1967–1972	−.47	−.00	−.10	−.33	−.21	.34
1973–1980	−.44	−.11	−.10	−.28	−.22	.39

rural or suburban, with a small minority population, a less educated electorate, a lower than average income, a heavily blue-collar labor force, and a high proportion of residents who own their own homes. Liberal districts, in contrast, would then be characterized by a heavily urbanized, heavily nonwhite, better-educated, wealthier, white-collar, renting population. In this respect, one fairly notable change in the 1970s as compared to the 1960s is the increased importance of race as a correlate of House conservatism.

The structure of constituency correlates in the Senate is substantially different from what has been described for the House. For the 1967–80 period, the single most important relationship is between Senate conservatism and median family income. Four other variables—percent urban, percent nonwhite, median years of

Table 5–9

Correlations between Conservative Coalition Support and
Constituency Variables: Senate

CC Support in Year	Percent Urban	Percent Nonwhite	Median Years of Education	Median Family Income	Percent White Collar	Percent Home- owners
1967	−.35	.22	−.17	−.44	−.34	.02
1968	−.32	.24	−.19	−.46	−.34	−.03
1969	−.25	.25	−.13	−.37	−.23	−.07
1970	−.30	.20	−.17	−.42	−.28	.06
1971	−.19	.32	−.21	−.35	−.20	−.12
1972	−.21	.25	−.18	−.35	−.21	−.01
1973	−.17	.39	−.35	−.34	−.14	−.04
1974	−.23	.35	−.37	−.45	−.23	.07
1975	−.16	.35	−.36	−.45	−.21	−.02
1976	−.10	.38	−.31	−.36	−.14	−.06
1977	−.09	.17	−.24	−.38	−.12	.02
1978	−.14	.15	−.25	−.41	−.16	.08
1979	−.27	.10	−.26	−.51	−.27	.16
1980	−.20	.06	−.17	−.45	−.22	.16

Mean
Correlations

1967– 1980	−.21	.24	−.24	−.41	−.22	.02
1967– 1972	−.27	.25	−.18	−.40	−.27	−.03
1973– 1980	−.17	.24	−.29	−.42	−.19	.05

education, and percent white collar—are moderately related to conservative coalition support, while percent homeowners bears essentially no connection to Senate ideological voting patterns.

The composite picture of a state likely to produce conservative senators would include lower income levels, a lesser degree of urbanization, lower educational attainment, a smaller proportion of white-collar workers, and a proportionately larger nonwhite population. This composite is different from the portrait of a conservative House district in that homeownership is no longer important, percent urban is much less relevant, the direction of percent nonwhite is reversed, and education and income are more important indicators of conservatism. Between the 1960s and 1970s, the relative importance of urbanization and

Table 5–10

Mean Correlations between Conservative Coalition Support and Constituency Variables, by Region

Dates and Region	Percent Urban	Percent Nonwhite	Median Years of Education	Median Family Income	Percent White Collar	Percent Home-owners
			SENATE			
1967–1972						
South	−.17	.46	−.15	−.12	−.25	−.37
West	.21	−.12	.06	−.14	−.04	.10
East	−.52	.03	−.01	−.33	−.30	.42
Midwest	−.20	−.16	.37	−.26	.06	−.18
1973–1980						
South	.06	.18	.28	.31	.19	−.28
West	−.02	−.14	−.02	−.25	−.10	.09
East	−.26	.09	−.27	−.26	−.21	.29
Midwest	−.06	−.08	.25	−.24	.10	−.14
1967–1980						
South	−.04	.30	.10	.13	.00	−.32
West	.08	−.13	.01	−.20	−.07	.09
East	−.37	.06	−.16	−.29	−.25	.35
Midwest	−.12	−.11	.30	−.25	.08	−.16
			HOUSE			
1967–1972						
South	−.17	.11	.13	.04	−.01	.00
West	−.19	−.36	.17	−.00	.08	.30
East	−.47	−.26	.05	−.08	−.18	.46
Midwest	−.52	−.43	.14	−.22	−.06	.39
1973–1980						
South	−.28	−.08	−.00	−.13	−.09	.38
West	−.19	−.20	.10	−.09	.02	.21
East	−.56	−.36	.19	−.01	−.24	.53
Midwest	−.41	−.38	.26	−.12	−.06	.32
1967–1980						
South	−.23	.00	.06	−.06	−.06	.22
West	−.19	−.27	.13	−.05	.05	.25
East	−.52	−.32	.13	−.04	−.21	.50
Midwest	−.46	−.40	.21	−.16	−.06	.35

white-collar work force have declined as correlates of Senate conservatism, whereas education has become a more meaningful indicator.

Controlling for regional differences, the results in Table 5–10 show some interesting departures from the overall national-level relationships between constituency traits and conservative support in Congress. Perhaps the single most meaningful result is the marked volatility in the magnitude, and even in the direction, of the constituency correlates. Urbanization is most consequential in the East and somewhat less so in the Midwest in both chambers. Nonwhite population for the Senate is most important in the South, where relatively larger minority populations are associated with more conservative voting records, though this relationship has declined in the 1970s relative to the 1960s. Major correlations in the opposite direction hold in the House for each region except the South. Education is of much consequence only in the Midwest, where more education is associated with greater conservatism. Income correlates positively with conservatism in the South, but negatively for the other regions, in the House. In the Senate, income is most important in the Midwest. White-collar employment is a distinctly eastern variable in both chambers, with more conservative legislators coming from districts and states having lesser proportions of white-collar workers. Homeownership is most important in the East, but for the House is nearly as relevant in the South. In the Senate, these correlations are in opposite directions for the South and East. The homeownership variable is at least moderately important in each region for the House, with a higher proportion of owners more likely to produce conservative representatives.

Summary

This chapter has thrust us into a thorny thicket of conceptual and measurement problems. The controversy over constituents' impact on legislative activity is perhaps unresolvable, but it is crucial for understanding the role of representation as a fundamental tenet of democratic theory. I have attempted here to contribute to that continuing dialogue by examining the impact of six constituency traits readily measured from published sources. Sharply varying regional patterns of the extent to which and the direction in which these sociodemographic characteristics help to explain patterns of congressional conservatism have appeared. Differences in the actual voting records of representatives and senators were also evaluated, controlling for region and party. Here the technique of time-series analysis proved essential in demonstrating differences in patterns of support for the conservative policy alliance over time and was an effective and revealing means of projecting likely future sources of conservative support.

6

Presidents and the Conservative Coalition

Congressional policy making does not take place within an institutional vacuum. In attempting to assess the impact that the congressional conservative coalition has on the form and quality of American public policy, it is necessary to keep in mind that this policy coalition participates in policy debates not simply within Congress but also between Congress and the president.

Several questions are relevant here. What impact, if any, does the occupant of the White House have on the activity of the conservative coalition? That is, to what extent do the positions taken by the president influence the distribution of the coalition's appearances and success across administrations? Reversing this line of causality, is there hard evidence that the conservative coalition has been either an effective help or a significant hindrance in a president's pursuit of his administration's programs? Finally, are there substantial differences over time in the nature of the interaction between the White House and the conservative coalition, as a function of split party control between the executive and the legislature, of shifting partisan control within either of the two institutions, or of the personalities and "styles" of individual presidents?

The connection between a president's policy initiatives or position taking on the one hand and congressional policy initiatives or disposition of presidential demands on the other hand has long been of interest to scholars investigating the behavior of the executive and legislative branches. Similarly, it has long been a favorite pastime of both journalists (notably those of Congressional Quarterly, Inc.) and academics to keep a running score regarding the relative degrees of initiative taken and success enjoyed by a president and by various partisan, regional, or policy groupings of the members of Congress.[1] The analysis presented in this chapter follows these well-established directions, but with a sharpened focus on the specific patterns of policy interaction between a readily identifiable ideological alliance in Congress and the expressed programmatic wishes of presidents of the United States over three decades.

Two related sets of data are employed in this evaluation of the dialectics of legislative-executive interaction. The time-series data on the frequency of conservative coalition appearances and successes introduced in Chapter 2 yield complete information on conservative coalition success and appearance for the administrations of eight presidents: Roosevelt, Truman, Eisenhower, Kennedy, Johnson, Nixon, Ford, and Carter. A briefer data set culled from Congressional Quarterly sources covering the time period 1953 to 1980[2] allows a more precise look at the interconnection between the activity of the conservative coalition and the policy position taken by the six presidents who followed Truman.

James MacGregor Burns, Joseph Clark, and James Patterson, among others, argue that the conservative coalition in Congress acts, and in a sense exists, chiefly to thwart the programmatic goals of liberal presidents.[3] That notion and some others will be tested in this chapter.[4] Roosevelt, Truman, Kennedy, Johnson, and Carter—all Democrats—are treated in this chapter as the ''liberal'' presidents. The Republican chief executives—Eisenhower, Nixon, and Ford—constitute the ''conservative'' presidents.

The appearance of the conservative coalition on legislative roll calls may be interpreted either as a defensive alliance designed to thwart liberal policy initiatives emanating from members of Congress or from the White House when it is in Democratic hands, or, alternatively, as a more aggressive policy bloc that is given extra impetus by the presence of a Republican administration. Findings of relatively higher rates of formation of the coalition under Republican administrations would substantiate the latter interpretation, whereas findings of greater coalition salience under Democratic administrations would lend support to the defense-reaction interpretation.

Given the evidently more conservative programmatic bent of Republican presidents relative to Democratic presidents, a significantly greater degree of agreement would be expected between the conservative coalition's policy positions and the stands taken by Republican presidents, as compared to that between the coalition and Democratic presidents. Of course, variations in president-coalition agreement over time and also across administrations that were under the control of the same party would be expected as a function of the varying personalities and policy thrusts of individual White House occupants. The position taken by the conservative coalition should be an important determinant of the success or failure of a president's policy preferences, assisting the goals of Republican presidents and reducing the chances for success of initiatives taken or supported by Democratic presidents.

Conservative Coalition Appearance and Success under Eight Presidents

The rates of occurrence and success of the conservative coalition in both the House and the Senate during the administrations of each of the eight presidents from Franklin Roosevelt to Jimmy Carter are presented in Table 6–1. Coalition appearances are expressed both as a proportion of all recorded votes and as a proportion of all nonunanimous roll calls that were taken in either chamber under each administration.[5]

The data within the table reflect the overall increase in the relative frequency with which the conservative coalition has appeared during the eight presidential administrations. A major jump in the coalition's rate of appearance in both

Table 6–1
Conservative Coalition Appearances and Success under Eight Presidents (n's for denominator are in parentheses)

President	CC Votes as Percent All Roll Calls		CC Votes as Percent Nonunanimous Roll Calls		Percent CC Success	
		HOUSE				
Roosevelt	9.21	(1,075)	10.55	(938)	84.85	(99)
Truman	19.81	(823)	25.15	(648)	89.63	(164)
Eisenhower	15.10	(669)	19.39	(521)	77.23	(101)
Kennedy	14.93	(335)	20.58	(243)	66.00	(50)
Johnson	20.71	(1,009)	30.96	(675)	49.76	(209)
Nixon	24.07	(1,969)	35.85	(1,322)	72.36	(474)
Ford	23.34	(1,474)	32.89	(1,046)	56.10	(344)
Carter	19.89	(2,816)	29.99	(1,867)	63.57	(560)
		SENATE				
Roosevelt	7.93	(1,311)	8.66	(1,201)	66.35	(104)
Truman	16.20	(1,222)	17.35	(1,141)	93.47	(199)
Eisenhower	17.67	(1,217)	22.37	(961)	82.33	(215)
Kennedy	21.94	(629)	24.73	(558)	52.90	(138)
Johnson	21.94	(1,422)	26.80	(1,164)	54.81	(312)
Nixon	26.92	(2,556)	35.39	(1,944)	63.66	(688)
Ford	26.11	(1,490)	33.19	(1,172)	54.76	(389)
Carter	23.08	(2,179)	28.43	(1,769)	66.20	(503)

chambers occurred between the Roosevelt and Truman administrations, with another major increase in the House under Johnson and in the Senate under Nixon. The relative frequency with which the conservative coalition has appeared declined somewhat under the Republican Ford and Democratic Carter administrations.

If these data on conservative coalition appearances are collapsed into a dichotomized comparison of the coalition's salience under all three Republican and all five Democratic administrations, sharp differences appear in patterns of White House control and congressional activity. The conservative coalition formed on 17.86 percent of the 6,058 House roll calls recorded during the five Democratic administrations, or on 24.75 percent of 4,371 nonunanimous votes. In contrast, the coalition in the House formed on 22.35 percent of all 4,112 Republican administration roll calls, or on 31.81 percent of 2,889 nonunanimous votes. The relative rate of coalition formation on nonunanimous roll calls in the House is thus nearly 30 percent greater under the three Republican presidents than under the five Democratic presidents. Controlling for the downward bias in the composite figure for Democratic presidents caused by the very low levels of House coalition formation under Roosevelt, however, makes this distinction based upon party control of the White House much less dramatic. More specifically, the conservative coalition appeared on 19.73 percent of the 4,983 House roll calls taken under Truman, Kennedy, Johnson, and Carter and on 28.63 percent of 3,433 nonunanimous votes. This rate is about 11 percent less than that found for the three Republican presidents.

The data in Table 6–1 show broadly similar patterns of increasing salience of the conservative coalition in congressional decision making since the 1930s in both the House and the Senate, although there are also some differences. The Senate data evidence a much smoother process of monotonic growth in the coalition's importance through the Nixon administration and then a subsequent slight decline. Aggregating the Senate coalition formation data according to presidential party results in sharper differences than those observed for the House. Under all five Democratic presidents combined, the coalition formed on 18.57 percent of 6,763 total Senate roll calls, or on 21.53 percent of 5,833 nonunanimous votes. In contrast, the conservative coalition formed on 24.55 percent of the 5,263 total Senate votes taken under the three Republican presidents, or on 31.69 percent of 4,077 nonunanimous roll calls. By the nonunanimous roll call measure, the Senate coalition formed about 47 percent more frequently under Republican than under Democratic administrations. Omitting results for the Roosevelt years does not eliminate this disparity in rates of coalition formation on nonunanimous votes as fully as in the House. The coalition under the three Republican presidents still formed over 27 percent more frequently in the Senate than it did under Truman, Kennedy, Johnson, and Carter.

Table 6–1 also indicates the distribution of conservative coalition success in both chambers across the last eight administrations. In the House, there is no clear distinction between levels of coalition success under Democratic as compared to Republican administrations. The low point of coalition success in the House came under the Johnson administration, but the highest levels of success were also recorded under Democratic administrations (Roosevelt and Truman). Overall, under the five Democratic presidents, the House coalition won on 66.9 percent of its appearances, almost identical to its 66.81 percent success rate under the three Republican presidents.

In the Senate, the coalition's success rate was greatest under Truman and lowest under Kennedy, both Democratic presidents. The conservative coalition was overall slightly more successful under Democratic (66.24 percent) than under Republican administrations (64.09 percent).

Measuring the Effects of Party Control of Congress and the White House on Coalition Activity and Success

The evidence presented thus far of presidential influence over the appearance and success of the conservative coalition is suggestive but not conclusive. There are important implications here for the making of public policy, particularly given the emphasis in American politics on the principle of the separation of political powers among distinct semiautonomous branches of government. The measurement of executive-legislative interaction in the context of programmatic coalitions is also important for assessing the role of both partisanship and ideology in shaping policy decisions.

A direct test of the nature of the relationship between the White House and the congressional conservative coalition may be made by controlling statistically for party differences in both the White House and Congress. That is, the activity and success of the conservative coalition under presidents of each party will be compared, as will coalition behavior under Democratic versus Republican control of Congress. The impact of split versus same-party control of the White House and Capitol Hill will also be considered. Through these measures, an attempt will be made to separate out the influence of party as a determinant of the frequency of coalition appearances and of the magnitude of coalition success.

In the forty-eight years covered in this analysis, a Republican-dominated Congress coincided with a Democratic administration only in the Eightieth Congress (1947–48); Republicans controlled both the White House and the Capitol during only the Eighty-third Congress (1953–54). Democratic presidents coincided with a Democratic Congress in the Seventy-third to Seventy-ninth, Eighty-first, Eighty-second, Eighty-seventh to Ninetieth, Ninety-fifth, and Ninety-sixth Congresses (1933–46, 1949–52, 1961–68, and 1977–80). Democrats controlled the Capitol while Republicans held the White House during the Eighty-fourth to Eighty-sixth and Ninety-first to Ninety-fourth Congresses (1955–60, 1969–76).

Under a Republican Congress and a Democratic administration (Truman), the conservative coalition formed on 26.56 percent of 128 nonunanimous House votes and on 18.39 percent of 223 nonunanimous Senate roll calls. When a Republican president (Eisenhower) interacted with a Republican Congress, the coalition formed on 22.64 percent of 106 nonunanimous House roll calls and on 22.67 percent of 225 nonunanimous Senate votes. When Democrats controlled both institutions, the coalition formed on 24.70 percent of 4,243 nonunanimous House votes and on 21.66 percent of 5,610 nonunanimous Senate roll calls. When Congress was organized by Democrats during Republican administrations, the conservative coalition appeared on 32.16 percent of 2,783 nonunanimous roll calls in the House and on 32.22 percent of 3,852 nonunanimous Senate votes.

Given the heavy disproportion in the four types of White House–Capitol Hill control, these results can be only indicative at best, although they do provide an interesting commentary on the effects of party ties in Congress and in the White House on the appearance of the conservative coalition. The striking difference is between levels of coalition appearance under a Republican president with a Democratic Congress and under the other three combinations of executive and legislative control. This result may be taken as evidence that the coalition in both chambers forms in large measure to support the conservative programs of Republican chief executives, as well as to foster the active pursuit of its own legislative initiatives that are more likely to succeed under the conservative climate generated by Republican administrations. More evidence on this point comes from the following set of correlations, which are based on annual observations beginning in 1933 (except for House coalition success, for which values are missing for 1933, 1936, and 1938).

A party-control variable can be set up that takes on the value of one when an institution is controlled by Democrats and the value of zero when that same institution is controlled by Republicans. When this is done, presidential party correlates $-.28$ with the appearance of the conservative coalition in the House and $-.45$ with coalition appearance in the Senate. Congressional party correlates only $-.04$ with coalition appearance in the House and .02 with appearances in the Senate. That is, on average, Republican presidencies portend higher rates of formation of the Republican–southern Democrat alliance, whereas congressional party control is essentially unrelated to coalition appearances. These results clearly demonstrate, in consonance with earlier findings, that the conservative coalition does not form merely as a reaction against the liberal programs of Democratic congresses or Democratic presidents.

Additional important information is provided by looking at levels of conservative coalition success under all four possible combinations of party power in the White House and in Congress. The rate of coalition success is 100 percent in both the House and the Senate with a Republican president and a Republican Congress, 68.85 percent in the House and 64.14 percent in the Senate when a Democratic Congress confronted a Republican president, 65.78 percent in the House and 65.10 percent in the Senate for the Democratic president–Democratic

Congress combination, and 100 percent in the House and 97.56 percent in the Senate when a Democratic president faced a Republican Congress. The most important result here is the virtually complete success during Republican Congresses enjoyed by the conservative coalition. This suggests that the coalition is in large measure a manifestation of Republican congressional policy needs, a point that is pursued further in Chapters 7 and 8. Coalition success is bound more closely to which party dominates Congress than to the party affiliation of the White House. This is the exact reverse of my earlier conclusion about the rate of appearance of the conservative coalition. The present finding is strengthened by the correlations between coalition success and party control. Success and presidential party are correlated only $-.001$ in the House and $-.14$ in the Senate, whereas success correlates $-.40$ with congressional party in the House and $-.38$ in the Senate. Higher rates of coalition success are expected under Republican control of Capitol Hill.

Time-Series "Intervention" Analysis of Presidential Effects

I have previously built and explored models of conservative coalition appearances and success in both the House and Senate. Now I will determine what additional effect beyond these basic results can be attributed to differences in a president's party. The results of this "intervention" analysis[6] of presidential effects are presented in Appendix E, as well as in Table 6–2, which summarizes the forecasts produced from each model. The models add a dichotomous "dummy" variable for presidential party, taking on a value of one during Democratic administrations and a value of zero for any year during a Republican presidential administration, to the models of coalition appearances and success discussed in Chapter 2.

The additional effect of presidential party on the rate of conservative coalition appearances as a percent of nonunanimous votes is negligible in both chambers. The important conclusion to be drawn from these models is that in neither chamber of Congress does a change in the party of the president have much statistical or substantive significance for the relative frequency with which the conservative coalition appears, above and beyond the previously determined patterns of serial correlation in levels of coalition appearance over time. Democratic administrations are associated with slightly higher rates of coalition formation in the House and very minimally lower rates of appearance in the Senate, after accounting for the autocorrelations within each of the two time series.

The effect of this presidential party "intervention" on conservative coalition success is also shown in Appendix E and in Table 6–2. According to these results, after controlling for patterns of serial dependence within the House and Senate coalition success data, the presence of a Democratic president is associated with a very small increase of about one percentage point in coalition success

Table 6–2

Time-Series Forecasts of Conservative Coalition
Appearances and Success Using Presidential Party and
Congressional Party as ''Interventions''

	Conditions of Party Control	Forecasts			
		1981	1982	1983	1984
House Conservative	Republican President	27.2	25.5	26.3	25.9
Coalition	Democratic President	28.3	27.8	29.7	30.5
Appearances	Republican House	27.1	25.4	26.2	25.8
	Democratic House	28.0	27.3	29.0	29.6
	Split/Same President and House	27.8	26.0	27.3	27.0
Senate Conservative	Republican President	23.4	24.2	23.8	24.0
Coalition	Democratic President	23.4	24.1	23.6	23.7
Appearances	Republican Senate	23.6	24.3	24.0	24.1
	Democratic Senate	24.0	25.0	25.1	25.5
	Split/Same President and Senate	24.3	25.9	26.3	27.3
House Conservative	Republican President	70.7	69.0	69.9	69.4
Coalition	Democratic President	71.5	70.6	72.3	72.6
Success	Republican House	69.7	68.5	69.1	68.8
	Democratic House	68.6	66.3	65.8	64.4
	Split/Same President and House	66.7	60.8	57.7	53.1
Senate Conservative	Republican President	64.2	63.7	69.3	67.5
Coalition	Democratic President	65.4	66.1	73.0	72.5
Success	Republican Senate	63.0	62.2	68.5	66.7
	Democratic Senate	62.8	61.8	68.0	66.0
	Split/Same President and Senate	65.5	66.7	74.1	73.7

Note: Republican presidents were in office 1953–60 and 1969–76; Democratic presidents
were in office 1933–52, 1961–68, and 1977–80; Republicans held a majority of seats in
the House and Senate 1947–48 and 1953–54; Democrats held a majority of seats in the
House and Senate 1933–46, 1949–52, and 1955–80.

rates in each chamber. Slightly higher forecasts of conservative coalition victory
rates are produced under the assumption of a Democratic administration than
under a Republican president from 1981–84.

The overall conclusion to be drawn from this analysis of marginal presidential
effects is that presidential party has very little additional influence over the rate of
conservative coalition appearance or the rate of its success beyond the recurring
historical factors reflected in the basic time-series models of Chapter 2. This
finding provides some interesting evidence of the relative insulation of Congress
from changes in presidential party.

If presidential party has little additional effect upon the success or the formation of the conservative coalition, are there significant influences upon coalition activity and its impact associated with party control of Congress above and beyond the underlying historical patterns revealed in the univariate models of Chapter 2? Again, a ready answer is available in Table 6–2 and in Appendix E, where the relevant results are produced by introducing a dummy variable that assumes the value of one for Democratic majority control and zero for years during which Republicans controlled Congress.

As just noted for the case of the negligible additional effects of changes in presidential party on coalition appearance, changing control of Congress has very little impact on the rate of formation of the southern Democrat–Republican alliance. The fact that these effects are positive, however, suggests that there is a slight tendency for the conservative coalition to form more frequently under Democratic than under Republican congressional control, beyond the underlying historical pattern. A reasonable interpretation of this result is that there is a residual tendency by the coalition to form more often when it must appear in order to oppose the generally liberal legislative agenda supported by Democratic majorities within Congress.

A reverse effect, although again one that is only minimal, appears when the residual effect of congressional party on coalition success is evaluated. Here, Republican control of Congress is associated with a small increase in the success rate enjoyed by the conservative coalition beyond what is expected from the internal dynamics of the historical performance of the coalition. This result is evident from the fact that the coefficients of the party control variable are negative in both chambers.

Finally, the relevance for appearance and success of the conservative coalition of split as opposed to same-party control over the White House and Capitol Hill must be considered. The results of this analysis are included in Table 6–2 and in Appendix E. In these models of party similarity and party differences, separate intervention terms are entered for each of the four logically possible circumstances of Republican House and Democratic president, Republican House and Republican president, Democratic House and Democratic president, and Democratic House and Republican president, and for the comparable situations in the Senate. The forecasts in Table 6–2 are based on the assumption that the years 1981–84 are characterized by a Democratic-controlled House, a Republican-controlled Senate, and a Republican White House.

Conservative coalition appearances in the House are residually affected the most by the combination of a Republican president and a Republican-controlled House. The additional influence of this combination of political power is to reduce the relative incidence of coalition appearances by about seven and one-half percentage points below what would be expected without considering the direction of party control in either the House or the presidency. Only very minor increases over expected levels of coalition activity occur in the House under conditions of a Democratic-controlled House and a Democratic president and under a majority Democratic House and a Republican chief executive. A negative influence is exercised by the combination of a Democratic White House and a Republican House of Representatives. The point of consistency here is the tendency for coalition appearance to be lower than otherwise expected when Republicans control the House and higher when Democrats are in charge. There is some tendency, then, for the appearance of the conservative coalition to be incrementally stimulated by opposition to the generally liberal proposals given a hearing under Democratic control of the House.

The rate of coalition appearances in the Senate shows a different pattern of party-control effects than was true in the House. The Senate results are strongest (and negative) for the combination of a Republican Senate and a Democratic president. The other effects of party sameness or party difference are negligible.

Coalition success at the margin is affected in the same direction in both the House and Senate. Success is greater than expected from the univariate base model for each party-control combination, except for a Republican White House and a Democratic-controlled chamber, although the magnitudes of these effects are widely different. These results suggest that the conservative elements in both chambers suffer lower levels of success when supporting the proposals of a Republican chief executive in the face of a more liberal Democratic majority.

Presidential Stands and Policy Interactions with the Conservative Coalition

We can get a somewhat more precise fix on the interrelationship between presidential position taking and the policy consequences of congressional coalition formation by examining the relative frequency with which the conservative coalition agreed and disagreed with the policy stands taken by each of the six presidents from Eisenhower to Carter. The necessary data (from Congressional Quarterly) are not available for the Roosevelt and Truman administrations. Table 6–3 shows the relative frequency with which the relevant presidents have taken a stand on all House and Senate roll call votes, as measured by Congressional Quarterly, as well as the proportion of all conservative coalition appearances in each administration on which the president also took a position. Each occasion in which a presidential stand coincides with an appearance of the conservative coalition is defined as a policy "interaction" between that president and the members of Congress who comprise the Republican–southern Democratic policy coalition. The table also shows the composite success rate enjoyed by each president, paralleling the conservative coalition success rate data for each administration reported in Table 6–1.

The critical issue here is the impact that the announcement or the awareness of presidential policy positions may have on the success of the conservative coalition and the reciprocal influence that the conservative coalition may exercise over

Table 6–3

Presidential Stands, Presidential Success, and
President-Conservative Coalition Interactions,
by Individual Presidents, 1953–1980
(n's for denominator are in parentheses)

President	Percent CC Votes Also Presidential Stands		Presidential Stands As Percent All Roll Calls		Percent Presidential Success	
	HOUSE					
Eisenhower	52.48	(101)	52.91	(669)	68.36	(354)
Kennedy	66.00	(50)	53.73	(335)	84.44	(180)
Johnson	57.42	(209)	50.84	(1009)	85.58	(513)
Nixon	27.00	(474)	19.50	(1969)	68.23	(384)
Ford	16.57	(344)	13.16	(1474)	51.03	(194)
Carter	26.07	(560)	16.09	(2816)	73.07	(453)
	SENATE					
Eisenhower	46.51	(215)	49.71	(1217)	70.74	(605)
Kennedy	49.28	(138)	55.01	(629)	84.68	(346)
Johnson	57.05	(312)	51.41	(1422)	80.03	(731)
Nixon	24.42	(688)	21.87	(2556)	61.54	(559)
Ford	14.91	(389)	14.36	(1490)	64.95	(214)
Carter	20.08	(503)	23.68	(2179)	79.65	(516)

the success of presidential programs.[7] The information essential to this analysis is contained in Table 6–4, which shows the relative frequency with which presidents have agreed with the positions taken by the conservative coalition (and vice versa) and the outcome of victory or defeat for both the coalition and the president.

Table 6–4 demonstrates that president-coalition interactions have occurred on a total of 537 House roll calls and on 673 Senate votes since 1953. Clearly, the dominant pattern in both chambers is one of generally higher rates of agreement between the conservative coalition and Republican presidents than between the coalition and Democratic presidents. President Eisenhower, however, disagreed with the coalition's position on a majority of its interactions in the House. Overall, the three Republican presidents agreed with the coalition's position in the House on 70.17 percent of its interactions. Nixon and Ford agreed with the coalition 80.54 percent of the time. In sharp contrast, the three Democratic presidents agreed with the coalition in the House on only 9.03 percent of their interactions, although Carter agreed with the coalition's position in the House a comparatively high 14.38 percent of the time. Kennedy and Johnson together agreed with the coalition only 3.92 percent of the time in the House.

Table 6–4

Presidential Stands and Conservative Coalition Vote Outcomes,
by Individual Presidents, 1953–1980
(n's for denominator are in parentheses)

President	Number CC Votes Also Pres. Stands	P and CC Agree, Both Win		P and CC Agree, Both Lose		P and CC Disagree, CC Wins		P and CC Disagree, P Wins	
HOUSE									
Eisenhower	53	30.19	(16)	3.77	(2)	47.17	(25)	18.87	(10)
Kennedy	33	3.03	(1)	0.00	(0)	60.61	(20)	36.36	(12)
Johnson	120	4.17	(5)	0.00	(0)	34.17	(41)	61.67	(74)
Nixon	128	62.50	(80)	19.53	(25)	9.38	(12)	8.59	(11)
Ford	57	36.84	(21)	40.35	(23)	5.26	(3)	17.54	(10)
Carter	146	12.33	(18)	2.05	(3)	41.10	(60)	44.52	(65)
SENATE									
Eisenhower	100	75.00	(75)	12.00	(12)	10.00	(10)	3.00	(3)
Kennedy	68	0.00	(0)	4.41	(3)	36.76	(25)	58.82	(40)
Johnson	178	18.54	(33)	3.37	(6)	34.83	(62)	43.26	(77)
Nixon	167	59.28	(99)	34.13	(57)	4.19	(7)	2.40	(4)
Ford	59	76.27	(45)	20.34	(12)	0.00	(0)	3.39	(2)
Carter	101	13.86	(14)	1.98	(2)	41.58	(42)	42.57	(43)

In the Senate, the three Republican presidents agreed with the coalition's position on 92.02 percent of all interactions, with no perceptible differences between Eisenhower and the other two Republican executives. As in the House, Democratic presidents agreed with the coalition on far fewer interactions (16.71 percent), but sharply different levels of agreement separate Johnson (21.91 percent) from Kennedy (4.41 percent), with Carter in between (15.84 percent).

In Table 6–4 the results of conservative coalition-president interactions are entered under four categories, representing the possible joint outcomes for each side. They may agree and jointly win, agree and jointly lose, disagree with the coalition winning, and disagree with the president winning. A glance at the data in the table suggests that dramatically different patterns of success and failure for both presidents and the conservative coalition have occurred on interactions under the six different administrations. In the House, Johnson and Ford enjoyed great success against the opposition of the conservative coalition, whereas executives and the conservative coalition working together were markedly successful under each president except Ford. In the Senate, Kennedy, Johnson, and Ford were highly successful against the opposition of the coalition, and the two working together were effective in every administration except Kennedy's.

"Presidential Effects" on Conservative Coalition Success

The discussion of the reciprocal impacts of congressional coalitions and presidential position taking can be focused more clearly by the use of appropriate indexes that measure the influence exercised by Congress over a president's positions and the extent to which presidents may determine the outcome of congressional decisions. Three such indexes of the impact of presidential stands on the success of the conservative coalition are developed. The numerical results of applying these indexes to the data from Tables 6–1 and 6–3 are summarized in Table 6–5.

These are collectively measures of what could be called differential coalition success. The first index, HURTCC, specifies the extent to which a president's

Table 6–5

Indexes of Differential Coalition Success
(cumulative n's from Table 6–4 are in parentheses)

President	HURTCC	HELPCC	NPE = HELPCC + HURTCC
Eisenhower			
House	− .0496 (35)	.0513 (18)	.0017 (53)
Senate	− .0085 (13)	.0410 (87)	.0325 (100)
Kennedy			
House	− .0514 (32)	.0156 (1)	− .0358 (33)
Senate	− .2609 (65)	− .0441 (3)	− .3050 (68)
Johnson			
House	− .2717 (115)	.0421 (5)	− .2296 (120)
Senate	− .1455 (139)	.1192 (39)	− .0263 (178)
Nixon			
House	− .0501 (23)	.0434 (105)	− .0067 (128)
Senate	− .0000 (11)	− .0029 (156)	− .0029 (167)
Ford			
House	− .1343 (13)	− .1152 (44)	− .2495 (57)
Senate	− .0339 (2)	.4268 (57)	.3929 (59)
Carter			
House	− .2097 (125)	.0501 (21)	− .1596 (146)
Senate	− .2135 (85)	.0510 (16)	− .1625 (101)

opposition to the roll call position eventually taken by the conservative coalition reduces the coalition's rate of success below its overall success recorded during that president's tenure. More formally, for the ith president

$$\text{HURTCC}_i = ((\frac{Dc}{D} - \frac{Cc}{C}) \times \frac{D}{A+D}) / \frac{Cc}{C}$$

where Dc =   the number of disagreements with the president that were won by
             the conservative coalition
    D =   the total number of disagreements between the conservative
             coalition and the president
    Cc =   the number of appearances won by the conservative coalition
    C =   the total number of conservative coalition appearances
    A =   the total number of agreements between the conservative coali-
             tion and the president.

This index can be interpreted as measuring the weighted incremental success enjoyed by the conservative coalition when it stands against the opposition of a president. The weight is simply the proportion of all interactions between that president and the conservative coalition that result in policy disagreements. The HURTCC index is positive if the coalition is more successful in the face of presidential opposition than its overall success rate during that administration. The index is negative if opposition from the White House lowers the coalition's success rate below its overall level. Expressed as a proportion of the coalition's overall rate of success, HURTCC indicates the percentage reduction (or increase) in conservative coalition success resulting from this form of policy interaction with the White House. A value of zero indicates no perceptible impact of presidential opposition on the coalition's pattern of success.

The HURTCC index is negative for all six presidents for both the Senate and the House, with the exception of the Nixon–conservative coalition interactions in the Senate. In that one case, there was no detectable difference between the coalition's overall success rate and the success enjoyed by the coalition when Nixon opposed its roll call position. The fact that this index is otherwise uniformly negative means that in the aggregate presidents have been successful in reducing the coalition's rate of success by expressing opposition to the stand that was eventually taken by a majority of voting Republicans and a majority of voting southern Democrats.

For the House, the degree of harm done to the conservative coalition by presidential opposition varies from a minimal reduction in its rate of success of less than 5 percent under Eisenhower to a reduction of over 27 percent under Johnson. Three presidents—Eisenhower, Kennedy, and Nixon—had only a minimal negative impact on the performance of the coalition on policy matters. Two presidents—Johnson and Carter—enjoyed comparative success in preventing the coalition from emerging victorious, and one—Ford—enjoyed moderate luck in holding coalition success against his programmatic preferences below its overall victory rate.

In the Senate, Kennedy and Carter showed the greatest amount of success in opposing the conservative coalition's roll call stands, whereas considerably less though still appreciable success was enjoyed by Johnson against the coalition in the Senate. None of the three Republican presidents had much luck in directly limiting the coalition's Senate success rate. The best Republican showing was by Ford, whose opposition reduced the coalition's Senate success rate by only about 3 percent.

In general, Democratic presidents have had more impact than Republican presidents in reducing the coalition's rate of success below its overall level by making known their opposition to the position later taken on roll call votes by the Republican-southern Democratic alliance.

An index very similar to the HURTCC index can be used to investigate the other side of the coin of presidential impact on coalition success. The extent to which a president can help the conservative coalition by expressing a position that is in agreement with the coalition's eventual voting stand is given for the ith president by the HELPCC index:

$$\text{HELPCC}_i = \left(\left(\frac{Ac}{A} - \frac{Cc}{C}\right) \times \frac{A}{A+D}\right) / \frac{Cc}{C}$$

where $Ac =$ the number of agreements with the president that were won by the conservative coalition

and the other variables in the equation are as defined for the HURTCC index above. This second index of differential coalition success can be interpreted as the weighted incremental success enjoyed by the conservative coalition when it has the support of the president, where the weight is the proportion of all interactions between the ith president and the conservative coalition that result in policy agreements. The HELPCC index is positive if the coalition is more successful when presidents agree with its stands and negative if presidential support fails to improve the coalition's overall rate of success. An index value of zero indicates no overall favorable presidential impact on coalition success.

Very different patterns than were evident for the HURTCC index emerge across the six presidencies on this index of presidential assistance. With the exception of Kennedy and Nixon in the Senate and Ford in the House, presidential support has always increased the coalition's success rate. But presidential agreement does not in general have a pronounced impact on the outcome of conservative coalition roll calls.

In the House, only Eisenhower's and Carter's agreement improved the coalition's success rate by as much as 5 percent, and the coalition's success was actually 11.5 percent less than its overall rate of success when President Ford agreed with its positions. The remarkable finding here is the consistency with which presidents fail to have much helpful effect on the coalition's success in the House. A somewhat more varied result emerges in the case of the Senate. Ford's support was a major impetus behind the success of the Senate coalition, which enjoyed a nearly 43 percent boost in its success rate when Ford agreed with its eventual roll call stand. The only other instance of presidential position taking having any perceptible helpful influence over coalition success in the Senate occurred under the Johnson administration. In both the Johnson and Ford cases, owing to the realities of parliamentary arithmetic reflecting poor election outcomes for the Republican party, the coalition's success rate was generally low and presidential support would have been more important in helping the coalition through to success on any given roll call.

The general conclusion following from this analysis of president–conservative coalition agreement is that neither Republican nor Democratic presidents systematically help to improve the coalition's overall success rate. The seemingly inevitable conclusion, then, is that regardless of party, presidents have a greater negative than a positive impact on the outcome of votes on which they interact with the conservative coalition.

A summary measure of the net impact that a president has on the policy success of the conservative coalition may be developed from the two preceding indexes of presidential impact. Each index separately shows the direction and magnitude of the harm or assistance that a president brings with his position taking. A meaningful measure of the net overall effect of presidential stands on conservative coalition success is simply the sum of the values of the two indexes of presidential harm and presidential helpfulness. This index of net presidential effect (NPE) is defined as

$$NPE = HELPCC + HURTCC.$$

A positive value of NPE indicates that a president was more effective in helping than in hurting the coalition's chances for success, whereas a negative value shows that a president had a greater impact in harming the coalition's programmatic stands. Intriguing distinctions between House and Senate patterns and also between Democratic and Republican presidential patterns emerge from this analysis, as may be seen from Table 6–5.

Comparing first the Senate results against results in the House, it becomes clear that Democratic presidents uniformly do more harm than good to the coalition's position in both the House and the Senate. Republican presidents, in contrast, do not show a consistent pattern. Only Eisenhower produced a very small net benefit for the coalition's success in the House; Ford had a substantial net negative impact; and Nixon had a minimal negative effect on the coalition's performance in the House. Looking at the Senate, again each of the three Democratic presidents harmed the coalition more than they helped it. Eisenhower and Ford produced net benefits for the coalition, and Nixon had a minimally adverse effect. Democratic administrations, then, are clearly associated with net harm to the programmatic intent of the conservative coalition, and Republican administrations may (Eisenhower in both chambers and Ford in the Senate) or may not (Nixon in both chambers and Ford in the House) assist the coalition's pursuit of its policy goals.

Comparing now across individual administrations, it is important to note that there are wide variations in both the magnitude and the direction of the impact that different presidents may have had on the outcome of this set of votes in Congress. Eisenhower and Nixon show only a very small impact on coalition success in either chamber, with Ike's effects on the positive side and Nixon's effects barely negative. Kennedy and Johnson had consistently negative impacts on coalition success in both the House and Senate, but with much greater effect in one chamber than in the other. Both Carter and Ford show consistently strong influence over the level of coalition success, with Ford having more impact in the Senate than in the House. The direction of the Ford and Carter effects is quite different, however, with Ford doing more harm than good in the House but the reverse in the Senate and Carter harming the coalition considerably in both chambers.

The Conservative Coalition and Presidential Programs

The reciprocal perspective in this analysis of patterns of executive-legislative interplay on policy making focuses on the impact that the conservative coalition has had on the outcome of presidential programs. Although the old saw that "the President proposes, Congress disposes" may not be fully valid, one would nonetheless expect to find in the roll call record substantial evidence of the conservative coalition (or of any other congressional coalition or voting bloc, for that matter) using its voting strength to attempt to alter, deflect, or destroy presidential policy preferences. Three indexes of the impact of conservative coalition voting activity on the success of a president's program are presented below, each of which exactly parallels the previously discussed indexes of presidential impacts on the performance of the conservative coalition.

These various indexes of the conservative coalition's impact on presidential performance collectively measure what could be called differential presidential success. The first index, HURTPRES, specifies the extent to which the formation of the conservative coalition on a roll call vote in opposition to the stated policy position taken by a president reduces that president's rate of success below his administration's overall success rate. That is, for the ith president,

$$\text{HURTPRES}_i = \left(\left(\frac{Dp}{D} - \frac{Pp}{P} \right) \times \frac{D}{A+D} \right) / \frac{Pp}{P}$$

where Dp = the number of disagreements with the conservative coalition that were won by the president

Pp = the number of presidential stands won by the president

P = the total number of presidential stands

and the other variables are as defined earlier. The HURTPRES index, then, is the weighted incremental success enjoyed by a president against the roll call opposition of the conservative coalition, where the weight is the same as in the HURTCC index. This index has the same properties as HURTCC, except, of course, that it reverses the logical direction of impact. Results from applying this index are presented in Table 6–6.

Table 6–6

Indexes of Differential Presidential Success
(cumulative n's from Table 6–4 are in parentheses)

President	HURTPRES		HELPPRES		NCE = HELPPRES + HURTPRES	
Eisenhower						
House	− .3844	(35)	.1020	(18)	− .2824	(53)
Senate	− .0876	(13)	.1903	(87)	.1027	(100)
Kennedy						
House	− .5391	(32)	.0056	(1)	− .5335	(33)
Senate	− .2612	(65)	− .0441	(3)	− .3053	(68)
Johnson						
House	− .2377	(115)	.0070	(5)	− .2307	(120)
Senate	− .2403	(139)	.0126	(39)	− .2277	(178)
Nixon						
House	− .0537	(23)	.0957	(105)	.0420	(128)
Senate	− .0270	(11)	.0291	(156)	.0021	(167)
Ford						
House	.1157	(13)	− .0499	(44)	.0658	(57)
Senate	.0183	(2)	.2082	(57)	.2265	(59)
Carter						
House	− .2469	(125)	.0249	(21)	− .2220	(146)
Senate	− .3071	(85)	.0156	(16)	− .2915	(101)

The HURTPRES index is negative in both chambers for five presidents, indicating that the dominant pattern is for presidential policy positions to be adversely affected by roll call opposition from the conservative coalition. The lone exception to this norm is Ford, whose success was not reduced by the opposition of the coalition. In general, the conservative coalition harmed the chances for success of presidents' programs to a considerable extent. In the House (ignoring the Ford results), the coalition's negative impact varies from a minimal 5 percent reduction in presidential success for Nixon to a nearly 54 percent reduction in Kennedy's rate of success. The conservative coalition in the House had only a moderately negative impact on Johnson and Carter programs and more strongly negative effects on Eisenhower. Comparing the results here with those presented in Table 6–5, we see that negative coalition impact is clearly greater than the reciprocal negative presidential effects on the coalition for Eisenhower and Kennedy in the House, but the coalition impact and presidential impact statistics are about equal for the other administrations (except that the direction of these compared effects is reversed for Ford).

Two tendencies regarding the harm done to presidential programs by the opposition of the conservative coalition are evident from Table 6–6. First, the coalition's opposition was generally more detrimental to a president's chances for success in the House than in the Senate. Across the six administrations, the coalition reduced presidential success rates by an average of about 22 percent in the House (34 percent for Democratic presidents, 11 percent for Republican presidents), and by a composite of just over 15 percent in the Senate (27 percent for Democratic presidents, 3 percent for Republican presidents). Second, as the figures in parentheses in the preceding sentence indicate, the coalition's policy disagreements with a president were in the aggregate more harmful for the policies of Democrats in the White House than for Republican executives.

The HELPPRES index serves the same analytical function as the HELPCC index discussed above. It is defined by

$$\text{HELPPRES}_i = \left(\left(\frac{Ap}{A} - \frac{Pp}{P}\right) \times \frac{A}{A+D}\right) / \frac{Pp}{P}$$

where Ap = the number of agreements with the conservative coalition that were won by the president

and the other variables are as previously defined. The HELPPRES index, then, measures the weighted incremental success enjoyed by the ith president when he has the roll call support of the conservative coalition. The weight is the same as for the HELPCC index. A positive value in Table 6–6 indicates that a president is more successful when the coalition agrees with his stands, and a negative value indicates that the coalition's support actually leads to a reduction in the president's overall rate of success. A value of zero indicates no overall favorable impact on presidential success when his position coincides with that of the conservative coalition.

The major conclusion to be drawn from this index of conservative coalition helpfulness for a president's program is that very little positive impact was manifested throughout these six administrations. The effects of coalition agreement were virtually nil in both chambers for the Kennedy, Johnson, and Carter administrations and approached substantial magnitudes only under Eisenhower in both chambers, under Nixon in the House, and under Ford in the Senate. Clearly, then, the conservative coalition's affirmative intervention on presidential stands is of any perceptible consequence only sporadically and only under Republican administrations.

In parallel with the summary measure of net presidential effect (NPE) presented earlier, an appropriate summary index of net coalition effect (NCE) may be constructed from the sum of the two indexes of conservative coalition harmfulness and helpfulness. This is defined as

$$\text{NCE} = \text{HELPPRES} + \text{HURTPRES}$$

A positive value of NCE indicates that the conservative coalition was more effective in helping a president's program than in blocking presidential-supported actions with which it was in disagreement, and a negative value indicates the reverse.

With the exception of the value of this index for Eisenhower in the House, there is a sharp distinction between the overall net negative consequences of conservative coalition interaction for the success of Democratic presidential stands, as compared against the net assistance given to the positions of Republican presidents. The magnitude of these effects, however, is widely varied, ranging from a barely visible positive impact on Nixon's success to a very profound negative impact on the success of President Kennedy. These results largely parallel the findings for the NPE index, in that the reciprocal impacts of presidents and the conservative coalition are more consistent and predictable for Democratic than for Republican administrations.

Summary and Conclusions

Markedly higher rates of agreement with the position taken by the conservative coalition are evident among Republican presidents than among the three Democratic presidents, although there was substantial variation within each presidential partisan grouping. The conservative coalition does have an important impact on the fate of a president's policy positions in most cases, although decidedly more so in the negative direction of harming the executive's programs than in providing significant assistance. The extent of coalition effects has been beneficial only to Republican presidents and then only sporadically.

The generally higher rate of conservative coalition activity under Republican administrations suggests that an interpretation of the coalition's appearance as a defensive reaction against liberal programmatic policy initiatives is overly simple. Emphasis should also be placed on the possibility that the conservative coalition operates with greater freedom, though not necessarily with greater success, when stimulated by the presence of a Republican president.

Congressional permeability to presidents' policy stands seems in the aggregate to be less than the degree to which presidential programmatic wishes are subject to congressional policy determination. Time-series ''intervention'' methods have indicated the effects of presidential party, congressional party, and same versus split control of Congress and the White House on the appearance and success of the southern Democrat–Republican alliance.

7

The Conservative Coalition and the Congressional Party System

The analysis in previous chapters has explored many of the circumstances under which the congressional conservative coalition has been an important determinant of the quality and the content of public policy in American society. An important remaining task is to evaluate the relationship of the conservative coalition to the American party system, through which members of Congress are elected to office and the formal distribution of legislative power is organized and structured.

The extent to which congressional decisions are structured by the influence of party is assessed here as the frequency with which party unity votes occur in each chamber. A party unity vote is a roll call on which a majority of voting Democrats, regardless of region, vote in opposition to the position taken by the majority of voting Republicans. The logical alternative to a party unity vote is a bipartisan vote, or a roll call on which a majority of voting Republicans agree with the position taken by a majority of voting Democrats. The number of party unity roll calls as a proportion of all nonunanimous votes cast in a given session provides a measure of the relative salience of party in congressional decision making.

It is also useful to examine the roll call record to measure the rate at which the Democratic party in Congress has split into two distinct blocs of southerners and nonsoutherners. A North-South Democratic split roll call is a recorded vote on which a majority of voting northern Democrats vote against the position of a majority of voting southern Democrats. The direction of Republican votes is not important for determining when a Democratic split has occurred, but if a majority of both Republicans and southern Democrats agree, then the conservative coalition has, of course, appeared.

The data yield some very important evidence about the causes and the rate of decomposition of the Democratic party. They also shed light on the origins of the conservative coalition as an alternative substantive congressional majority that emerged as the Democratic party's unity began to shatter. The frequency of North-South Democratic splits as a proportion of all nonunanimous roll calls for a given session is used as an indicator of the magnitude of the breakup of the Democratic party coalition and of the establishment of preconditions for the emergence of the new, cross-party alliance of southern Democrats and Republicans.

Finally, the relationship between the conservative coalition and the congressional party system may also be explored by analyzing the extent to which North-South Democratic splits coincide with the appearance of the conservative coalition. These data are especially important as a measure of the level of "maturation," or the degree of "articulation," of the conservative coalition. The coalition may be said to have "matured" or become more fully "articulated" over time to the extent that an increasing proportion of all splits between northern and southern Democrats have also been conservative coalition votes.

George Galloway believes that the conservative coalition emerged during the 1910–41 period, when the party caucus disintegrated and disciplined congressional party government was supplanted by loose and unstable alliances. He further argues that the coalition's influence was consolidated during the Seventy-ninth Congress (1945–46).[1] The exact time, at least since 1933, when the coalition became most influential on the congressional party system is assessed in this chapter. The exact nature of the long-term trends of party unity voting is evaluated by the method of time-series analysis.

Time-series analysis of the level of party unity voting in this chapter allows a direct evaluation of the Hinckley and Li finding that the conservative coalition is more stable than the coalition of southern and northern Democrats.[2] The time-series method is also used to assess the comparative stability of the party coalition and of the cross-party conservative coalition in each chamber.

It is reasonable to expect that, as the conservative coalition has matured into a stable and more regularly occurring legislative alliance, the rate of North-South Democratic splits has also increased over time and has recently stabilized at a fairly high level. Similarly, the maturation of the conservative coalition should be reflected in an increased rate of coincidence of Democratic regional splits with the formation of the coalition.

Before investigating these historical patterns, however, it is worthwhile to consider the foundations of both party unity and party divisions within the United States Congress. Although the following excerpt from the *Congressional Record* deals with events of the long-ago 1960s, it presents a thorough outline of the basis for party cohesiveness and the reasons for cross-party cooperation.

Parties and Coalitions: A Congressional Commentary

Although the floor of the House of Representatives is not the usual locale for discussions of electoral strategy or for the airing of intraparty disputes, the following colloquy among three House leaders provides an interesting perspective on congressional parties and the legislature's cross-party groupings. The participants in this discussion of Republican party strategy for the 1968 elections were Gerald R. Ford (R-Michigan), then House minority leader, Omar Burleson (D-Texas), a leader among conservative southern Democratic congressmen, and Hale Boggs (D-Louisiana), at the time the House majority whip. The three-way discussion reveals much about the norms of congressional activity and presents a picture of both the tenuous nature of Republican–southern Democratic cooperation and the gap separating Dixie Democrats from their northern party colleagues. The verbal floor action on May 15, 1967, was precipitated by a speech on May 10 delivered by Ford regarding the different goals of Republicans and southern Democrats in the upcoming congressional elections of 1968. Particulars of that speech are given in Burleson's opening statement.

Mr. BURLESON. Mr. Speaker, one of the most remarkable and amazing statements was made by the distinguished minority leader in Ohio last week. I have a copy of his speech, and I would like to quote that portion which, it seems to me, is one of the most irresponsible statements made by a distinguished leader of this great institution. If the minority leader wants to respond, I shall be glad, as I have told him personally, to ask for a special order this afternoon at the close of legislative business, or any other day which might be more convenient to him. In part this is what the gentleman from Michigan, the able minority leader, said in a speech at Bowling Green University, Bowling Green, Ohio, on last Wednesday, May 10:

"House Republicans also are making a record for Republican congressional candidates to run on. We need 31 more seats to take over the House—and I think there's a good chance we'll make it. We have a good chance for many reasons. One of these is what might be called my Southern Strategy."

This is a quote:

"The strategy is to drive Southern Democrats in the House into the arms of the Administration—where they belong—on votes that will hurt them in their home congressional districts.

"This strategy runs exactly counter to the old pattern of a Southern Democrat–Republican coalition that often prevailed over Administration forces in the House in years past.

"But I think it is far better to lose a few legislative battles and win the next election. Besides, in following my Southern Strategy we Republicans in the House are staking out positions in which we believe—responsible, constructive positions.

"There will be times when Republicans will win in the 90th Congress. We won't win as many legislative fights as we could if we resorted to the old coalition tactics, but it's the Big Prize that counts, and that's what we're after.

"The Big Prize is control of at least one House of Congress and control of the White House. We want that prize not because we relish power for the sake of power but because we sincerely believe that our course, our program, is a better way than LBJ."

Mr. Speaker, I want to inform the minority leader that he is not "driving" anyone anywhere on this side of the aisle, and particularly this Member. I do not think very many other Members of a like mind will be driven from doing that which they believe to be best for our country regardless of party or politics. I would think that my distinguished colleague from Michigan would have enough difficulty and be concerned and occupied enough in leading the various factions on his own side of the House. It would seem to me that you would have enough to do in leading from 21 to 26 liberal Republicans who helped inaugurate many of the programs that are under question and debate and of very questionable nature during the last 2 years, and it would seem to me that you would have enough to do in leading your conservatives who, I think, put the good of this country ahead of party. Some of these two factions in your own party may have difficulty in finding that "middle of road" to which you referred in your speech last week.

I can only interpret the minority leader's remarks as saying that the party comes first, and that the good of the country, constructive legislation, is not a matter of first concern. That is the only interpretation I can place on it, Mr. Speaker, and I say again it is one of the most amazing and astounding statements attributed to one in the responsible position of minority leader. In fact it would be surprising coming from any Member but especially so under the circumstances. It is disappointing but I doubt will be discouraging to efforts of those on both sides who are concerned with the future welfare of our Nation.

Mr. GERALD R. FORD. Mr. Speaker, I ask unanimous consent to address the House for 1 minute and to revise and extend my remarks.

The SPEAKER. Is there objection to the request of the gentleman from Michigan?

There was no objection.

Mr. GERALD R. FORD. Mr. Speaker, I appreciate the gentleman from Texas notifying me in advance that he intended to make the remarks that he just made. The speech or excerpts from it that I made the gentleman quoted exactly.

I happen to feel that those of us on this side of the aisle, in our own process of policy determination, should develop and enunciate Republican policy. We do not believe we should determine our policy by letting those on the other side of the aisle, whether they are southern or northern, liberal or conservative, have an impact on our policy decision. Our policy decisions are predicated on what the Republican Party decides in its best judgment what [*sic*] is best for the country. We welcome the support of anybody, but we are not going to have a Democrat or a segment of the Democratic Party determine our policy.

Mr. BURLESON. Mr. Speaker, will the gentleman yield?

Mr. GERALD R. FORD. I yield to the gentleman from Texas.

Mr. BURLESON. Mr. Speaker, the gentleman mentions the old Democratic and Republican coalition. This is something I believe should be brought out very clearly and distinctly. In the first place, there is no such thing, and there never has been. Men of like mind have gravitated together to exchange views and discuss strategy. Good Members on both sides of the aisle interested in seeing the welfare of our country served best have something great in common. Those of us on the Democratic side who subscribe to what is commonly known as the conservative view have often met to compare opinions, to exchange ideas, to determine tactics for offering certain amendments, and what the chances are for success. Of course, that is the reason they make doors, so we will not have to run our heads into a brick wall. Now, that is the extent of the so-called Republican–Democratic coalition.

We have had some great leaders in the past, men who were interested first in doing what they thought was the best thing for the country at large. Contrary to the opinion of some, and particularly some members of the press, there are no joint meetings of Democrats and Republicans but is there any reason why there should not be rapport between those seeking common goals? There is nothing surreptitious about it. We do not get together in the back room. That has never happened. A lot of people believe we sneak around someplace, behind the leadership's back, and contrive and scheme, and come in here with the idea of sinking somebody's boat, just because we might be able to.

That is not the point at all, and it never has been. But when we cannot have rapport, when we cannot know what may be the course of action, then I believe this House of Representatives is pretty weak in serving the American people.

Mr. GERALD R. FORD. My position, as I said a moment ago—and this has been the position of the leadership at least for the last 2½ years—is that we, as a Republican Party, as one of the two great major political parties, must evolve our own policy decisions. It may be that in the final analysis, when that position has been taken by the Republican Party, we will get some help on the other side of the aisle. We welcome Democratic support for our policy position regardless of whether it is liberal or conservative, north or south.

But the point I was trying to make, and I want to reemphasize it, is this: We will make our own policy decisions in our own way through our policy committee, the Republican conference, and by our leadership. When the bill gets to the floor of the House, involving a legislative matter, then it is up to the House as a whole—435 of us, 258 [*sic*] Democrats and 187 Republicans—who must make the final decision. Your vote and my vote on occasion may be the same. They may be different, but in the initial stage, the Republican Party must make up its own mind without any influence in any way whatsoever as far as the Democratic Party is concerned.

Mr. BURLESON. Mr. Speaker, will the gentleman from Michigan yield further?

Mr. GERALD R. FORD. I yield to the gentleman from Texas.

Mr. BURLESON. Mr. Speaker, I would just like to ask the gentleman one question. Does the gentleman put the policy of the Republican Party before the good of the country?

Mr. GERALD R. FORD. Mr. Speaker, we happen to believe that the party decisions of the Republican Party are in the national interest, and we do not take a position for any partisan purpose.

Our party position, in our judgment, is in the national interest; just as I am sure the administration believes its decisions are in the party interest.

But those decisions by us will be predicated on our own determination, not influenced by what a segment of the Democratic Party may believe to be right.

Mr. BURLESON. If the gentleman will yield further, I cannot interpret his speech in Ohio on last Wednesday in that way. The gentleman said that the purpose was to do that which it takes to elect a President of the United States. The gentleman said "southerners," but there are some people here who are conservative who are not from the Deep South. I use that word advisedly, as it means all things to all people.

As I interpret it, the gentleman said that the first consideration of all those actions was for that purpose and no other; that there might be times when good legislation was defeated and bad legislation enacted but that did not matter. What mattered was what is good for the Republican Party.

If the speech can be interpreted any other way, I fail to see it and the gentleman has failed to defend his intemporate [*sic*] words.

Mr. GERALD R. FORD. I am sorry; it was not intended that way.

I say again, as I said before, we construe Republican Party positions to be in the national interest. We hope they prevail despite the fact that we are still a minority in the House, 187 to 258 [*sic*].

If we build a record on those policies, I still believe we will win in 1968.

Mr. BOGGS. Mr. Speaker, I ask unanimous consent to address the House for 1 minute and to revise and extend my remarks.

The SPEAKER. Is there objection to the request of the gentleman from Louisiana?

There was no objection.

Mr. BOGGS. Mr. Speaker, I have listened with, shall I say, more than passing interest to the exchange which has just occurred here between two of my very distinguished friends; between my distinguished Democratic friend the gentleman from Texas and the distinguished minority leader of the House of Representatives.

The only point I want to make is that despite the great respect I have for the gentleman from Texas, I am not surprised at the statement made by the gentleman from Michigan. I should like to compliment and congratulate the gentleman from Michigan because he has made a very honest statement about the Republican Party. He does not want Democrats. He never has wanted them, over all these years. He wants to defeat Democrats wherever they live.

I discovered a long time ago: No. 1, that I did not help my people or the nation by voting for negative Republican measures; and, No. 2, that if I did it would not mean I would not have Republican opposition.

Some of my dear friends on this side have somehow or other felt that perhaps if they voted for this type of negative government the opposition party would not oppose them.

But I have noted that some of the—and I put this in quotation marks, because I never like to categorize anyone or use labels—"most conservative" Members on this side have been opposed by Republicans who have called them bad names, in describing their legislative activities.

So I say to the gentleman from Michigan that he has made an honest statement. I believe he is absolutely right when he says he wants to win a measure and win it only with Republican votes, not Democratic votes.

The Democratic Party, I am happy to say, does not require conformity. We expect our members to vote as their own consciences dictate. We hope our programs are in the best interests of our country and deserve support on that basis.

On Tuesday and Wednesday of this coming week we will have a test of affirmative Government. We will have under consideration a bill that affects every school-child in the United States.

From the point of view of the Democratic Party, the bill which the committee has reported is a bill that continues to help these children in schools all over our country.

From the point of view of the Republican Party, they say, ''No, we want to do it another way.''

We feel that what they propose will wreck the program.

I would hope that when the vote comes on next Wednesday my good friends from the South will follow the wise admonition of the gentleman from Michigan and not vote with the Republicans.

Mr. BURLESON. Mr. Speaker, will the gentleman yield now?

Mr. BOGGS. Surely. I yield.

Mr. BURLESON. Let me say that those of us over here who do not always vote with the leadership never vote with the Republicans—they vote with us.

Mr. BOGGS. Excuse me. Let me say to the gentleman I do not want him to feel for 1 minute that I think he or anyone else does not have a right to vote any way he likes. I have always believed that the Democratic Party encompasses many people. I consider the gentleman from Texas as good a Democrat as the Speaker of the House and the majority leader and myself. I am happy to have him in the Democratic Party.

Mr. BURLESON. Does the gentleman mean to tell me he would always expect every Member on our side of the aisle to vote exactly as the administration and the leadership tells him to vote? If that is so, I will stay back home where I can enjoy living a great deal more than I can here.

Mr. BOGGS. I said exactly the opposite. I said I welcome the gentleman, regardless of how he votes. I am happy to have him. He is one of the ablest and most valuable Members of this body. I admire and respect him and have for many years both as a person and as a sincere legislator of great conviction.[3]

Party Unity Voting and Formation of the Conservative Coalition

As can be seen in Table 7–1, there has been considerable variation over time in the rate at which majorities of Democrats and Republicans annually have voted in opposition to one another's recorded positions on nonunanimous roll calls. There is no clearly consistent trend over time in the rate at which the two parties come into conflict on the floor of the House and Senate, although there was a noticeable decline in the appearance of party coalitions, beginning about 1967, to a fairly stable lower plateau.

The exceptionally low rate of party unity voting in the Senate in 1964, about 39 percent, is a consequence of the sharp divisions between northern and southern Democrats sparked by legislative maneuverings associated with passage of the Civil Rights Act of 1964. The extent of party unity in the House, in contrast, was

Table 7–1

Party Unity Votes, 1933–1980

Year	Number of Party Unity Roll Calls		Party Unity Votes as Percent All Roll Calls		Party Unity Votes as Percent Nonunanimous Votes	
	House	Senate	House	Senate	House	Senate
1933	46	69	75	70	81	74
1934	58	91	71	70	77	72
1935	85	71	65	54	70	57
1936	43	31	53	51	61	53
1937	59	62	61	67	67	73
1938	41	46	67	57	72	61
1939	70	69	74	61	84	67
1940	92	93	69	61	78	67
1941	47	65	59	66	68	75
1942	19	34	26	36	36	45
1943	42	66	54	54	56	60
1944	29	50	45	51	56	55
1945	50	53	50	49	68	54
1946	60	72	46	53	59	55
1947	39	95	46	69	59	76
1948	36	55	46	50	58	56
1949	66	148	55	63	69	67
1950	72	148	47	65	60	69
1951	65	116	60	58	71	63
1952	42	75	58	66	71	71
1953	37	46	52	51	66	56
1954	29	85	38	47	58	59
1955	30	27	39	31	54	44
1956	33	69	45	53	61	62
1957	59	39	59	36	66	52
1958	37	87	40	44	55	52
1959	48	103	55	48	63	61
1960	49	76	53	37	67	49
1961	58	127	50	62	64	69
1962	57	92	46	41	67	46
1963	58	108	49	47	67	55
1964	62	109	55	36	75	39
1965	105	108	52	42	71	50
1966	80	118	41	50	68	61
1967	89	109	36	35	57	48
1968	82	90	35	32	54	41
1969	55	89	31	36	49	45
1970	72	147	27	35	44	48

	Number of Party Unity Roll Calls		Party Unity Votes as Percent All Roll Calls		Party Unity Votes as Percent Nonunanimous Votes	
Year	House	Senate	House	Senate	House	Senate
1971	121	176	38	42	55	54
1972	89	194	27	36	43	51
1973	226	237	42	40	57	54
1974	158	241	29	44	45	55
1975	296	288	48	48	63	57
1976	237	256	36	37	53	49
1977	298	269	42	42	64	52
1978	277	233	33	45	53	57
1979	318	232	47	47	66	56
1980	227	243	38	46	56	57

not affected by the civil rights debate, and in fact party unity voting in the House during the mid-1960s held steady at a high level. The low levels of party unity in both chambers in 1942 may be attributed to a surge of bipartisan cooperation in light of the threats to national survival occasioned by entry into World War II. Overall, party unity held on about 56 percent of all nonunanimous Senate votes, which is slightly less frequently than was the case in the House (just under 60 percent). Perhaps the single most significant finding that emerges from these data is that the congressional party, as measured by the relative frequency of party unity votes as a proportion of nonunanimous roll calls, has declined in salience but has not completely disintegrated with the passing of time and events.

Time-series analysis using the models described in Appendix F reveals that the relative frequency of House party unity voting is characterized by a strong pattern of dependency of values one year apart throughout the data. The series, in other words, is highly stable, with strong session-to-session similarities. Furthermore, the current level of House party unity voting is closely related to past levels over the most recent three years, that is, for the preceding Congress plus one adjacent session.

Somewhat different dynamics of party unity voting operate in the Senate than in the House. In the Senate, there is a significant relationship among all first sessions and among all second sessions. The model shows that the incidence of party unity voting in the Senate follows a stable long-term process, though one that differs from the historical pattern of party unity in the House.

Forecasts of future levels of party unity voting in the House suggest fairly little variation from the recent patterns over the 1981–84 period. The forecasted levels of partisan divisions separating Republican representatives from both northern and southern Democrats are about 62 percent in 1981, 59 percent in 1982, 64 percent in 1983, and 63 percent in 1984. These results indicate perhaps a slight future increase in the extent of House party unity compared to the levels of the past decade.

In the Senate, forecasts of party unity divisions as a proportion of nonunanimous votes are approximately 57 percent for each year from 1981 to 1984. This suggests very little variation in the early 1980s from preceding levels of Senate party unity in conformity with the fact that Senate party unity voting varied only slightly from year to year over the decade of the 1970s.

Is there any direct relationship between the rise in appearance of the cross-party southern Democrat–Republican coalition and the decline in party unity? The product-moment correlation between the incidence of conservative coalition appearances as a percentage of all nonunanimous roll call votes in the House and the level of party unity voting is a very strong $-.53$. The comparable correlation in the Senate is a more modest but still strong $-.39$. These results lend considerable support to the argument that the decline in party solidarity has been related to and in part caused by the increased rate of appearance of the conservative coalition.[4] But the correlation between coalition success and party unity voting is nearly zero in both chambers ($r = -.05$ in the House; $r = .01$ in the Senate). There is essentially no association over time between the coalition's success rate and the strength of party ties, in contrast to the finding of a strongly negative relationship between the rate of coalition formation and party unity.

The Bifurcation of the Democratic Party in Congress

Table 7–2 demonstrates the dramatic variation over time in the relative frequency with which northern and southern Democrats have parted ways on recorded votes in the House and Senate. The overall pattern is one of sharp increases in the relative frequency of North-South Democratic splits as a proportion of all roll calls and as a proportion of nonunanimous votes.

The pattern of these data generally parallels the pattern of conservative coalition appearances over time in each chamber. An early period of irregular and relatively low incidence was followed by a World War II–induced phase of much more frequent occurrence. The time series culminates in a higher and even more regular coincidence of Democratic regional divisions with the introduction of significant civil rights and Great Society legislation in the 1960s. In the late 1970s, however, the intraparty split lessened. Overall, the Democratic party in the Senate split somewhat more frequently, on just under 37 percent of all nonunanimous votes, than in the House, where the Democrats split along regional lines on a bit over 34 percent of all nonunanimous votes since 1933.

Levels of Democratic splits in the House show a strong pattern of serial dependence among successive changes in the values of the time series, as seen in

Table 7–2

North-South Democratic Splits, 1933–1980

Year	Number of North-South Democratic Splits		Democratic Splits as Percent of All Roll Calls		Democratic Splits as Percent Nonunanimous Votes	
	House	Senate	House	Senate	House	Senate
1933	2	20	3	20	4	22
1934	6	15	7	12	8	12
1935	17	18	13	14	14	15
1936	4	6	5	10	6	10
1937	18	19	19	20	20	22
1938	4	18	7	22	7	24
1939	11	13	12	11	13	13
1940	25	36	19	24	21	30
1941	18	10	22	10	26	11
1942	19	20	26	21	36	26
1943	25	22	27	18	33	20
1944	19	44	29	45	37	48
1945	19	16	19	15	26	16
1946	42	54	32	40	42	42
1947	21	28	25	20	32	22
1948	21	33	27	30	34	34
1949	34	46	28	20	36	22
1950	45	54	29	24	28	25
1951	26	36	24	18	29	19
1952	23	25	32	22	39	24
1953	25	24	35	27	45	29
1954	14	46	18	25	28	32
1955	12	13	16	15	21	21
1956	17	29	23	22	31	26
1957	30	33	30	31	34	44
1958	26	59	28	30	39	36
1959	20	63	23	29	26	37
1960	34	85	37	41	47	55
1961	26	81	22	40	29	44
1962	22	52	18	23	26	26
1963	19	65	16	28	22	33
1964	16	169	14	55	19	60
1965	61	99	30	38	41	46
1966	42	82	22	35	36	42
1967	67	81	27	26	43	36
1968	66	107	28	38	43	48
1969	56	97	32	40	50	49
1970	70	163	26	39	43	53

Table 7–2 continued

Year	Number of North-South Democratic Splits		Democratic Splits as Percent of All Roll Calls		Democratic Splits as Percent Nonunanimous Votes	
	House	Senate	House	Senate	House	Senate
1971	122	157	38	37	55	48
1972	115	215	35	40	55	56
1973	158	160	29	27	40	37
1974	116	210	22	39	33	48
1975	189	220	31	37	40	43
1976	159	219	24	32	36	42
1977	163	212	23	33	35	41
1978	188	135	23	26	36	33
1979	154	115	23	23	32	28
1980	106	127	18	24	26	30

Appendix F. The negative sign of this term in the model reflects the fact that smaller fluctuations in Democratic splits between the two sessions of a Congress were followed by larger changes between successive congresses. That is, Democratic splits in the House have followed a predictable, nonrandom pattern in the first difference.

The time series of North-South Democratic splits in the Senate follows a model that is similar to that of the process that underlies the time series of House Democratic splits, in that it is also nonstationary with the same overall pattern of serial dependence among successive changes in the level of Democratic splits from session to session. Smaller and larger magnitudes of change tend to alternate throughout the data set. This negative correlation among changes in the level of Democratic splits in the Senate is stronger than the corresponding parameter in the model for House Democratic splits, indicating that this tendency is more pronounced in the Senate. An interesting difference between the House and the Senate models of Democratic splits lies in the fact that the most recent level of Senate Democratic splits is closely determined by the number of splits in the comparable session of the immediately preceding Congress.

A forecast of future levels of House Democratic splits yields the following almost invariant values: 28 percent in 1981, 27 percent in 1982, 28 percent in 1983, and 28 percent in 1984. These projections suggest very steady, perhaps slightly declining, future rates of North-South Democratic splits in the House to a level of under 30 percent. The Senate model produces essentially constant forecasts of future levels of Democratic splits of approximately 34 percent of nonunanimous roll calls for each of the years 1981–84.

North-South Democratic splits are very highly correlated with the rate of conservative coalition appearances, at levels of .92 in the House and .83 in the Senate. This result provides strong evidence of the coincidence over time of Democratic party splits with the appearance of the southern Democrat–Republican cross-party alliance. Coalition success and the incidence of Democratic splits are correlated only $-.15$ in the House and $-.08$ in the Senate. There is thus a slight negative relationship between Democratic bifurcation and victory for the conservative coalition. A much stronger negative relationship, $r = -.59$ in the House and $r = -.57$ in the Senate, holds between Democratic splits and the relative frequency of party unity votes. There is, then, a clear connection between the heightened tendency of the Democratic party to divide into northern and southern liberal and conservative wings and the declining salience of party on roll call votes.

Democratic Splits and "Articulation" of the Conservative Coalition

Given the divergence of northern and southern Democratic voting patterns, it is still necessary for southern Democrats to articulate a voting alliance with Republicans in order for the conservative coalition to appear. The rate at which Democratic party splits coincide with the appearance of the conservative coalition provides a useful measurement of the extent to which the coalition has "matured" into a cross-party alliance that regularly and predictably links Republicans with the conservative wing of the Democratic party.

Table 7–3 presents the historical pattern of the conjunction between Democratic splits and appearance of the conservative coalition in Congress. The data demonstrate that the magnitude of this conjunction has increased markedly, though somewhat irregularly, since the 1930s. This result signifies what might be called the maturation or regularization over time of the programmatic split within Democratic ranks into an increasingly frequent and more predictable cross-party alliance. Overall, just over 80 percent of all Democratic House splits have also been conservative coalition votes, as were about 70 percent of Democratic divisions in the Senate. These rates are far greater than would be expected if the coalition were only the casual product of occasional and random interaction of the two voting blocs of which it consists.

Since the mid-1970s, a very high proportion of all Democratic splits have seen Republicans and southern Democrats join forces, particularly in the House, where it is now very rare for a North-South Democratic division not to result simultaneously in formation of the conservative coalition. But there has never been a session of Congress in which all Democratic splits were also conservative coalition votes. This finding suggests that the articulation of the southern Democrat–Republican alliance is as yet incomplete, even though it has become a given of congressional decision making.

Table 7–3

Percent of North-South Democratic Splits and
Conservative Coalition Votes, 1933–1980

Year	Percent All House Splits	Percent All Senate Splits
1933	0	65
1934	33	60
1935	47	28
1936	0	17
1937	56	28
1938	0	29
1939	55	38
1940	64	28
1941	50	30
1942	58	25
1943	72	68
1944	89	57
1945	63	62
1946	83	74
1947	81	75
1948	81	61
1949	59	76
1950	69	50
1951	85	78
1952	87	80
1953	64	75
1954	57	72
1955	83	54
1956	41	72
1957	53	36
1958	54	64
1959	55	63
1960	56	54
1961	88	80
1962	73	65
1963	79	66
1964	75	30
1965	84	62
1966	88	85
1967	81	69
1968	77	65
1969	80	71
1970	63	66
1971	81	76

Year	Percent All House Splits	Percent All Senate Splits
1972	71	71
1973	84	77
1974	88	77
1975	90	75
1976	90	82
1977	96	88
1978	87	88
1979	94	79
1980	90	83

The correlation between conservative coalition appearances and Democratic splits that are also coalition votes is .81 in the House and .73 in the Senate. This high correlation indicates that there is a very strong relationship over time between the disintegration of the Democratic party coalition and the rise of the cross-party conservative coalition. In the Senate, but not in the House, the heightened articulation of the conservative coalition has led to greater coalition success. The values of these correlations are $-.17$ in the House and .24 in the Senate. As would be expected, the increased conjunction of Democratic splits with the appearance of the conservative coalition is strongly negatively correlated ($r = -.34$) with the incidence of party unity voting in the House. In the Senate, however, where the comparable correlation is just $-.02$, the salience of party has not suffered noticeably from the greater coalescence of conservative elements in both parties. The level of articulation of the Republican–southern Democrat coalition is correlated .62 with the relative frequency of Democratic splits in the House and a substantially lower .31 in the Senate. This last finding strongly suggests that, particularly in the House, as the bifurcation of the Democratic party has progressed, so, too, has the articulation of the southern Democrat–Republican alliance.

A time-series analysis of the degree of articulation of the conservative coalition, based on the models in Appendix F, reveals that essentially identical processes have characterized the historical coincidence of Democratic splits with the appearance of the cross-party conservative bloc in the House and in the Senate. In the House, there is a strongly negative relationship between successive changes in the relative frequency of North-South Democratic splits that are also conservative coalition votes. Large or positive changes in one session tend to be followed by smaller or negative changes in the next session. This model produces forecasted levels of coalition articulation for the House of about 93 percent in 1981, 91 percent in 1982, 92 percent in 1983, and 91 percent in 1984.

The important point here is that there is every reason to expect continued high rates of formation of the conservative coalition when House Democrats bifurcate into liberal northern and conservative southern wings.

A comparable historical process has been at work in the Senate, with a similar pattern of changes within congresses alternating in sign and magnitude with changes between congresses. Forecasts of future levels of coalition articulation in the Senate are about 81 percent in 1981, 82 percent in 1982, 82 percent in 1983, and 82 percent again in 1984. The evidence, then, is that without dramatic changes in the process of coalition formation in the Senate, there should be little change in the rate at which Democratic splits translate into the appearance of the conservative coalition. In both chambers, nearly all North-South Democratic disagreements ought to result in formation of the Republican–southern Democrat alliance.

Summary and Implications

This chapter has traced the patterns of congressional party unity, of North-South divisions within the Democratic party, and of the degree of "articulation" of the conservative coalition, where "articulation" is defined as the incidence of Democratic party splits on which Republicans form an alliance with southern Democrats. Time-series analysis has been used to explore the distinct stochastic processes underlying these various time series in each chamber. Forecasts of each of the time series up to 1984, or the second session of the Ninety-eighth Congress, suggest very stable levels of party unity voting, North-South Democratic splits, and coalition articulation.

The importance of the findings in this chapter for understanding decision-making processes within Congress cannot be overstated. A long-term pattern of irregular decline in congressional party unity has been noted, especially in the House during the 1970s. The finding of strongly negative correlations between the level of party unity and the relative frequency of conservative coalition appearances in both chambers is critical evidence of the interplay between party and policy in Congress. Similarly, the finding of strong negative correlations between party unity and Democratic splits supports George Galloway's vision of party decline in Congress, as do the findings of strong positive correlations between Democratic splits and both the rate of formation of the conservative coalition and the high and increasing level of articulation of the coalition.[5]

An examination of the Hinckley-Li finding that the conservative coalition has become a more stable alliance than the party coalition of southern Democrats and northern Democrats can be made by comparing the models developed in Chapter 2 of levels of conservative coalition appearance with the models developed in this chapter of the relative frequency of party unity voting. The evidence on this score is mixed.

On the one hand, the conservative coalition appearance data in both chambers follow nonstationary time-series processes, whereas the party unity structure is stationary for both House and Senate. The Democratic party coalition has, then, been more stable overall than the cross-party conservative coalition, at least in the sense that party unity voting could be said to fluctuate around a fixed mean whereas conservative coalition appearances have had a more volatile history of an overall sharply increased rate of incidence.

On the other hand, the more recent historical record of, say, the sixteen years from 1965 to 1980 tells a different story. The post-1965 data provide essentially no evidence of any difference in the sample variances, s^2, of Senate party unity voting ($s^2 = 5.03$) and Senate conservative coalition formation ($s^2 = 5.05$), where both variables are measured as percentages of nonunanimous roll calls. In the House, variability of conservative coalition appearances ($s^2 = 4.94$) is considerably less than among party unity percentages ($s^2 = 8.25$). The evidence, then, is that since the emergence of domestic issues related to the Great Society and foreign issues sparked by the war in Vietnam, the conservative coalition has been at least as consistent a factor in congressional decision making on roll call votes as the party coalitions that pit Democrats against Republicans. This statement should be tempered, however, by noting that when we control for the different average levels of party unity and conservative coalition appearances, there is no difference in the relative degree of variability of these two types of coalitions in the House, and the party coalition appears to be very slightly more stable than the southern Democrat–Republican alliance against liberal northern Democrats.

8

Measuring the Strength of the Conservative Coalition: Size, Cohesion, and Defections

Previous chapters have examined trends over time in the rates of appearance and success of the conservative coalition, the issue content of conservative coalition votes, the nexus between the presidency and the behavior of the conservative coalition, the relationship between the activity of the coalition and the declining salience of American legislative parties, and the importance of committees and constituencies.

The precise cause of the conservative coalition's overall high rate of success and fluctuations in its victory rate has not yet been fully explained. This can be done in two ways. First, this chapter explores the magnitude of cohesion within each of the three voting blocs of Republicans, southern Democrats, and northern Democrats. Second, the frequency with which members of each bloc defect regularly to the opposition is determined as a means of developing a refined measure of the operational strength of congressional conservative forces.

The results of the analysis in Chapters 1 through 7 generally substantiate William Riker's perspective on coalition formation as the product of conscious decision-making processes occurring within and among political groups.[1] The conservative coalition is a purposive and consciously constructed legislative alliance, not a randomly occurring, unpredictable chance combination of political elements. Further, the appearance of the southern Democrat–Republican coalition is a consequence of uniquely congressional forms of the joint use of resources to determine the outcome of conflicts among groups whose members' motives are mixed.[2] The resource that is most clearly measurable here is, of course, the single vote available to each member of Congress. The complete range of motives underlying every congressional action cannot be specified in precise detail because we lack hard data on the impact of pressure groups or of constituency beliefs on congressmen's voting decisions, or of the relationship between members' decisions in committees and their behavior on the floor, or of the psychology of legislative elite behavior. These shortcomings necessitate a focus on something that is more readily observable—the policy consequences of congressional coalition activity.

Ultimately, the most important question is perhaps this: what will the strength of the conservative coalition likely be in the foreseeable future, if past trends continue? This question is addressed through the now familiar means of time-series analysis. First, the long-term pattern of growth and decline in support for the conservative coalition will be examined, identifying supporters and nonsupporters within each of the three voting blocs. Past history is then projected into the near future to ascertain what the expected strength of the conservative coalition would be in the absence of dramatic departures from previous trends. The stage is set for this analysis by looking at electoral patterns since 1933.

The Coalition Elements in the House

The pattern of changes over time in the relative size of the three voting blocs of southern Democrats, Republicans, and northern Democrats in the House is presented in Table 8–1. The table also includes information on the number of seats held by third-party members or congressional independents. These data were compiled from appropriate volumes of the *Congressional Directory*. The total number of House seats shown may exceed 435 for some years because allowances have been made for shifts in party control of individual districts within each session. The dominant tendency has been for Republicans to constitute the single largest voting bloc and for southern Democrats to constitute the smallest bloc. The middle-sized bloc of northern Democrats follows a pattern of fluctuating strength that is, of course, almost the exact inverse of trends in the size of the Republican bloc.

The number of southern Democrats in the House has varied relatively little over time, reflecting throughout the 1930s and 1940s the truthfulness of the "solid South" appellation. Since the early 1950s, however, there has been a slow but distinct decline in the number of southern Democratic representatives. Clearly, the explanation for this decline lies in the rising fortunes of the Republican party in the thirteen states that are defined to constitute the South. By the late 1970s, however, about two-thirds of all southern House seats were still held by Democrats.[3] Ordinarily, southern Democrats have constituted the smallest of the three voting blocs, but during the Seventy-eighth, Eightieth, and Eighty-third Congresses (1943–44, 1947–48, and 1953–54), the majority of Democrats in the House were southerners. Furthermore, southern Democratic representatives were more numerous than House Republicans from 1933 to 1938.

House Republican strength has fluctuated widely over the past half century.

Table 8–1

Potential Strength of the Conservative Coalition in the House, 1933–1980

Year	Southern Democrats	Repub- licans	Potential CC	Northern Democrats	Others	Percent Potential CC
1933	118	117	235	195	5	54.02
1934	118	116	234	196	5	53.79
1935	117	105	222	204	10	50.92
1936	117	105	222	203	10	51.03
1937	117	89	206	217	13	47.25
1938	117	89	206	216	13	47.36
1939	117	169	286	145	4	65.75
1940	117	170	287	144	4	65.98
1941	116	163	279	152	5	63.99
1942	116	167	283	149	5	64.76
1943	118	210	328	105	4	75.06
1944	117	212	329	103	4	75.46
1945	117	191	308	125	2	70.80
1946	117	191	308	126	2	70.64
1947	115	246	361	73	1	82.99
1948	115	246	361	73	2	82.80
1949	118	172	290	145	1	66.51
1950	118	172	290	145	1	66.51
1951	116	200	316	118	1	72.64
1952	116	202	318	116	1	73.10
1953	111	221	332	102	1	76.32
1954	111	219	330	104	1	75.86
1955	110	203	313	122	0	71.95
1956	110	203	313	122	0	71.95
1957	110	200	310	124	0	71.43
1958	110	200	310	125	0	71.26
1959	110	153	263	173	0	60.32
1960	110	155	265	170	0	60.92
1961	111	174	285	152	0	65.22
1962	111	174	285	152	0	65.22
1963	105	178	283	153	0	64.91
1964	105	178	283	152	0	65.06
1965	100	141	241	194	0	55.40
1966	100	141	241	195	0	55.28
1967	91	187	278	156	0	64.06
1968	91	188	279	156	0	64.14
1969	88	192	280	158	0	63.93
1970	88	189	277	158	0	63.68
1971	88	180	268	167	0	61.61

Year	Southern Democrats	Republicans	Potential CC	Northern Democrats	Others	Percent Potential CC
1972	88	179	267	168	0	61.38
1973	84	192	276	159	0	63.45
1974	84	189	273	164	0	62.47
1975	91	145	236	199	0	54.25
1976	90	145	235	200	0	54.02
1977	91	146	237	201	0	54.11
1978	90	147	237	198	0	54.48
1979	86	159	245	190	0	56.32
1980	87	160	247	189	0	56.65

Republican congressmen have regularly constituted the single largest bloc in the House, even though they organized the House only in 1947–48 and again in 1953–54. Republicans were the smallest of the three blocs only in the early Roosevelt years (1933–38) and have constituted the middle-sized bloc in scattered periods (1959–60, 1965–66, and 1975–80).

The number of northern Democrats in the House varies greatly over time. The strength of the northern Democratic bloc was greatest in the Seventy-fifth Congress (1937–38), following the Republican electoral debacle of 1936, and was lowest in 1947–48 (the Eightieth Congress), when the Republican party organized the House in the wake of its successes in the 1946 postwar congressional elections. Northern Democrats constituted the single largest voting bloc in the House during the Seventy-third to Seventy-fifth, Eighty-sixth, Eighty-ninth, Ninety-fourth, and Ninety-fifth Congresses (1933–38, 1959–60, 1965–66, and 1975–78), always following major Republican electoral defeats. House northern Democrats were the weakest of the three blocs in the Seventy-eighth, Eightieth, and Eighty-third Congresses (1943–44, 1947–48, and 1953–54). On the two latter occasions, the northern Democratic decline was accompanied by Republican control of the House.

The "potential conservative coalition" in the House, defined as the sum of congressional seats held by Republicans and those held by southern Democrats, has constituted a majority of the House for all but two years in this time series. In 1937 and 1938, or during the Seventy-fifth Congress, the potential conservative coalition in the House was outnumbered by northern Democrats as a consequence of the near extermination of the Republican party in the election of 1936. The House potential coalition was strongest during the Eightieth Congress (1947–48), after Republicans swamped the Democratic party outside the South in the 1946 election. Overall, since 1933 the potential conservative coalition has held an average of nearly two-thirds (about 64 percent) of all seats in the House.

Table 8–2

Potential Strength of the Conservative Coalition in the Senate, 1933–1980

Year	Southern Democrats	Repub- licans	Potential CC	Northern Democrats	Others	Percent Potential CC
1933	26	35	61	34	1	63.54
1934	26	35	61	34	1	63.54
1935	26	25	51	44	2	52.58
1936	26	24	50	44	3	51.55
1937	26	16	42	50	4	43.75
1938	26	16	42	51	4	43.30
1939	26	23	49	43	4	51.04
1940	26	25	51	43	4	52.04
1941	26	28	54	40	2	56.25
1942	26	30	56	39	2	57.73
1943	25	38	63	33	1	64.95
1944	25	39	64	33	1	65.31
1945	25	41	66	33	1	66.00
1946	24	39	63	32	1	65.63
1947	24	51	75	21	0	78.12
1948	24	51	75	21	0	78.12
1949	26	44	70	28	0	71.43
1950	26	42	68	28	0	70.83
1951	26	47	73	24	0	75.26
1952	26	46	72	24	0	75.00
1953	25	48	73	23	1	75.26
1954	25	49	74	24	1	74.75
1955	26	47	73	23	0	76.04
1956	26	47	73	23	0	76.04
1957	24	47	71	26	0	73.20
1958	24	47	71	26	0	73.20
1959	24	35	59	41	0	59.00
1960	24	35	59	42	0	58.42
1961	24	36	60	41	0	59.41
1962	23	36	59	41	0	59.00
1963	23	33	56	44	0	56.00
1964	22	34	56	44	0	56.00
1965	22	33	55	46	0	54.46
1966	22	32	54	46	0	54.00
1967	21	36	57	43	0	57.00
1968	21	37	58	43	0	57.43
1969	19	43	62	38	0	62.00
1970	19	43	62	39	0	61.39

Year	Southern Democrats	Republicans	Potential CC	Northern Democrats	Others	Percent Potential CC
1971	18	45	63	37	0	63.00
1972	18	45	63	37	0	63.00
1973	16	43	59	41	0	59.00
1974	16	43	59	42	0	58.42
1975	18	39	57	44	0	56.44
1976	18	38	56	44	0	56.00
1977	19	38	57	43	0	57.00
1978	19	38	57	43	0	57.00
1979	19	41	60	40	0	60.00
1980	19	41	60	40	0	60.00

The Coalition Elements in the Senate

Table 8–2 presents the pattern of variations over time in the relative size of each of the three voting blocs in the Senate. In general, the Senate data repeat the House pattern of greatest cumulative bloc strength among Republicans and least overall strength among southern Democrats. These figures, again derived from the *Congressional Directory,* may exceed the maximum number of seats in some years because of partisan shifts during those sessions.

As in the House, the strength of the Senate southern Democratic bloc has generally declined over time and in fact decreased steadily from 1956 to 1974. As late as 1956, all twenty-six southern senators were Democrats. Southern Democrats have been regularly the smallest of the three Senate voting blocs, although they outnumbered northern Democratic senators in 1947–48 and again from 1951 to 1956 and outnumbered Senate Republicans in the 1935–40 period.

The strength of the Republican bloc in the Senate has varied greatly over time, from a low of just sixteen in the Seventy-fifth Congress (1937–38) to a pre-Reagan maximum of fifty-one in the Eightieth Congress (1947–48), when Republicans organized the Senate. Republicans constituted the single largest of the three blocs in the Senate during the Seventy-third, Seventy-eighth to Eighty-fifth, Ninety-first to Ninety-third, and Ninety-sixth Congresses (1933–34, 1943–58, 1969–74, and 1979–80). Senate Republicans were the weakest of the three blocs in the Seventy-fourth to Seventy-sixth Congresses (1935–40). During the Seventy-seventh, Eighty-sixth to Ninetieth, and Ninety-fourth to Ninety-fifth Congresses (1941–42, 1959–68, and 1975–78), Republicans were the middle-ranked bloc, with northern Democrats the largest single bloc.

Northern Democratic strength in the Senate has also varied markedly, from a low of twenty-one in the Eightieth Congress (1947–48) to an absolute majority in the Seventy-fifth Congress (1937–38). Northern Democrats were the largest of the three voting blocs in the Senate during the Seventy-fourth to Seventy-seventh, Eighty-sixth to Ninetieth, Ninety-third, and Ninety-fourth Congresses (1935–42, 1959–68, and 1975–78). Northern Democrats were the least numerous of the three blocs in the Eightieth and Eighty-second to Eighty-fourth Congresses (1947–48 and 1951–56).

The "potential conservative coalition" in the Senate, or the sum of Republican and southern Democratic senators, has held a majority of all Senate seats in every year covered in this study, with the exception of 1937 and 1938 (the Seventy-fifth Congress). This result is identical to that found earlier for the House. Clearly, in both chambers the "potential conservative coalition" has regularly constituted a clear majority of the national legislative elite. The Senate potential coalition was strongest during the Eightieth Congress (1947–48), coinciding with the Republican victory in the 1946 congressional elections. This high point of the Senate strength of conservative forces occurred at exactly the same time as the apex of potential coalition strength in the House. Overall, from 1933 to 1980 the potential conservative coalition has held an average of about 62 percent of all Senate seats, or slightly less than its overall potential strength in the House.

In each chamber, the variation over time in the potential strength of the conservative coalition is much more strongly related to the size of the Republican bloc ($r = .95$ in the House; $r = .92$ in the Senate) than to the relatively invariant size of the southern Democratic contingent ($r = .30$ in the House; $r = .24$ in the Senate). As would be expected simply from the definition of the conservative coalition, the potential coalition is very strongly related inversely to the size of the northern Democratic bloc ($r = -.92$ in the House; $r = -.99$ in the Senate). These last correlations fail to equal minus one only because of minor year-to-year fluctuations in relative bloc sizes caused by third-party victories.

Size as an Explanatory Variable

It is important to determine the influence of the relative size of the potential conservative coalition and of each of the three voting blocs (Republicans, southern Democrats, northern Democrats) on the coalition's rate of appearance and on its rate of success. Such an assessment will indicate the structural forces within Congress that explain greater or lesser levels of coalition appearance and success, which in turn influence the content of public policy.

In the House of Representatives, the proportionate size of the potential conservative coalition bears only a weak positive relationship to the coalition's rate of appearance over time ($r = .21$). This modest association masks very different relationships between each of the two coalition partners separately and the magnitude of coalition formation. The relative size of the Republican bloc over time is strongly correlated ($r = .44$) with the relative frequency of coalition appearances, whereas the size of the southern Democratic bloc is strongly negatively related ($r = -.66$) to the appearance of the conservative coalition in the House.

This finding is clearly consistent with earlier results in suggesting that conservative coalition activity is largely focused around Republican-sponsored initiatives, which increase in frequency as an expansion in their voting strength increases the likelihood of success and hence the attractiveness of coalition formation with conservative Democrats. The strong negative correlation between the level of coalition appearances and the size of the southern Democratic bloc in part simply reflects the decline in the number of southern Democratic congressmen occasioned by increased two-party competition in the South. More important, however, this negative association perhaps also indicates that the articulation of the conservative coalition is still incomplete. The coalition's activity is very much dominated by Republican issue concerns, and southern Democrats generally tag along on issues with which they are in agreement with the GOP.

The relationship in the House between the relative frequency of conservative coalition appearance and the relative size of the northern Democratic bloc is weakly negative ($r = -.15$). This finding is expected, given the presumption that the coalition is in important ways an aggressive policy grouping that does not form exclusively as a blocking alliance whose only goal is to thwart the adoption of liberal legislative initiatives. The relatively small magnitude of the correlation, however, suggests that the level of activity of the conservative coalition in the House is very nearly unrelated to the size of the bloc opposing the coalition. At any rate, the activity of the conservative coalition is clearly not limited to voting against northern Democrats' policy proposals.

The rate of success of the conservative coalition in the House is, of course, strongly related to the relative size of the potential House coalition ($r = .67$). Clearly, and predictably, as the potential coalition in the House grows numerically stronger, it is increasingly likely to win when it forms. Within the coalition, the size of the Republican bloc is somewhat more strongly related to coalition success ($r = .59$) than is the size of the southern Democratic bloc ($r = .40$).

The potential voting strength of the northern Democratic bloc is, of course, strongly negatively correlated with the success rate of the conservative coalition in the House ($r = -.69$). The larger the bloc of potential opponents of the conservative coalition, then, the lower will be the coalition's likelihood of success.

The associations between bloc size and rates of both conservative coalition appearances and success in the Senate are broadly similar to the comparable correlations in the House. The time series of Senate coalition appearances as a proportion of nonunanimous roll calls bears only a very weakly positive relationship to the size of the potential conservative coalition ($r = .06$). Republican bloc size and coalition appearances are fairly strongly correlated in a positive direction ($r = .39$), and the size of the southern Democratic bloc is very strongly negatively related ($r = -.79$) to the relative frequency of coalition appearances. The voting strength of Senate northern Democrats is only very weakly correlated ($r = .04$) with the rate of conservative coalition appearances.

In the Senate, coalition success depends strongly on the proportionate size of the potential conservative coalition ($r = .68$). Republican bloc size is a much more significant factor in determining the Senate coalition's rate of success ($r = .58$) than is the size of the southern Democratic bloc ($r = .26$). Northern Democratic strength bears a very strong negative relationship ($r = -.69$) to coalition success.

The above results suggest that over time in both chambers the number of Republicans has much more to do with coalition success than does the number of southern Democrats. The more northern Democrats in Congress, the poorer are the chances for congressional conservatives to win. This is all very simple, but it is possible to develop a more sophisticated assessment of the relevance of a "size principle" to the activity and policy impact of the conservative coalition. This will be done by evaluating the patterns of defections from expected voting patterns by members of each of the three blocs.

Voting Bloc Cohesion and Defections

Table 8–3 presents the levels of cohesion of each of the three voting blocs in the House and Senate. No index of cohesion is computed for the three House sessions in which the coalition did not appear. These levels of cohesion are important indicators of the intensity with which support for and opposition to the position taken by the conservative coalition forms. Furthermore, an examination of the magnitude of cohesion among expected conservative coalition supporters and anticipated opponents serves as an explanatory variable of potentially great value for explaining the magnitude of conservative coalition appearances and success.

The important point in Table 8–3 is the general stability of annual levels of cohesion in each chamber over time within all three voting blocs, broken by some periods of change. Single-session cohesion among House Republicans was generally low in the earliest years of the time series, increased to substantially higher levels from 1943 to 1954, with the peak intensity of Republican unity coming in 1948, and has fluctuated substantially since the mid-1950s. Southern Democratic cohesion was very high in the first House session in which the conservative coalition made an appearance (1934), but since then has with rare exceptions (1941, 1947, and 1959) hovered well below the 80 percent mark. Northern Democratic cohesion on conservative coalition roll calls in the House was initially low and failed to exceed 80 percent until 1946. From 1949 to 1968,

Table 8–3

Average Cohesion on Conservative Coalition Votes, by Bloc

Year	House			Senate		
	Repub- licans	Southern Democrats	Northern Democrats	Repub- licans	Southern Democrats	Northern Democrats
1933	–	–	–	69	62	63
1934	66	93	58	58	65	60
1935	77	68	69	66	59	62
1936	–	–	–	56	56	62
1937	80	72	73	76	63	61
1938	–	–	–	80	72	61
1939	89	71	75	78	67	63
1940	86	72	70	65	62	64
1941	79	81	71	75	78	73
1942	80	74	67	62	69	58
1943	87	80	75	69	78	70
1944	86	78	77	81	72	79
1945	83	77	80	84	71	71
1946	86	78	83	80	77	74
1947	90	82	75	93	68	81
1948	96	80	73	84	72	77
1949	83	71	86	77	71	73
1950	81	75	83	75	70	76
1951	82	76	87	85	74	71
1952	81	73	89	83	72	73
1953	89	76	82	85	76	76
1954	87	75	80	92	66	69
1955	76	71	81	83	67	70
1956	68	70	80	71	71	70
1957	74	67	87	90	70	73
1958	71	76	86	76	75	73
1959	87	86	83	80	69	77
1960	77	66	91	74	77	78
1961	83	69	85	75	73	84
1962	74	65	86	79	77	71
1963	77	71	87	75	73	80
1964	76	72	86	72	78	80
1965	81	68	89	81	71	81
1966	82	69	86	79	75	83
1967	81	75	85	73	75	76
1968	74	77	84	74	76	70
1969	75	79	79	73	77	75
1970	77	78	80	74	75	78
1971	79	76	76	78	80	73

Table 8–3 continued

Year	House			Senate		
	Repub-licans	Southern Democrats	Northern Democrats	Repub-licans	Southern Democrats	Northern Democrats
1972	80	75	76	74	77	80
1973	77	70	78	77	74	83
1974	75	72	76	69	79	81
1975	80	69	78	70	79	81
1976	79	72	75	77	73	79
1977	82	68	75	80	75	74
1978	80	68	75	69	71	77
1979	84	70	72	73	76	71
1980	81	68	73	75	71	74
Means	80.4	73.8	79.2	75.9	72.0	73.1

northern Democratic cohesion was strong, peaking at over 90 percent in 1960. Since the late 1960s, cohesion among House northern Democrats has declined markedly.

Overall, the average level of Republican cohesion on House conservative coalition votes is substantially higher (80.4 percent) than that among southern Democrats (73.8 percent), but is essentially identical to the magnitude of cohesion among northern Democrats (79.2 percent). There is, then, a modest tendency for Republicans to be the bloc which is the most intensely interested in conservative coalition votes in the House. The pattern of relatively weak cohesion among House southern Democrats is presumably a consequence of the cross-pressure exerted on them through conservative ideological and constituency predilections on the one hand and through the impact of party leadership and their northern colleagues' demands for party regularity on the other hand.

Levels of cohesion on conservative coalition votes in the Senate generally follow the same pattern that obtains on House coalition votes. Republican cohesion in the Senate averages 75.9 percent, which is somewhat below the average level of cohesion among House Republicans. Senate Republican cohesion was generally low and highly unstable until the mid-1940s. From that time until 1959, with the exception of 1956, cohesion among Republicans was consistently over 75 percent. The peak of Republican intensity occurred in 1954. Since 1960, Senate Republican cohesion has noticeably declined. Southern Democratic Senate cohesion has fluctuated at levels generally well below 80 percent, but shows some evidence of both increasing in magnitude and becoming more stable since 1960. Overall, an average of about 72.0 percent of southern Democratic votes were cast in support of the conservative coalition. Southern Democratic cohesion in the Senate, like the comparable Republican figure, falls short of the degree of unity attained by that bloc in the House.

Cohesion among northern Democratic senators on conservative coalition votes has generally risen over time, although the unity of this bloc was strongest (at 84 percent) in 1961. Northern Democratic cohesion on all Senate conservative coalition votes averages 73.1 percent, substantially below the level of northern Democrats' cohesion in the House.

These annual summary measures of cohesion tend to obscure sharp variations in the intensity of bloc voting across the individual roll calls on which the conservative coalition has appeared. The distribution of degrees of cohesiveness within each voting bloc on all conservative coalition roll calls from 1933 to 1980 is presented in Table 8–4. Some important conclusions are evident from these results.

Of particular importance is the concentration of comparatively high proportions of conservative coalition roll calls producing very intense (90% + to 100%) levels of cohesion in the House among Republicans and northern Democrats. House southern Democrats' levels of cohesion tend to concentrate at lesser levels of intensity. In the Senate, southern Democrats cohere with somewhat greater frequency at higher levels of intensity than do their regional party brethren in the House. Also, the proportion of highly intense cohesion scores is less in the Senate than in the House for Republicans and for northern Democrats.

Table 8–4
Distribution of Cohesion Intensity on
Conservative Coalition Roll Calls, 1933–1980, by Bloc

Bloc	50% + – 60%	60% + – 70%	70% + – 80%	80% + – 90%	90% + – 100%
			HOUSE		
Republicans	10.1	13.0	20.6	29.3	27.0
Southern Democrats	26.0	21.6	23.0	17.4	11.9
Northern Democrats	14.1	16.3	21.0	25.1	23.6
			SENATE		
Republicans	15.3	24.7	22.9	20.6	17.3
Southern Democrats	19.4	20.7	23.6	21.4	15.0
Northern Democrats	15.5	19.0	21.9	22.5	21.0

It is a sign both of the incomplete articulation of the conservative coalition and of the importance of interbloc defections that the coalition has never formed with 100 percent cohesion among all three blocs simultaneously in either chamber. All three blocs rarely enter into programmatic conflict with cohesion levels over 90 percent for each bloc.

This is, of course, not to say that levels of voting bloc cohesion are unimportant to the frequency of conservative coalition success. Coalition success in the House bears a moderately negative relationship to northern Democratic cohesion ($r = -.27$) and shows a much stronger positive association with southern Democratic cohesion ($r = .62$). House coalition success covaries somewhat less markedly with Republican cohesion ($r = .39$).

In the Senate, conservative coalition success depends only minimally on both northern Democratic cohesion ($r = -.14$) and on the magnitude of cohesion among southern Democrats ($r = .16$) but depends very strongly on cohesion among Republicans ($r = .53$). These considerable cross-chamber differences in the relevance of the cohesion of individual blocs for coalition success seem to reflect different structures of bloc interaction, with the extent of Democratic coalescence more important in the House and Republican unity more salient in the Senate.

There are significant differences between the House and Senate in the relationship between bloc size and bloc cohesion. In the House, cohesion declines as bloc size increases among northern Democrats ($r = -.22$), but increases with bloc size among both southern Democrats ($r = .26$) and Republicans ($r = .33$). In the Senate, bloc size and cohesion are essentially unrelated among northern Democrats ($r = -.10$) but are strongly negatively related among southern Democrats ($r = -.56$) and strongly associated positively among Republicans ($r = .48$). There is no consistent tendency for cohesion to decline as the size of these voting blocs increases. This is an interesting finding, because it is not what would be expected if there were a pronounced tendency for ideological divisions in Congress to result in the formation of "minimum winning coalitions."

The magnitude of Republican cohesion on conservative coalition votes increases markedly in both chambers when Republicans control Congress. This is true both when a Democratic president sits in the White House (1947–48) and when Republicans dominate both the legislature and the executive branch (1953–54). There are no comparable changes in southern Democratic or northern Democratic cohesion when either of these two forms of Republican control of Congress obtains.

A more precise indicator of the operational size of the conservative coalition in the House is presented in Table 8–5. This refined measure of coalition strength defines a conservative coalition supporter as a member who agrees with the position adopted by the conservative coalition on a majority of votes on which the coalition appears in a given session. There is some double counting in this table because all members who have cast at least one vote on a conservative

Table 8–5

Refined Conservative Coalition: House

Year	Republicans CC	Republicans Not CC	Northern Democrats CC	Northern Democrats Not CC	Southern Democrats CC	Southern Democrats Not CC	Total CC	Total Not CC	Percent Refined CC
1933	–	–	–	–	–	–	–	–	–
1934	57	41	55	118	93	11	207	172	54.62
1935	91	19	40	162	82	32	313	216	49.65
1936	–	–	–	–	–	–	–	–	–
1937	87	12	28	190	96	20	211	227	48.17
1938	–	–	–	–	–	–	–	–	–
1939	163	6	23	115	86	26	273	150	64.54
1940	160	9	30	113	92	24	283	149	65.51
1941	136	31	32	116	106	10	275	159	63.36
1942	152	16	34	110	98	17	285	145	66.28
1943	202	12	16	87	106	11	325	112	74.37
1944	205	9	16	85	104	13	327	108	75.17
1945	178	16	15	111	101	16	294	143	67.28
1946	185	9	13	110	100	17	298	136	68.66
1947	241	3	13	60	110	5	364	69	84.06
1948	242	2	15	57	103	12	360	72	83.33
1949	162	10	5	139	95	22	262	172	60.37
1950	159	11	7	137	94	25	260	174	59.91
1951	178	22	4	117	97	20	279	159	63.70
1952	177	25	6	110	83	31	266	166	61.57
1953	210	11	8	94	97	15	315	120	72.41
1954	195	23	6	98	87	24	288	145	66.51
1955	178	25	7	114	86	23	271	162	62.59
1956	153	49	7	115	88	21	248	185	57.27
1957	150	49	6	117	80	30	236	196	54.63
1958	152	45	4	121	89	20	245	186	56.84
1959	139	14	15	158	105	5	259	177	59.40
1960	120	33	3	167	70	40	193	240	44.57
1961	163	11	3	150	78	32	244	193	55.84
1962	133	41	9	138	75	36	217	215	50.23
1963	160	16	6	147	79	26	245	189	56.45
1964	143	34	10	141	74	30	227	205	52.55
1965	123	17	5	190	73	27	201	234	46.21
1966	124	16	10	184	73	26	207	226	47.81
1967	174	13	9	146	75	16	258	175	59.58
1968	159	28	8	147	73	17	240	192	55.56
1969	165	27	10	145	75	13	250	185	57.47
1970	166	23	12	143	77	10	255	176	59.16

Table 8–5 continued

Year	Republicans		Northern Democrats		Southern Democrats		Total CC	Total Not CC	Percent Refined CC
	CC	Not CC	CC	Not CC	CC	Not CC			
1971	162	18	27	140	73	15	262	173	60.23
1972	162	16	18	148	75	13	255	177	59.03
1973	170	22	14	142	67	17	251	181	58.10
1974	159	29	14	145	67	17	240	191	55.68
1975	129	15	11	187	76	15	216	217	49.88
1976	132	13	13	187	76	14	221	214	50.80
1977	134	12	19	180	70	20	223	212	51.26
1978	133	14	25	173	66	24	224	211	51.49
1979	147	12	28	161	69	18	244	191	56.09
1980	145	14	29	160	69	18	243	192	55.86

coalition roll call in a given session are included in the relevant bloc. All Republicans and southern Democrats who vote against their intrabloc colleagues on at least one-half of the votes they cast on conservative coalition appearances, and all northern Democrats who cast a majority of their votes with the conservative coalition, are treated as "defectors," or "ideological mavericks."

The data demonstrate the widespread and consistent tendency within all three blocs for sizable numbers of congressmen to deviate from the voting pattern associated with conservative coalition support among Republicans and southern Democrats or opposition to the coalition among northern Democrats. In every session of Congress each of the three blocs had at least one defector. The proportion of defectors within each bloc has varied widely over time, as a function of changing issues, the varying strength of party leadership, and altered patterns of executive-legislative control.

Overall, the tendency is for defections in the House to be most common within the southern Democratic bloc, among whom an average of about 19 percent have opposed the position of the conservative coalition. An average of only 11 percent of House Republican congressmen are ideological mavericks, as are just over 10 percent of northern Democrats. These results are readily explainable in terms of the cross-pressures exerted on southern Democrats. They also suggest the relative liberalism of southern Democrats in the House on certain issues and further indicate the scope of Republican domination of conservative coalition activities.

It is interesting, in light of coalition theory literature regarding group size and group solidarity, that the smallest of the three blocs is the most defection-ridden. Given the thrust of much of the literature that is critical of the policy thrust and antipartisan behavior of the conservative coalition and of the ineffectiveness of liberal programmatic efforts, it is also interesting that northern Democrats are the least divided bloc. Finally, minor party congressmen generally opposed the conservative coalition but were never sufficiently numerous to have a major impact on the outcome of coalition votes. On average, about 25 percent of minor party congressmen regularly supported the coalition.

It is very important to note that the net effect of defections almost invariably reduced the effective strength of the conservative coalition. Only in 1934, 1937, 1942, and 1947–48 did the pattern of defections among the three blocs result in a net increase in the proportionate size of the coalition. This finding clearly signifies that the coalition's operational strength is nearly always less, and sometimes much less, than its potential strength as assessed through the naive definition of the coalition as the sum of all Republicans and all southern Democrats. By the refined measure, the coalition was in a minority position in the House in 1935, 1937, 1960, 1965, 1966, and 1975. Overall, the effective strength of the conservative coalition averaged just over 59 percent of all House seats.

The tendency to widespread defections in the House is basically duplicated in the Senate, as indicated in Table 8–6. In the 1973 Senate session, however, no northern Democrats regularly supported the conservative coalition. As in the House, Senate defections are greatest within the southern Democratic bloc, among whom an average of 23 percent regularly opposed the coalition. Again as in the House, there is no appreciable difference in the extent of Senate defections among Republicans (18 percent) as compared to northern Democrats (17 percent). In each case, the lack of solidarity among each of the three Senate blocs exceeds the defection rates of the blocs in the House. As in the House, minor party and independent senators generally opposed the conservative coalition.

Table 8–6
Refined Conservative Coalition: Senate

Year	Republicans CC	Republicans Not CC	Northern Democrats CC	Northern Democrats Not CC	Southern Democrats CC	Southern Democrats Not CC	Total CC	Total Not CC	Percent Refined CC
1933	27	8	8	26	18	8	53	43	55.21
1934	22	13	13	21	16	10	51	45	53.12
1935	18	7	11	31	15	11	45	50	47.37
1936	9	7	15	19	8	5	32	33	49.23
1937	14	4	18	31	14	11	46	48	48.94
1938	13	5	16	35	22	4	53	44	54.64
1939	16	7	13	31	15	8	45	47	48.91
1940	16	9	10	34	19	7	45	52	46.39
1941	20	7	5	34	21	6	46	47	49.46

Table 8–6 continued

Year	Republicans CC	Republicans Not CC	Northern Democrats CC	Northern Democrats Not CC	Southern Democrats CC	Southern Democrats Not CC	Total CC	Total Not CC	Percent Refined CC
1942	19	12	13	26	17	9	49	47	51.04
1943	27	11	8	25	20	4	55	40	57.89
1944	36	5	5	28	19	6	60	39	60.61
1945	34	7	6	28	17	6	57	41	58.16
1946	34	5	7	27	21	3	62	35	63.92
1947	49	2	2	19	17	6	68	27	71.58
1948	48	3	4	16	20	5	72	24	75.00
1949	38	6	5	23	20	6	63	35	64.29
1950	33	8	6	22	21	5	60	35	63.16
1951	44	2	5	19	23	4	72	25	74.23
1952	40	6	4	20	19	7	63	33	65.62
1953	45	4	3	19	20	6	68	29	70.10
1954	49	2	8	15	20	6	77	23	77.00
1955	45	3	6	16	17	9	68	28	70.83
1956	35	13	4	19	22	6	61	38	61.62
1957	45	2	5	20	19	7	69	29	70.41
1958	41	6	5	20	21	4	67	30	69.07
1959	32	3	4	37	16	8	52	48	52.00
1960	27	7	3	39	19	5	49	51	49.00
1961	30	5	1	41	17	6	48	52	48.00
1962	32	4	6	35	20	3	53	42	58.00
1963	28	5	1	43	16	7	45	55	45.00
1964	25	8	4	40	19	4	48	52	48.00
1965	30	2	3	43	15	7	48	52	48.00
1966	27	5	4	42	15	7	46	54	46.00
1967	26	10	4	39	18	3	48	52	49.00
1968	31	6	7	35	18	3	56	44	56.00
1969	34	9	3	35	15	4	52	48	52.00
1970	34	7	3	37	15	4	52	48	52.00
1971	38	7	8	29	16	2	62	38	62.00
1972	36	9	5	32	16	2	57	43	57.00
1973	36	7	0	41	13	3	49	51	49.00
1974	30	12	3	39	14	2	47	53	47.00
1975	27	11	4	39	15	3	47	54	46.53
1976	31	7	4	40	14	4	49	51	49.00
1977	33	5	8	35	16	3	57	43	57.00
1978	27	11	4	39	18	1	49	51	49.00
1979	31	10	7	33	19	0	57	43	57.00
1980	33	8	4	36	17	2	54	46	54.00

The strength of the operational Senate conservative coalition, like that in the House, has nearly always been below the potential size of the Senate coalition. The effective strength of the southern Democrat–Republican alliance was enhanced by net defections among the three blocs only in 1937, 1938, and 1954. The operational coalition was in a minority position in the Senate in 1935–37, 1939–41, 1960–61, 1963–67, 1973–76, and 1978, considerably more frequently than in the House. Overall, the operational conservative coalition has held an average of about 56 percent of all Senate seats, which is slightly below the average effective strength of the coalition in the House.

Time-Series Analysis of Coalition Size

If the past is a good predictor of the future, this information about historical levels of both the potential and operational strength of the conservative coalition can be used to project the likely degree of future support that the coalition may enjoy in Congress. The data used in this exercise are the actual number of seats held by the "potential conservative coalition" of all Republicans and all southern Democrats and the percent of members during each session who have generally supported the informal southern Democrat–Republican alliance. In the latter case of the refined conservative coalition, the House data are available on a continuous basis only since 1939.

In the House, the historical pattern of potential conservative coalition strength follows a nonstationary model (see Appendix G for details on the structure of the model), a fact that reflects the changing long-term average value of potential coalition strength as combined Republican and southern Democratic numbers increased markedly after the 1930s and declined precipitously following the 1946 election. House conservative coalition strength shows a strongly consistent pattern of very small changes within a Congress alternating with much larger changes between Congresses. This is, of course, simply a function of the election calendar. When this model is used to forecast future potential conservative coalition strength in the House, it produces the following results: 243 in 1981, 242 in 1982, 244 in 1983, and 245 in 1984. (There were actually 270 Republicans and southern Democrats at the beginning of the Ninety-seventh Congress in 1981, considerably more than this set of projections would have predicted under more "normal" conditions.) What the forecasted results say is that, absent dramatic electoral transformations such as that of 1980, there is little reason to expect a sharp growth or decline in the potential size of conservative forces in the House of Representatives.

The parallel model of coalition strength in the Senate is rather different from that in the House. The magnitude of coalition size follows a very consistent pattern, both within a Congress and between sessions of different Congresses, varying about a constant mean of about 65.5 seats, unlike the nonstationary process characterizing potential conservative coalition power in the House. This result is reasonable because only one-third of the Senate, but all members of the House, must stand for reelection every two years, and hence the magnitude of change should be less in the Senate. The Senate model of potential coalition strength projects sixty Republican and southern Democratic seats for each of the years 1981–84, barring unexpectedly dramatic electoral events. (The actual number of Republicans and southern Democrats was 68 at the opening of the Ninety-seventh Congress in 1981, reflecting the much greater than usual gains by conservative forces in the 1980 elections.)

The analysis that has just been done for potential coalition size is done next for the operational strength of congressional conservatives. The most important result of this phase of the analysis is that the two time series of refined coalition strength follow practically identical stochastic processes.

In each case, there is a very strong pattern of similar levels of coalition strength from session to session, both within a Congress and between the second session of one Congress and the first session of the following Congress. That is, both time series are highly stable and vary about a fixed long-run mean. The mean for the House operational coalition is about 60 percent from 1939 to 1980, which translates into about 261 seats out of 435. For the Senate, the long-run mean strength of the refined conservative coalition since 1933 is roughly 56 to 57 seats out of 100.

Forecasts of the expected future operational strength of the conservative coalition in each chamber show at least modest growth in the proportion of conservative coalition supporters. In the House, the historical record projects about 248 supporters in 1981, 252 in 1982, 254 in 1983, and 256 in 1984. More important than the actual numbers is the overall trend, which is toward increased support for the conservative position.

A similar set of projections for the Senate produces the following results: 55 conservative coalition supporters in 1981, 55 in 1982, 55 in 1983, and 56 in 1984. The important point again is the overall (slight) increase in expected future operational strength of the conservative coalition in the Senate. Both sets of forecasts of future coalition strength are, of course, meant only to suggest what the future would look like if past patterns were to continue and are not prognostications of the actual future.

It is logical to presume that when there are more pro-conservative votes than contrary votes in a given session of Congress, the success of the conservative coalition should rise. Whether such an effect is visible, on top of the already established pattern of coalition success in each chamber, can be determined by the use of intervention methods. The dummy variable in this model takes on the value of one for years of conservative numerical superiority in a session of Congress and zero when nonconservatives are in the majority. The precise models are given in Appendix G.

The basic conclusion is that in neither chamber is the "intervention" of conservative control a statistically significant determinant of coalition success, beyond the serial correlations that exist within each time series. The additional influence of conservative control is sufficient to account for an increase of only about four-tenths of 1 percent in conservative coalition success in the House and just under two percentage points in the Senate.

With the dummy variable for ideological control taken into account, forecasted levels of conservative coalition success in the House are approximately 71 percent in 1981, 70 percent in 1982, 71 percent in 1983, and 71 percent in 1984, assuming a conservative majority in each of those years. For the Senate, again assuming conservative majorities for 1981–84, forecasted levels of coalition success are about 67 percent in 1981, 68 percent in 1982, 75 percent in 1983, and 75 percent in 1984.

Summary and Conclusions

The Brams model of coalition behavior emphasizing the significance of bloc defections has proved to be a very useful point of departure for studying the behavior of the conservative coalition. In the aggregate, the net tendency of the direction of defections is to reduce the effective strength of the conservative coalition to a level somewhat closer to what theorists of coalition behavior would regard as a "minimum winning size." Furthermore, analysis of the magnitude of bloc cohesion suggests that each of the three groupings of southern Democrats, northern Democrats, and Republicans departs considerably from ideological purity. It is this tendency for slippage in coalition support that perhaps best explains the necessity for the conservative coalition to operate with a great deal of "slack," or potential surplus members. Time-series analysis of the operational strength of the coalition is suggestive of increased future support in Congress for conservative policy positions and reveals overall stability in patterns of coalition strength over time.

The basic thesis of this book—that the conservative coalition exists as an essentially permanent cross-party majority in Congress—has generally been supported by the data, but important variations on this theme are indicated by the pattern of bloc defections. The persistence of the conservative coalition over time and its increased rate of formation are counterbalanced by the sharply varying pattern of conservatives' cohesion on individual roll calls and by the faint tendency for northern Democrats to be the most cohesive of the three blocs.

The complex relationship between the magnitude of conservative coalition success and the degree of voting bloc cohesion has been noted. Coalition size has been shown to be a significant determinant of its success but seems to be of much less importance for its magnitude of appearance. The data also support the belief that Republicans on the whole are far more supportive of the conservative coalition than are southern Democrats, a finding that is readily explained in terms of the cross-pressures to which southern Democrats are subject.

The ramifications of the 1980 electoral triumph for the Republican party specifically and for congressional conservatives more generally were felt very sharply in the 1981 session of Congress.[4] Republican congressional election victories ate into the southern Democratic ranks in both chambers, but the net effect was to produce a potential coalition strength of 68 Republicans and southern Democrats in the Senate and 270 in the House. Cohesion rose among Republicans and southern Democrats on conservative coalition votes but fell among northern Democrats voting against the conservative tide. The coalition's great success (95.19 percent of 104 votes in the Senate and 88.00 percent of 75 House votes) largely reflected the new parliamentary arithmetic and the strong support shown for President Reagan's economic and defense proposals. Coalition successes in the Senate included reductions in food stamps, maintenance of tobacco price supports, limiting federal funding for abortions, and limiting the use of school busing for purposes of racial desegregation. House victories were highlighted by restraints on the Legal Services Corporation, curbs on abortion and busing, and blocking reduced criminal penalties proposed for sex-related offenses in the District of Columbia.

9

Other Directions and Current Events

Where does the study of ideological blocs in Congress go from here? The findings and conclusions in this study do not constitute a complete predictive model of the behavior and policy impact of the conservative coalition. Neither can this book explore fully all the possibly momentous developments of the early 1980s in the patterns of congressional policy making. Some ways of obtaining the additional information necessary for a more detailed understanding of the future direction of the conservative policy coalition can be suggested, however.

One aspect of congressional structure influencing the activity and policy impact of the conservative coalition that has necessarily remained largely unexplored is the role of the formal congressional leadership in aiding or harming the coalition's prospects for success. Such a study should be undertaken of both major parties' leaders under circumstances of both majority and minority party status. To ascertain the precise nature of the relationship between formal leadership and ideological voting, it is important to go beyond previous impressionistic assessments of the role of the congressional leadership. In particular, what part is played by the leadership of each party in agenda setting for the issues that lead to the appearance of the conservative coalition? What is the impact of leadership pressure and position taking on cohesion both for and against the position taken by congressional conservatives? We must ultimately try to understand the exact mechanisms and magnitude of party leadership effects on ideological voting, separate from the influence of senior committee members, the White House, or the informal legislative power structure.

The precise effect of both formal and informal groups on the activity and success of the conservative coalition in congressional decision making is another major task remaining for future research. One aspect of this work must involve the impact of congressional delegations in the House and of informal friendship networks throughout both chambers. The crucial issue here involves the development of a framework for the future possible emergence of more formalized groups among both southern Democrats and conservative Republicans. Such a structured tying together of the cross-party interests of congressional conservatives would constitute a very strong signal presaging a future formal institutionalization of the conservative coalition.

Such a structured framework for conservative cross-party cooperation may in time evolve from the so-called Western Coalition in the Senate, from the Democratic Research Organization serving southern Democrats in the House, or, more realistically because it is more institutionalized already, the House Republican Study Committee. Moderate and liberal House Democrats, perhaps because of a felt need for closer cooperation to maximize their usually inferior voting strength, have a much more deeply entrenched institutional base in the Democratic Study Group. Also, the bipartisan Northeast-Midwest Congressional Coalition provides a more pork-barrel, constituent-need-oriented foundation for cooperation among liberals and moderates along regional lines in the House. Will congressional conservatives, perhaps out of a need to assure greater cohesion if their numerical support or control of key resources declines, also seek out an institutionalized form to attempt to ensure their programmatic success? To answer that question, evidence is needed of the appearance of more formalized channels of coordination and communication among conservative leaders or among the rank and file through elements such as the Republican Study Committee or the Democratic Research Organization in the House, or their successors.

Two intriguing developments in the Ninety-seventh Congress (1981–82) marked a potential watershed in the development of a more formal structure among conservative Democrats in both chambers. The first of these omens was the emergence of a nameless grouping of roughly a dozen moderate to conservative Democrats in the Senate, most of whom were from southern states. Officially formed as of April 8, 1981, this assemblage of antiliberal elements in combination with the Republican Senate majority of 1980 was a possible forerunner of more regular and formal cooperation among Senate Republicans and Democratic Senate conservatives. Led initially by David L. Boren of Oklahoma, such a bloc of generally pro-Reagan Democratic votes suggested that structural changes in patterns of congressional policy making might be afoot.

The second structural change came in the House of Representatives. There, a group of almost fifty conservative Democrats constituted themselves into the Conservative Democratic Forum[1] and gave strong support to the early phases of President Reagan's economic and social counterattack against the New Deal and the Great Society. The leadership of this House grouping spoke with a heavy Texas accent. Its organizers and principal Democratic sponsors of Republican-initiated legislative proposals included Charles W. Stenholm, Kent Hance, and Phil Gramm, all of Texas districts. Gramm co-sponsored the famous Gramm-

Latta Republican/bipartisan substitute to the package of budget cuts favored by the House Democratic leadership in June 1981. The Conservative Democratic Forum, though its membership was not drawn entirely from southern states, could serve as a vehicle for a future more or less permanent conservative Democratic organizational structure. Unabashedly courted by the new Republican White House, a large bloc of mostly southern House Democratic conservatives broke openly with their party on a wide range of fundamental social and economic principles and avowed support for Republican solutions to the nation's problems. This pattern of Democratic defections in the House was in this respect substantially different from the "Southern Manifesto" of the late 1950s when the North-South cleavage among House Democrats was caused by civil rights issues on which Republicans only occasionally agreed with their cross-party fellow conservatives.

The attention of analysts in the future will certainly be turned to the effects on election outcomes and on congressional policy decisions produced by a constellation of prominent conservative special-interest groups.[2] The one group of greatest immediate interest is the National Conservative Political Action Committee (NCPAC). In 1978 the NCPAC targeted for defeat several liberal Democratic and Republican members of the Senate. Its successes included the primary defeat of Republican Clifford Case of New Jersey and the general election defeat of Democrat Dick Clark of Iowa. In 1980, the NCPAC and its allied pressure groups successfully targeted liberal Democratic Senators John Culver of Iowa, George McGovern of South Dakota, Frank Church of Idaho, and Birch Bayh of Indiana, but failed to unseat Senators Alan Cranston of California and Thomas Eagleton of Missouri.

Plans for the 1982 elections indicated that twenty senators, including three liberal Republicans, and several Democratic House leaders, were similarly targeted. Heading the 1982 list were Senators Edward Kennedy of Massachusetts, Donald Riegle of Michigan, Howard Metzenbaum of Ohio, Paul Sarbanes of Maryland, Harrison Williams of New Jersey, and Henry Jackson of Washington.[3]

Other conservative activist pressure groups also focused their efforts more on the Senate than on the House, presumably because senators historically have been more vulnerable than representatives in reelection contests and because fewer seats need to be won in any given election in order to swing control of the entire chamber to the desired party. These right-wing citizens' groups included, besides the NCPAC, the Life Amendment Political Action Committee, which is concerned primarily with the passage of an antiabortion constitutional amendment, the National Rifle Association Political Victory Fund, the Fund for a Conservative Majority, the American Conservative Union, the Conservative Caucus headed by Howard Phillips, and the Committee for the Survival of a Free Congress.

Appearing on the political scene well after the advent of liberal pressure groups such as Americans for Democratic Action or the Council for a Livable World, these New Right groups provided negative advertisements against liberal incumbents and awarded substantial financial support to candidates who adopted the accepted position on such issues as foreign policy, abortion, gun control, economic policies, the commodity straddle, or the Equal Rights Amendment. What long-run impact the efforts of these groups have had and will have on the composition, and, more important, the policy outputs, of Congress remains to be investigated. One consequence of the mass mobilization of conservative interests was the emergence of counterforce elements on the political left, such as George McGovern's Americans for Common Sense group or People for the American Way headed by former television writer and creator of Archie Bunker, Norman Lear. The extension of ideological debates to the mass public through these grass-roots efforts of pressure groups working both ends of the political spectrum portends interesting and potentially system-transforming possibilities for American politics.

The various conservative political action groups collectively seemed to want a fundamental change in the American electoral process. Whether through a partisan critical realignment or a slower ingathering of what is commonly perceived as a conservative "real majority,"[4] the aim was clearly to achieve a cohesive and programmatic electoral base that could sustain in office strong majorities of conservative Republicans or Democrats. Chapter 5 has indicated where this putative conservative majority may find its greatest constituency support. These constituency indicators, however, are muddled by regional differences and by different patterns between states and congressional districts. In general, though, I think an advocate of this potential conservative anti–New Deal majority would be well advised to concentrate on those areas characterized by traits of "backwardness" rather than by traits of "postindustrialization." One wonders, though, if this is a good short-run and a bad long-term strategy, if a continued "greening" of the population also gives the nation a somewhat more pinkish tinge on certain issues.

Even barring a large-scale electoral transformation, the creation of a more unified conservative majority in Congress may still proceed apace. This seemed to be the goal of such New Right senators as Jesse Helms (R-South Carolina), Orrin Hatch and Jake Garn (R-Utah), or Paul Laxalt (R-Nevada) and of such members of the House as Larry McDonald (D-Georgia), Charles Stenholm (D-Texas), or Philip Crane (R-Illinois). The force of common partisan identification, combined with a touch of remaining neopopulist economic progressivism and a desire to hold onto the spoils of victory enjoyed by those who organize the House or Senate, may prevent southern Democrats from ever joining in a formalized alliance with Republicans, but the conservative coalition as discussed in these pages represents a highly successful informal effort to create what is essentially a permanent bipartisan policy majority.

The broad policy goals of extracongressional conservatives, particularly those goals pursued by New Right proponents, have been clearly expressed since the later 1970s. These are the views of one of the leaders of the religious Right, Jerry Falwell:

> It is now time for moral America to band together in a collective voice and make the difference in America by exerting an effort to make their feelings known. The godless minority of treacherous individuals who have been permitted to formulate national policy must now realize they do not represent the majority. They must be made to see that moral Americans are a powerful group who will no longer permit them to destroy our country with their godless, liberal philosophies.[5]

Richard Viguerie, mass-mail and computer data bank expert for the New Right, has presented the following version of a credo for the rising generation of conservatives:

> We are the people who reject the liberal line that America has had her day in the sun. We believe that America is still the land of opportunity, of optimism, of progress. We know that while the truths that made America great may have suffered an eclipse, they still blaze as brightly as ever.
> We believe in God and the importance of the traditional family. We believe that the way to peace is to be stronger than any country that wants to conquer us. We believe in fiscal prudence, and in helping those—but only those—who truly cannot help themselves.
> We are Christian and Jewish. We are Republican, Democratic, and independent. Our first commitment is to political principles, not to political parties.
> We are mostly middle and working class. We wear a blue as well as a white collar.
> We care about the social and cultural index of this nation as well as the Consumer Price Index.
> We live and work mostly on Main Street, not Wall Street. We're more at home on the front porch than in the boardroom.
> We are aggressive, committed, confident.
> We don't give a darn about yesterday's defeats. We're interested in tomorrow's victories.[6]

Although there is no automatic mechanism by which New Right pressure must result in its intended outcomes, and even though grass-roots organizational efforts to unite conservatives from all partisan persuasions do not have the same influence on public policy as a congressional alliance of conservatives, the New Right also had direct plans for the party system. Again, Richard Viguerie writes:

> Coalition politics was being considered in the early 1970s by the Nixon White House. It was aimed at persuading Southern Democrats to change parties and thus take over the U.S. House of Representatives. But then Watergate came along, and coalitions fell victim to Nixon's problems as did a lot of other plans.

In the 1980s, the New Right is determined to do away with old-style politics.

In the past, liberals practiced coalition politics successfully while conservatives limited themselves to the Republican Party. No wonder we were such a small minority.

To put it bluntly, we were snookered. The liberals said what is ours is ours—the Democratic Party—and what is yours—the Republican Party—is negotiable.

So the liberals for many years have had almost 100% of the national Democratic Party and about 40% of the national Republican Party—giving the liberals about 70% of the political elections.

How can conservatives ever expect to govern if we concede 100% of the larger of the two major parties to the liberals without any fight and limit our fight to the political party which represents about 20% of the voters?

But the New Right is not willing to play by the liberals' rules. We are more than willing to support Democrats as long as they are Democrats who are basically right of center. It's a matter of simple arithmetic and common sense.

I want to make it clear that coalition politics does not necessarily mean a third party. . . .

Coalition politics includes working within the Republican and Democratic parties to nominate conservative candidates, promote conservative positions and create conservative majorities in both parties. . . .

Conservatives have the strength, the resources and the ability to operate in both major parties. In fact, because the Democratic Party is so much larger, there are many more conservative Democrats than conservative Republicans when you add up all the blue collar, ethnic, Catholic and other social conservative Democrats.

To sum it up, conservatives should neither abandon the Republicans nor ignore the Democrats.

We do not seek to eliminate the present political structures but to influence them to adopt the conservative point of view which we believe to be that of the majority of the American people.[7]

The future shape of coalition politics in the United States Congress will certainly be affected if these strategies are successfully pursued. Together with countertrends among political liberals, these proposals should make the politics of late twentieth-century America interesting, volatile, and heavily charged with policy and ideological debate.

Although the congressional elections of 1982 failed to add to the ranks of House and Senate conservatives, the long-run nature of Republican and conservative Democratic policy agreement together with continued pressure group support for the political right should extend the working life of the conservative coalition. For the Ninety-eighth Congress (1983–84) and perhaps for succeeding legislative sessions as well, the most important effect of the 1982 elections was the shift of some two dozen House seats to the Democratic party. The conservative political action committees had little to boast about, as very few of their Senate and House targets succumbed at the ballot box and earlier grandiose plans for a Republican House majority and a stronger Senate Republican advantage were aborted by rising unemployment and by Democratic voters returning to the fold. When congressional conservatives must face the reality of a narrowed potential majority, and especially when they confront a potential liberal-to-moderate voting advantage, they must alter their legislative strategies accordingly. Even the presence of a strongly conservative president cannot ensure continued conservative policy success, especially success on the dramatic scale of the Ninety-seventh Congress, when parliamentary arithmetic and the policy agenda change against the permanent majority.

Appendix A

A time series is defined as a set of observations taken at equally spaced intervals, $z_t, t = 1, 2, \ldots, n$. The analysis of such longitudinal data sets is undertaken with the assumption that the observations in the series are serially correlated, that is,

$$E \left((z_t - \mu)(z_{t+i} - \mu) \right) \neq 0.$$

Here, E denotes the "expected value," or the long-run average, of the products of each z_t and z_{t+i}, which are individual observations in the series located i time periods apart and calculated with respect to the mean of the series, μ. This assumption directly contradicts the traditional assumption in regression and other linear methods of independence among observations. The nonlinear modeling strategy followed in the approach of George E. P. Box and Gwilym M. Jenkins incorporates this pattern of serial correlation. The strategy involves a process of identifying, estimating, and checking the components of a model that specify any relationships of serial dependence within the data.

The details of model building are left for the reader to find in other sources. What is important here is a discussion of the types of models that are appropriate for the task at hand. First, it is useful to distinguish a stationary time series, which remains in equilibrium about a constant mean level, from a nonstationary time series having no natural mean. For the latter case, the appropriate model is a member of the class of autoregressive integrated moving average (ARIMA) processes. We will initially consider models appropriate to stationary time series.

Two broad types of stochastic models, autoregressive and moving average, are of great practical importance in representing an observed time series. In the case of the autoregressive (AR) model, the current value of the time series is expressed as a finite, linear combination of previous values of the series, plus a shock, a_t. The values of a time series occurring at equally spaced intervals, $t, t - 1, t - 2, \ldots$ are denoted as $z_t, z_{t-1}, z_{t-2}, \ldots$ and the values of their deviations from the mean of the series are $\tilde{z}_t, \tilde{z}_{t-1}, \tilde{z}_{t-2}, \ldots,$ where $\tilde{z}_t = z_t - \mu$. Then an autoregressive process of order p, AR(p), is given by the equation

$$\tilde{z}_t = \emptyset_1 \tilde{z}_{t-1} + \emptyset_2 \tilde{z}_{t-2} + \ldots + \emptyset_p \tilde{z}_{t-p} + a_t.$$

The terminology "autoregressive" signifies that we may interpret the above result to be a regression equation in which the variable z is regressed on previous values of itself. If we define an autoregressive operator of order p by

$$\emptyset(B) = 1 - \emptyset_1 B - \emptyset_2 B^2 - \ldots - \emptyset_p B^p$$

where B is the backshift operator given by $B^m z_t = z_{t-m}$, then the autoregressive model may be written economically in the form $\emptyset(B)\tilde{z}_t = a_t$.

A finite moving average process of order q, MA(q), expresses $\tilde{z}_t$ as linearly dependent on a finite number, q, of previous a_t's, in the form

$$\tilde{z}_t = a_t - \theta_1 a_{t-1} - \theta_2 a_{t-2} - \ldots - \theta_q a_{t-q}.$$

If we define a moving average operator of order q by

$$\theta(B) = 1 - \theta_1 B - \theta_2 B^2 - \ldots - \theta_q B^q$$

then the MA model may be written economically as $\tilde{z}_t = \theta(B)a_t$.

A more flexible modeling approach than accepting a pure AR or a pure MA model as the proper specification may be obtained by including both AR and MA terms in the model. Such a model is known as mixed autoregressive-moving average (ARMA), and has the form

$$\tilde{z}_t = \emptyset_1 \tilde{z}_{t-1} + \ldots + \emptyset_p \tilde{z}_{t-p} + a_t - \theta_1 a_{t-1} - \ldots - \theta_q a_{t-q}$$

or, more succinctly, $\emptyset(B)\tilde{z}_t = \theta(B)a_t$.

In practice, we frequently achieve an adequate representation of nonseasonal stationary time series with AR, MA, or ARMA models in which the number of AR and MA parameters, p and q respectively, do not exceed two.

For nonstationary time series, that is, series that do not vary about a fixed mean, we may represent the underlying process by a generalized autoregressive operator $\underline{\emptyset}(B)$, which is defined by

$$\underline{\emptyset}(B) = \emptyset(B)(1 - B)^d.$$

We may develop a general model representing nonstationary behavior of the form

$$\underline{\emptyset}(B)z_t = \emptyset(B)(1 - B)^d z_t = \theta(B)a_t$$

which can be expressed more compactly as

$$\emptyset(B)w_t = \theta(B)a_t$$

where $w_t = \nabla^d z_t$ and $\nabla z_t = z_t - z_{t-1} = (1 - B)z_t$ for $d = 1$. What this says is that in order to make an initially nonstationary time series more manageable, take its d'th difference, which is $(1 - B^d)z_t$ or $\nabla^d z_t$, where d usually has a value of 1 or 2. In practical terms, then, we would take the difference between each value in the time series and its appropriate neighbor(s), in order to reveal what underlies a pattern of growth or decline.

The appropriate model to handle nonstationary time series is then the autoregressive integrated moving average process of order p, d, q, or ARIMA (p, d, q), which is defined by

$$w_t = \emptyset_1 w_{t-1} + \ldots + \emptyset_p w_{t-p} + a_t - \theta_1 a_{t-1} - \ldots - \theta_q a_{t-q}$$

where $w_t = \nabla^d z_t$. If we replace w_t by $z_t - \mu$, when $d = 0$, the ARIMA (p, d, q) model includes the stationary mixed model as a special case, as well as the pure autoregressive and pure moving average models.

These basic models, in both stationary and nonstationary forms, are used in this and succeeding chapters to elucidate underlying historical patterns of the coalition process in Congress and to make forecasts based on those models for the near-term future. Forecast results are produced from the conditional expectation of some future value, z_{t+1}, given knowledge of all the z's in the time series up to time t. Details of forecasting procedures are explained in sources available to the interested reader, as discussed in footnote 2 to Chapter 2.

Appendix B

The univariate time series models that are appropriate for each issue dimension in each chamber are as follows:

HOUSE

Civil Liberties
$$(1 - B)(1 + .67B)z_t = a_t$$
Government Management
$$(1 - B)(1 + .40B)z_t = a_t$$
International Involvement
$$(1 - .65B)z_t = a_t$$
Social Welfare
$$(1 - B)(1 + .80B)z_t = (1 - .63B^2)a_t$$

SENATE

Civil Liberties
$$(1 - B)(1 + .55B)z_t = a_t$$
Government Management
$$(1 - .51B)z_t = a_t$$
International Involvement
$$(1 - .59B)z_t = a_t$$
Social Welfare
$$(1 - .30B)z_t = a_t$$

Appendix C

The univariate time-series models that are appropriate for each bloc of committee chairmen or ranking minority members are given below.

HOUSE
(1939–1980)

Southern Democrats
$$(1 - .42B)z_t = 36.09 + a_t$$
Northern Democrats
$$(1 - .62B)z_t = 7.23 + a_t$$
Republicans
$$(1 - .23B - .30B^2)z_t = 32.50 + a_t$$

SENATE
(1933–1980)

Southern Democrats
$$(1 - .44B)z_t = 35.26 + a_t$$
Northern Democrats
$$(1 - .35B)z_t = 17.56 + (1 + .40B^3)a_t$$
Republicans
$$(1 - .33B)z_t = 40.41 + (1 + .62B^2)a_t$$

Appendix D

The time-series models that adequately represent levels of support for the conservative coalition for each regional and partisan group are shown below.

House Eastern Democrats
$$(1 - B)(1 + .44B)z_t = (1 - .46B^4)a_t$$

House Western Democrats
$$(1 - B)z_t = (1 - .38B - .35B^2)a_t$$

House Southern Democrats
$$z_t = 62.57 + (1 - .88B^7)a_t$$

House Midwestern Democrats
$$(1 - B)z_t = (1 - .42B)a_t$$

House Eastern Republicans
$$(1 - B)(1 + .33B)z_t = (1 - .35B^3)a_t$$

House Western Republicans
$$z_t = 72.10 + (1 - .46B^3)a_t$$

House Southern Republicans
$$(1 + .30B)z_t = 109.89 + a_t$$

House Midwestern Republicans
$$(1 - B)(1 + .55B)z_t = (1 - .60B^3)a_t$$

Senate Eastern Democrats
$$(1 - B)(1 + .72B)z_t = a_t$$

Senate Western Democrats
$$z_t = 24.77 + (1 - .92B^8)a_t$$

Senate Southern Democrats
$$(1 - .57B)z_t = 25.26 + a_t$$

Senate Midwestern Democrats
$$(1 - B)z_t = (1 - .70B)a_t$$

Senate Eastern Republicans
$$z_t = 18.55 + (1 - .66B)a_t$$

Senate Western Republicans
$$z_t = 68.40 + (1 + .59B + .32B^6)a_t$$
Senate Southern Republicans
$$(1 - .65B)z_t = a_t$$
Senate Midwestern Republicans
$$z_t = 65.10 + (1 + .78B^2)a_t$$

Appendix E

The following models were used in producing the results shown in Table 6–2. The variables employed were:

I_p = 0 for Republican presidents (1953–60, 1969–76)

I_p = 1 for Democratic presidents (1933–52, 1961–68, 1977–80)

I_c = 0 for Republican control of Congress (1947–48, 1953–54)

I_c = 1 for Democratic control of Congress (1933–46, 1949–52, 1955–80)

I_{RHRP} = 1 for Republican control of the House and of the presidency (1953–54)

= 0 otherwise

I_{RHDP} = 1 for Republican control of the House and Democratic control of the presidency (1947–48)

= 0 otherwise

I_{DHDP} = 1 for Democratic control of the House and of the presidency (1933–46, 1949–52, 1961–68, 1977–80)

= 0 otherwise

I_{DHRP} = 1 for Democratic control of the House and Republican control of the presidency (1955–60, 1969–76)

= 0 otherwise

I_{RSRP} = 1 for Republican control of the Senate and of the presidency (1953–54)

= 0 otherwise

I_{RSDP} = 1 for Republican control of the Senate and Democratic control of the presidency (1947–48)

= 0 otherwise

I_{DSDP} = 1 for Democratic control of the Senate and of the presidency (1933–46, 1949–52, 1961–68, 1977–80)

= 0 otherwise

I_{DSRP} = 1 for Democratic control of the Senate and Republican control of the presidency (1955–60, 1969–76)

= 0 otherwise

The model for conservative coalition appearances in the House under varying conditions of presidential control was
$$(1 - B) (1 + .49B)z_t = a_t + 1.15I_p.$$
The model for conservative coalition appearances in the House under varying conditions of party control of the House was
$$(1 - B) (1 + .48B)z_t = a_t + 0.94I_c.$$
The model for conservative coalition appearances in the House under varying conditions of split versus same-party control of the House and the presidency was
$$(1 - B) (1 + .52B)z_t = a_t - 2.02I_{RHDP} - 7.56I_{RHRP} + 1.44I_{DHDP} + 0.02I_{DHRP}.$$
The model for conservative coalition appearances in the Senate under varying conditions of presidential control was
$$(1 - B) (1 + .51B)z_t = a_t - 0.07I_p.$$
The model for conservative coalition appearances in the Senate under varying conditions of party control of the Senate was
$$(1 - B) (1 + .51B)z_t = a_t + 0.36I_c.$$
The model for conservative coalition appearances in the Senate under varying conditions of split versus same-party control of the Senate and the presidency was
$$(1 - B) (1 + .52B)z_t = a_t - 2.80I_{RSDP} + 0.81I_{RSRP} + 0.10I_{DSDP} + 0.96I_{DSRP}.$$
The model for conservative coalition success in the House under varying conditions of presidential control was
$$(1 - B) (1 + .53B)z_t = a_t + 0.81I_p.$$
The model for conservative coalition success in the House under varying conditions of party control of the House was
$$(1 - B) (1 + .53B)z_t = a_t - 1.10I_c.$$
The model for conservative coalition success in the House under varying conditions of split versus same-party control of the House and the presidency was
$$(1 - B) (1 + .55B)z_t = a_t + 3.67I_{RHDP} + 4.70I_{RHRP} + 0.63I_{DHDP} - 4.07I_{DHRP}.$$
The model for conservative coalition success in the Senate under varying conditions of presidential control was
$$(1 - B) (1 + .36B + .48B^2)z_t = a_t + 1.25I_p.$$
The model for conservative coalition success in the Senate under varying conditions of party control of the Senate was
$$(1 - B) (1 + .35B + .48B^2)z_t = a_t - 0.18I_c.$$
The model for conservative coalition success in the Senate under varying conditions of split versus same-party control of the Senate and the presidency was
$$(1 - B) (1 + .36B + .49B^2)z_t = a_t + 2.05I_{RSDP} + 1.51I_{RSRP} + 1.46I_{DSDP} - 3.32I_{DSRP}.$$

Appendix F

The appropriate model for party unity voting in the House is
$$(1 - .73B)z_t = 17.03 + (1 - .52B^3)a_t$$
while Senate party unity voting is well represented by the ARIMA $(1, 0, 0)$ process
$$(1 - .38B^2)z_t = 35.52 + a_t.$$
North-South Democratic splits in the House follow the time series model
$$(1 + .40B)(1 - B)z_t = a_t$$
and the corresponding model for the Senate is
$$(1 + .84B)(1 - B)z_t = (1 - .43B^2)a_t.$$
The appropriate models for the relative frequency of North-South Democratic splits which result in the formation of the conservative coalition are
$$(1 - B)(1 + .63B)z_t = a_t$$
in the House and
$$(1 - B)(1 + .41B)z_t = a_t$$
in the Senate.

Appendix G

Potential conservative coalition strength follows the ARIMA $(1, 1, 0)$ model
$$(1 - B)(1 + .48B^2)z_t = a_t$$
in the House, and the ARIMA $(1, 0, 0)$ process
$$(1 - .88B)z_t = 1.62 + a_t$$
in the Senate.
The House model for the operational strength of the conservative coalition is
$$(1 - .72B)z_t = 16.98 + a_t$$
while the corresponding model in the Senate is
$$(1 - .74B)z_t = 14.41 + a_t.$$
Intervention models for the impact of conservative control of Congress on success of the conservative coalition are
$$(1 - B)(1 + .52B)z_t = a_t + 0.42I_c$$
for the House and
$$(1 - B)(1 + .35B + .47B^2)z_t = a_t + 1.87I_c$$
in the Senate, where
$I_c = 1$ for years when conservatives outnumber liberals
$ = 0$ for years in which liberals are more numerous than conservatives.

Notes

Notes to Chapter 1

1. Much of the anlaysis that follows is distilled from postelection issues of Congressional Quarterly's *Weekly Report*.

2. The six states carried by Carter in 1980 were Georgia, Hawaii, Maryland, Minnesota, Rhode Island, and West Virginia.

3. Cleveland lost the electoral vote count, despite commanding a slender popular vote plurality over Benjamin Harrison.

4. All the members of this group have served in the House of Representatives. For a useful discussion of the Republican Senate class of 1980, see Gerald M. Pomper et al., *The Election of 1980: Reports and Interpretations* (Chatham, New Jersey: Chatham House, 1981), pp. 126–32.

5. On the mathematical underpinnings of time-series analysis, see George E. P. Box and Gwilym M. Jenkins, *Time Series Analysis: Forecasting and Control* (San Francisco: Holden-Day, 1976), and Charles R. Nelson, *Applied Time Series Analysis for Managerial Forecasting* (San Francisco: Holden-Day, 1973). Social science applications of the technique are discussed in Richard McCleary and Richard A. Hay, Jr., *Applied Time Series Analysis for the Social Sciences* (Beverly Hills, California: Sage Publications, 1980). A very brief discussion of time-series models is presented in Appendix A.

6. The early work in the area of legislative cohesion by A. Lawrence Lowell and Stuart Rice has been brought to fruition in the studies of congressional behavior undertaken by Julius Turner, David B. Truman, Aage R. Clausen, David R. Mayhew, and Duncan MacRae, Jr., among others (see Bibliography).

7. For a discussion of the development of the concept of "responsible parties," see Austin Ranney, *The Doctrine of Responsible Party Government: Its Origins and Present State* (Urbana: University of Illinois Press, 1962).

8. William H. Riker, *The Theory of Political Coalitions* (New Haven: Yale University Press, 1962).

9. See Arthur G. Stevens, Jr., Arthur H. Miller, and Thomas E. Mann, "Mobilization of Liberal Strength in the House, 1955–1970: The Democratic Study Group," *American Political Science Review* 68 (1974): 667–81; and Kenneth Kofmehl, "The House Democratic Study Group: The Institutionalization of a Voting Bloc," *Western Political Quarterly* 17 (1964): 256–72.

10. William Gamson, "Experimental Studies of Coalition Formation," in *Advances in Experimental Psychology,* ed. Leonard Berkowitz (New York: Academic Press, 1964), p. 85.

11. Riker, *Theory of Political Coalitions.*

12. On the subject of the costs of coalition-building, see Charles R. Adrian and Charles Press, "Decision Costs in Coalition Formation," *American Political Science Review* 62 (1969): 556–63. They specify these costs as information, responsibility, intergame, division of payoffs, dissonance, inertia, time, and persuasion.

13. For Leiserson's approach, see Sven Groennings, E. W. Kelly, and Michael Leiserson, *The Study of Coalition Behavior* (New York: Holt, Rinehart, and Winston, 1970).

14. See, for example: Gabriel A. Almond, Scott C. Flanagan, and Robert J. Mundt, *Crisis, Choice, and Change* (Boston: Little, Brown & Co., 1973); Michael Leiserson, "Coalitions in Politics: A Theoretical and Empirical Study" (Ph.D. dissertation: Yale University, 1966); Abraham de Swann, "An Empirical Model of Coalition Formation as an N-Person Game of Policy Distance Minimization," in Groennings, Kelly, and Leiserson, *Study of Coalition Behavior,* pp. 424–44; and Abraham de Swann, *Coalition Theories and Cabinet Formations* (Amsterdam: Elsevier, 1974).

15. Scott C. Flanagan, "Models and Methods of Analysis," in Almond, Flanagan, and Mundt, *Crisis, Choice, and Change,* pp. 43–102, especially p. 72.

16. Steven J. Brams, "Positive Coalition Theory: The Relationship between Postulated Goals and Derived Behavior," in *Political Science Annual IV: Conflict, Competition, and Coalitions,* ed. Cornelius Cotter (Indianapolis: Bobbs-Merrill, 1972), pp. 3–40. See also Brams, "A Cost/Benefit Analysis of Coalition Formation in Voting Bodies," in *Probability Models of Collective Decision Making,* ed. Richard G. Niemi and Herbert F. Weisberg (Columbus, Ohio: Charles E. Merrill Publishing Company, 1972), pp. 101–24.

17. Richard G. Niemi and Herbert F. Weisberg, "The Effects of Group Size on Collective Decision Making," in Niemi and Weisberg, ed., *Probability Models,* pp. 125–48.

18. David H. Koehler, "The Legislative Process and the Minimal Winning Coalition," in Niemi and Weisberg, ed., *Probability Models,* pp. 149–64. For a strong critique of Koehler, see Russell Hardin, "Hollow Victory: The Minimum Winning Coalition," *American Political Science Review* 70 (1976): 1202–14.

19. Stephen K. Bailey, *The New Congress* (New York: St. Martin's Press, 1966).

20. Charles O. Jones, "Joseph G. Cannon and Howard W. Smith: An Essay on the Limits of Leadership in the House of Representatives," *Journal of Politics* 30 (1968): 617–46.

21. Daniel Berman, *In Congress Assembled: The Legislative Process in the National Government* (New York: The Macmillan Company, 1964).

22. George Blair, *American Legislatures: Structure and Process* (New York: Harper and Row, 1967).

23. Charles L. Clapp, *The Congressman: His Work as He Sees It* (Washington, D.C.: The Brookings Institution, 1963).

24. James MacGregor Burns, *The Deadlock of Democracy: Four-Party Politics in America* (Englewood Cliffs, New Jersey: Prentice-Hall, 1967).

25. Joseph S. Clark, *The Senate Establishment* (New York: Hill and Wang, 1963).

26. Joseph S. Clark, *Congress: The Sapless Branch,* rev. ed. (New York: Harper and Row, 1965).

27. Morris P. Fiorina, *Representatives, Roll Calls, and Constituencies* (Lexington, Massachusetts: Lexington Books, 1974).

28. William J. Keefe and Morris S. Ogul, *The American Legislative Process: Congress and the States,* 2d ed. (Englewood Cliffs, New Jersey: Prentice-Hall, 1968).

29. George B. Galloway, *History of the House of Representatives* (New York: Thomas Y. Crowell Company, 1961), p. 142.

30. Ibid., p. 227.

31. Richard Bolling, *Power in the House: A History of the Leadership of the House of Representatives* (New York: E. P. Dutton and Co., 1968), p. 195. See also his *House Out of Order* (New York: E. P. Dutton and Co., 1965).

32. Bolling, *House Out of Order,* p. 80. A similar point is made by Richard Fenno, *Congressmen in Committees* (Boston: Little, Brown & Co., 1973), who, in characterizing the conservative coalition in the House as a House-led policy coalition, in contrast to executive-led, party-led, or clientele-led coalitions, argues that the conservative coalition, as is true for all House-led coalitions, is "strictly a sometime thing" as the prime mover and shaper of national policy.

33. Fenno, *Congressmen in Committees,* p. 159. See also John F. Manley, *The Politics of Finance* (Boston: Little, Brown & Co., 1970), p. 297.

34. Aage R. Clausen, *How Congressmen Decide: A Policy Focus* (New York: St. Martin's Press, 1973), pp. 32–33.

35. Richard P. Y. Li and Barbara Hinckley, "Time Series, Systems Analysis, and Serial Dependence in Coalition Formation," *Political Methodology* 3 (1976): 523–44. The quotation is from p. 524. See also Hinckley, "Coalitions in Congress: Size in a Series of Games," *American Politics Quarterly* 30 (1973): 339–59; Hinckley, "Coalitions in Congress: Size and Ideological Distance," *Midwest Journal of Political Science* 16 (1972): 197–207; and Hinckley, *Coalitions and Politics* (New York: Harcourt Brace Jovanovich, 1981).

36. Joel Paul Margolis, "The Conservative Coalition in the United States Senate, 1933–1968" (Ph.D. dissertation: University of Wisconsin-Madison, 1973).

37. James T. Patterson, *Congressional Conservatism and the New Deal: The Growth of the Conservative Coalition in Congress, 1933–1939* (Lexington, Kentucky: University of Kentucky Press, 1967).

38. John F. Manley, "The Conservative Coalition in Congress," *American Behavioral Scientist* 17 (1973): 223–47.

39. Some intriguing signs of the emergence of similar groupings among conservative congressmen are considered in Chapter 9.

40. V. O. Key, *Southern Politics in State and Nation* (New York: Alfred A. Knopf, 1949).

41. David W. Brady and Charles S. Bullock III, "Is There a Conservative Coalition in the House?" *Journal of Politics* 42 (1980): 549–59. See also their chapter "Coalition Politics in the House of Representatives," in *Congress Reconsidered,* 2d ed., edited by

Lawrence C. Dodd and Bruce I. Oppenheimer (Washington, D.C.: Congressional Quarterly Press, 1981), pp. 186–203.

42. Notably Margolis, "Conservative Coalition."

43. Especially Manley, "Conservative Coalition in Congress," and Patterson, *Congressional Conservatism and the New Deal.* Recent exceptions to some of these criticisms are Brady and Bullock, "Is There a Conservative Coalition in the House?" and "Coalition Politics in the House of Representatives."

44. The term "conservative" is explained in detail in Chapter 3. Generally, I take conservatism to represent a philosophy of free enterprise, self-help, minimal government intervention, restrictive fiscal and monetary policies, and maintenance of traditionalist religious and social norms.

45. ADA scores are computed as the percentage of times a senator or representative agrees with the "liberal" position on selected roll call votes or enters a live pair agreeing with the ADA's preferred position, and failure to vote lowers the scores. ACA ratings are similarly based on percentage agreement with the preferred "conservative" issue position on selected votes, but failure to vote does not lower the scores. For a single session of Congress, each organization typically selects between twenty and thirty key roll calls which they believe to be critical tests of ideological consistency.

46. *Congressional Record,* June 30, 1958, p. 12612.

47. Fenno, *Congressmen in Committees.*

48. For an excellent recent discussion of the role of ideology in congressional decision making, see Jerrold Schneider, *Ideological Coalitions in Congress* (Westport, Connecticut: Greenwood Press, 1979). See also William R. Shaffer, *Party and Ideology in the United States Congress* (Lanham, Maryland: University Press of America, 1980).

49. This is the "index of relative cohesion," as discussed in Lee F. Anderson, Meredith W. Watts, Jr., and Allen R. Wilcox, *Legislative Roll Call Analysis* (Evanston: Northwestern University Press, 1966), especially pp. 32–40.

50. For definitions of a conservative coalition vote, the South, the North, and conservative coalition support scores, see Congressional Quarterly, Inc., *Congressional Quarterly Almanac,* in the section devoted to coverage of the conservative coalition in any issue.

Notes to Chapter 2

1. The major reference is Box and Jenkins, *Time Series Analysis.*

2. Recommended for the reader who is unacquainted with time-series methods is McCleary and Hay, *Applied Time Series Analysis for the Social Sciences.* The Box and Jenkins text is recommended for an advanced discussion of univariate and multivariate methods. A good intermediate-level presentation is in Robert B. Miller and Dean W. Wichern, *Intermediate Business Statistics: Analysis of Variance, Regression, and Time Series* (New York: Holt, Rinehart and Winston, 1977).

3. The incidence of "unanimous" or "noncontroversial" roll calls has increased in both the House and the Senate. In some sessions of Congress, the frequency of such votes is extraordinarily high. A maximum of just over 39 percent of all House roll calls in 1970 were "noncontroversial," as against the Senate maximum of nearly 30 percent in 1957. The great increase in total roll calls in both chambers, especially in the House, is some-

what less significant when the recent increase in the incidence of "unanimous" roll calls is taken into consideration. The incidence of "noncontroversial" roll calls should be factored into any assessment of congressional activity that relies on this form of "hard" data. The substantive implications of this roll call vote problem are evident from comparing the magnitude of conservative coalition activity as measured in the last two columns of Tables 2–1 and 2–2.

4. By using the term "pluralist," I mean to relate this discussion to the broader issue in democratic theory of the locus on institutional power. This is the terminology used by Schneider, in *Ideological Coalitions in Congress*.

Notes to Chapter 3

1. Clausen, *How Congressmen Decide*.

2. Clausen succeeded in including approximately 75 percent of all roll calls taken in either chamber between 1953 and 1964 in his set of issue dimensions. Here, I have determined a unique issue dimension for all roll calls on which the conservative coalition formed in each chamber. In so doing, it was necessary at times to overlook the multidimensionality of individual roll calls and perhaps artificially to categorize a roll call under what appeared to be the single most important issue dimension underlying that particular vote. This technique cannot be fully defended against charges that votes have been assigned to one category as opposed to an alternative category that may also seem appropriate.

3. Jones, "Joseph G. Cannon and Howard W. Smith."

4. Bailey, *The New Congress;* Blair, *American Legislatures;* Thomas P. Murphy, *The New Politics Congress* (Lexington, Massachusetts: D.C. Heath and Company, 1974); Norman J. Ornstein and David W. Rohde, "Seniority and Future Power in Congress," in *Congress in Change: Evolution and Reform,* ed. Norman J. Ornstein (New York: Praeger, 1975); Clapp, *The Congressman*.

5. Berman, *In Congress Assembled*.

6. Clark, *The Senate Establishment* and *Congress*.

7. Galloway, *History of the House of Representatives*.

8. Margolis, "Conservative Coalition."

9. Lewis A. Froman, Jr., *Congressmen and Their Constituencies* (Chicago: Rand McNally and Co., 1963).

10. Undated letter from the National Committee for an Effective Congress, p. 1. Punctuation and capitalization are as in the original.

Notes to Chapter 4

1. See, in particular, Barbara Hinckley, *The Seniority System in Congress* (Bloomington: Indiana University Press, 1971).

2. The point about coalition success is addressed, for example, by Keefe and Ogul, *The American Legislative Process,* and by Brady and Bullock, "Is There a Conservative Coalition in the House?"

3. Clark, *The Senate Establishment*.

4. This section and the one following owe much to Larry M. Schwab, *Changing Patterns of Congressional Politics* (New York: D. Van Nostrand Co., 1980), pp. 106–15.

5. The same question is handled in a more limited way by Keefe and Ogul, *The American Legislative Process*, pp. 187–91.

6. The role of the conservative coalition on the House Rules Committee is well summarized in Congressional Quarterly, Inc., *Congressional Quarterly's Guide to Congress*, 2d ed. (Washington, D.C.: Congressional Quarterly, Inc., 1976), pp. 51–52, 55–56, 90–91. The ensuing discussion relies heavily on this source. For discussions of the struggle to break conservative control of the committee, see Robert L. Peabody, "The Enlarged Rules Committee," and Milton C. Cummings, Jr., and Robert L. Peabody, "The Decision to Enlarge the Committee on Rules: An Analysis of the 1961 Vote," both in *New Perspectives on the House of Representatives*, ed. Robert L. Peabody and Nelson W. Polsby (Chicago: Rand McNally and Co., 1963), pp. 129–64 and pp. 167–94, respectively. See also Bruce I. Oppenheimer, "The Rules Committee: New Arm of Leadership in a Decentralized House," in *Congress Reconsidered*, ed. Lawrence G. Dodd and Bruce I. Oppenheimer (New York: Praeger Publishers, 1977).

Notes to Chapter 5

1. Keefe and Ogul, *The American Legislative Process*.

2. A thorough conceptualization of different perspectives on the meaning of representation is provided in Hanna F. Pitkin, *The Concept of Representation* (Berkeley and Los Angeles: University of California Press, 1967).

3. The term is meant to separate out those people who are part of a "special public," or those for whom a particular single issue or set of issues are particularly salient, as distinct from the "general public."

4. On this topic, see Leroy N. Rieselbach, *Congressional Reform in the Seventies* (Morristown, New Jersey: General Learning Press, 1977), especially pp. 8–10.

5. David R. Mayhew, *Congress: The Electoral Connection* (New Haven: Yale University Press, 1974).

6. The classic study, using 1958 data, is Warren Miller and Donald Stokes, "Constituency Influence in Congress," *American Political Science Review* 57 (1963): 45–56. The authors found marked agreement between 116 representatives and their constituents on social welfare and particularly on civil rights issues, but very little correspondence on foreign policy, on which congressmen tend to act in accordance with the president's views. An important early study of the constituency correlates of conservative coalition support is Froman, *Congressmen and Their Constituencies*. See also Margolis, "Conservative Coalition."

7. Clausen, *How Congressmen Decide*.

8. The regions are defined as follows: East: Connecticut, Delaware, Maine, Maryland, Massachusetts, New Hampshire, New Jersey, New York, Pennsylvania, Rhode Island, Vermont, and West Virginia; West: Alaska, Arizona, California, Colorado, Hawaii, Idaho, Montana, Nevada, New Mexico, Oregon, Utah, Washington, and Wyoming; South: Alabama, Arkansas, Florida, Georgia, Kentucky, Louisiana, Mississippi, North

Carolina, Oklahoma, South Carolina, Tennessee, Texas, and Virginia; Midwest: Illinois, Indiana, Iowa, Kansas, Michigan, Minnesota, Missouri, Nebraska, North Dakota, Ohio, South Dakota, and Wisconsin.

9. All constituency data were collected from United States Bureau of the Census, *Congressional District Data Book (Districts of the 88th Congress)* (Washington, D.C.: U.S. Government Printing Office, 1963), and *Congressional District Data Book: 93rd Congress* (Washington, D.C.: U.S. Government Printing Office, 1973). Reapportionment supplements for the mid-1960s were used to update constituency characteristics in the wake of court-enforced redrawing of congressional districts. A very useful recent discussion of the many difficulties inherent in attempts to infer a legislator-constituent relationship is Walter J. Stone, "Measuring Constituency-Representative Linkages: Problems and Prospects," *Legislative Studies Quarterly* 4 (1979): 623–39. On the defects of demographic traits as indicators of constituency political characteristics, see also Richard Fenno, *Home Style: House Members in Their Districts* (Boston: Little, Brown & Co., 1978).

10. See Christopher H. Achen, "Measuring Representation: Perils of the Correlation Coefficient," *American Journal of Political Science* 21 (1977): 805–15, for a lucid discussion of the limitations of comparing correlational results across variables. Correlations are used here, rather than unstandardized regression coefficients, because of the easier and clearer interpretability of correlation results and also because of severe problems of multicollinearity for any multiple regression analysis run with this mix of variables.

Notes to Chapter 6

1. For some scholarly examples of this genre, see: Wilfred E. Binkley, *President and Congress,* 3d rev. ed. (New York: Vintage Books, 1962); Louis Fisher, *President and Congress* (New York: Free Press, 1972); Nelson W. Polsby, *Congress and the Presidency* (Englewood Cliffs, New Jersey: Prentice-Hall, 1976); and Steven A. Shull, *Presidential Policy Making: An Analysis* (Brunswick, Ohio: King's Court Communications, 1979).

2. This data set, derived from Congressional Quarterly's familiar compilation of roll call votes on which presidents take a position, reflects the universe of conservative coalition roll calls on which a president has taken a stand. Presidential position taking is determined by CQ's assessment of the clarity of a president's position on individual roll calls as manifested in press conferences, official statements, or messages to Congress. This evaluation is used by CQ in determining its presidential support scores.

3. Burns, *Deadlock of Democracy;* Clark, *The Senate Establishment* and *Congress;* Patterson, *Congressional Conservatism and the New Deal.*

4. A related concept is that of congressional "impermeability." See Barbara Hinckley, "Party as Coalition in Legislative Settings: Possible 'Impermeability' to External Effects," paper presented at the Annual Meeting of the American Political Science Association, 1975.

5. In these and all succeeding calculations, the total number of votes taken during an administration are figured from the first vote taken in Congress after that president's initial election or ascension to office until the last vote taken before that president's term ended or until he resigned (Nixon) or died in office (Roosevelt and Kennedy).

6. The seminal article is George E. P. Box and G. C. Tiao, "Intervention Analysis with Applications to Economic and Environmental Problems," *Journal of the American Statistical Association* 70 (1975): 70–79.

7. No attempt is made here to distinguish between presidential "success" and "support," as identified by Shull, *Presidential Policy Making*.

Notes to Chapter 7

1. Galloway, *History of the House of Representatives*.

2. Li and Hinckley, "Time Series, Systems Analysis, and Serial Dependence in Coalition Formation."

3. *Congressional Record*, May 15, 1967, pp. 12611–13.

4. Conservative coalition votes are a mixture of both party unity and bipartisan votes. Since 1933, the trend has been toward a heightened coincidence of coalition appearances with party unity votes. This transformation in the partisan content of conservative coalition votes doubtless is due mostly to the declining strength of the southern Democrats in both chambers and the consequent domination of the "potential conservative coalition" by Republicans.

5. On the general topic of the decline of party in Congress and its policy consequences, see, for example, David Brady, Joseph Cooper, and Patricia Hurley, "The Decline of Party in the House of Representatives," *Legislative Studies Quarterly* 4 (1979): 381–409. Also see Barbara Sinclair, "Party Realignment and the Transformation of the Political Agenda," *American Political Science Review* 71 (1977): 940–54.

Notes to Chapter 8

1. Riker, *Theory of Political Coalitions*.

2. Gamson, "Experimental Studies of Coalition Formation."

3. As of the 1970 census, the thirteen states of the South were allocated a total of 121 House seats. This figure represents virtually no net change from the 120 southern House seats as of the 1930 census. The following redistribution of congressional power occurred between these two censuses among the southern states.

State	1930	1970	Net Gain/Loss
Alabama	9	7	− 2
Arkansas	7	4	− 3
Florida	5	15	+ 10
Georgia	10	10	0
Kentucky	9	7	− 2
Louisiana	8	8	0
Mississippi	7	5	− 2
North Carolina	11	11	0
Oklahoma	9	6	− 3
South Carolina	6	6	0

State	1930	1970	Net Gain/Loss
Tennessee	9	8	−1
Texas	21	24	+3
Virginia	9	10	+1

4. The following discussion is based on *Congressional Quarterly Weekly Report,* January 9, 1982, pp. 50–51.

Notes to Chapter 9

1. For a discussion of both Senate and House conservative Democratic groupings of the Ninety-seventh Congress, see *Congressional Quarterly Weekly Report,* June 13, 1981, pp. 1023–26.

2. For a general discussion of many of the ''New Right'' pressure groups and their tactics, see Alan Crawford, *Thunder on the Right: The ''New Right'' and the Politics of Resentment* (New York: Pantheon Books, 1980).

3. *Los Angeles Times,* November 12, 1980.

4. The term, if not the point of view, is taken from Richard M. Scammon and Ben J. Wattenberg, *The Real Majority* (New York: Coward, McCann & Geogegan, 1970).

5. In the Introduction to Richard A. Viguerie, *The New Right: We're Ready to Lead* (Falls Church, Virginia: The Viguerie Company, 1981), no page number.

6. Ibid., p. 26.

7. Ibid., pp. 87–88.

Bibliography

Achen, Christopher H. "Measuring Representation: Perils of the Correlation Coefficient." *American Journal of Political Science* 21 (1977): 805–15.

Adrian, Charles R., and Charles Press. "Decision Costs in Coalition Formation." *American Political Science Review* 62 (1969): 556–63.

Almond, Gabriel A., Scott C. Flanagan, and Robert J. Mundt. *Crisis, Choice, and Change.* Boston: Little, Brown & Co., 1973.

Anderson, Lee F., Meredith W. Watts, Jr., and Allen R. Wilcox. *Legislative Roll Call Analysis.* Evanston: Northwestern University Press, 1966.

Bailey, Stephen K. *The New Congress.* New York: St. Martin's Press, 1966.

Berkowitz, Leonard. *Advances in Experimental Psychology.* New York: Academic Press, 1964.

Berman, Daniel. *In Congress Assembled: The Legislative Process in the National Government.* New York: The Macmillan Company, 1964.

Binkley, Wilfred E. *President and Congress.* 3d rev. ed. New York: Vintage Books, 1962.

Blair, George. *American Legislatures: Structure and Process.* New York: Harper and Row, 1967.

Bolling, Richard Walker. *House Out of Order.* New York: E. P. Dutton and Co., 1965.

———. *Power in the House: A History of the Leadership of the House of Representatives.* New York: E. P. Dutton and Co., 1968.

Box, George E. P., and Gwilym M. Jenkins. *Time Series Analysis: Forecasting and Control.* San Francisco: Holden-Day, 1976.

Box, George E. P., and G. C. Tiao. "Intervention Analysis with Applications to Economic and Environmental Problems." *Journal of the American Statistical Association* 70 (1975): 70–79.

Brady, David W., and Charles S. Bullock III. "Coalition Politics in the House of Representatives." In *Congress Reconsidered,* 2d ed., edited by Lawrence C. Dodd and

Bruce I. Oppenheimer, pp. 186–203. Washington, D.C.: Congressional Quarterly Press, 1981.

———. "Is There a Conservative Coalition in the House?" *Journal of Politics* 42 (1980): 549–59.

Brady, David W., Joseph Cooper, and Patricia Hurley. "The Decline of Party in the House of Representatives." *Legislative Studies Quarterly* 4 (1979): 381–409.

Brams, Steven J. "A Cost/Benefit Analysis of Coalition Formation in Voting Bodies." In *Probability Models of Collective Decision Making,* edited by Richard G. Niemi and Herbert F. Weisberg. Columbus, Ohio: Charles E. Merrill Publishing Company, 1972.

———. "Positive Coalition Theory: The Relationship between Postulated Goals and Derived Behavior." In *Political Science Annual IV: Conflict, Competition, and Coalitions,* edited by Cornelius Cotter. Indianapolis: Bobbs-Merrill, 1972.

Burns, James MacGregor. *The Deadlock of Democracy: Four-Party Politics in America.* Englewood Cliffs, New Jersey: Prentice-Hall, 1967.

Clapp, Charles L. *The Congressman: His Work as He Sees It.* Washington, D.C.: The Brookings Institution, 1963.

Clark, Joseph S. *Congress: The Sapless Branch.* Rev. ed. New York: Harper and Row, 1965.

———. *The Senate Establishment.* New York: Hill and Wang, 1963.

Clausen, Aage R. *How Congressmen Decide: A Policy Focus.* New York: St. Martin's Press, 1973.

Congressional Quarterly, Inc. *Congressional Quarterly Almanac.* Washington, D.C.: Congressional Quarterly, Inc., various years.

———. *Congressional Quarterly Weekly Report.* Washington, D.C.: Congressional Quarterly, Inc., various issues.

———. *Congressional Quarterly's Guide to Congress.* 2d ed. Washington, D.C.: Congressional Quarterly, Inc., 1976.

Cotter, Cornelius. *Political Science Annual IV: Conflict, Competition, and Coalitions.* Indianapolis: Bobbs-Merrill, 1972.

Crawford, Alan. *Thunder on the Right: The "New Right" and the Politics of Resentment.* New York: Pantheon Books, 1980.

Cummings, Milton C., Jr., and Robert L. Peabody. "The Decision to Enlarge the Committee on Rules: An Analysis of the 1961 Vote." In *New Perspectives on the House of Representatives,* edited by Robert L. Peabody and Nelson W. Polsby. Chicago: Rand McNally and Company, 1963.

de Swann, Abraham. *Coalition Theories and Cabinet Formations.* Amsterdam: Elsevier, 1974.

———. "An Empirical Model of Coalition Formation as an N-Person Game of Policy Distance Minimization." In *The Study of Coalition Behavior,* edited by Sven Groennings, E. W. Kelly, and Michael Leiserson. New York: Holt, Rinehart, and Winston, 1970.

Fenno, Richard. *Congressmen in Committees.* Boston: Little, Brown & Co., 1973.

———. *Home Style: House Members in Their Districts.* Boston: Little, Brown & Co., 1978.

Fiorina, Morris P. *Representatives, Roll Calls, and Constituencies.* Lexington, Massachusetts: Lexington Books, 1974.

Fisher, Louis. *President and Congress.* New York: Free Press, 1972.

Flanagan, Scott C. "Models and Methods of Analysis." In *Crisis, Choice, and Change,* edited by Gabriel A. Almond, Scott C. Flanagan, and Robert J. Mundt. Boston: Little, Brown & Co., 1973.

Froman, Lewis A., Jr. *Congressmen and Their Constituencies.* Chicago: Rand McNally and Company, 1963.

Galloway, George B. *History of the House of Representatives.* New York: Thomas Y. Crowell Company, 1961.

Gamson, William. "Experimental Studies of Coalition Formation." In *Advances in Experimental Psychology,* edited by Leonard Berkowitz. New York: Academic Press, 1964.

Groennings, Sven, E. W. Kelly, and Michael Leiserson. *The Study of Coalition Behavior.* New York: Holt, Rinehart, and Winston, 1970.

Hardin, Russell. "Hollow Victory: The Minimum Winning Coalition." *American Political Science Review* 70 (1976): 1202–14.

Hinckley, Barbara. *Coalitions and Politics.* New York: Harcourt Brace Jovanovich, 1981.

_____. "Coalitions in Congress: Size and Ideological Distance." *Midwest Journal of Political Science* 16 (1972): 197–207.

_____. "Coalitions in Congress: Size in a Series of Games." *American Politics Quarterly* 1 (1973): 339–59.

_____. "Party as Coalition in Legislative Settings: Possible 'Impermeability' to External Effects." Paper presented at the Annual Meeting of the American Political Science Association, 1975.

_____. *The Seniority System in Congress.* Bloomington: Indiana University Press, 1971.

Jones, Charles O. "Joseph G. Cannon and Howard W. Smith: An Essay on the Limits of Leadership in the House of Representatives." *Journal of Politics* 30 (1968): 617–46.

Keefe, William J., and Morris S. Ogul. *The American Legislative Process: Congress and the States.* 2d ed. Englewood Cliffs, New Jersey: Prentice-Hall, 1968.

Key, V. O. *Southern Politics in State and Nation.* New York: Alfred A. Knopf, 1949.

Koehler, David H. "The Legislative Process and the Minimal Winning Coalition." In *Probability Models of Collective Decision Making,* edited by Richard G. Niemi and Herbert F. Weisberg. Columbus, Ohio: Charles E. Merrill Publishing Company, 1972.

Kofmehl, Kenneth. "The House Democratic Study Group: The Institutionalization of a Voting Bloc." *Western Political Quarterly* 17 (1964): 256–72.

Leiserson, Michael. "Coalitions in Politics: A Theoretical and Empirical Study." Ph.D. dissertation, Yale University, 1966.

Li, Richard P. Y., and Barbara Hinckley. "Time Series, Systems Analysis, and Serial Dependence in Coalition Formation." *Political Methodology* 3 (1976): 523–44.

Lowell, A. Lawrence. "The Influence of Party upon Legislation in England and America." In *Annual Report of the American Historical Association for 1901.* Washington, D.C., 1902.

McCleary, Richard, and Richard A. Hay, Jr. *Applied Time Series Analysis for the Social Sciences.* Beverly Hills, California: Sage Publications, 1980.

MacRae, Duncan, Jr. *Dimensions of Congressional Voting.* Berkeley: University of California Press, 1958.

Manley, John F. "The Conservative Coalition in Congress." *American Behavioral Scientist* 17 (1973): 223–47.

_____. *The Politics of Finance.* Boston: Little, Brown & Co., 1970.

Margolis, Joel Paul. "The Conservative Coalition in the United States Senate, 1933–1968." Ph.D. dissertation, University of Wisconsin-Madison, 1973.

Mayhew, David R. *Congress: The Electoral Connection.* New Haven: Yale University Press, 1974.

Miller, Robert B., and Dean W. Wichern. *Intermediate Business Statistics: Analysis of Variance, Regression, and Time Series.* New York: Holt, Rinehart and Winston, 1977.

Miller, Warren, and Donald Stokes. "Constituency Influence in Congress." *American Political Science Review* 57 (1963): 45–56.

Murphy, Thomas P. *The New Politics Congress.* Lexington, Massachusetts: D. C. Heath and Company, 1974.

Nelson, Charles R. *Applied Time Series Analysis for Managerial Forecasting.* San Francisco: Holden-Day, 1973.

Niemi, Richard G., and Herbert F. Weisberg. "The Effects of Group Size on Collective Decision Making." In *Probability Models of Collective Decision Making,* edited by Richard G. Niemi and Herbert F. Weisberg. Columbus, Ohio: Charles E. Merrill Publishing Company, 1972.

———. *Probability Models of Collective Decision Making.* Columbus, Ohio: Charles E. Merrill Publishing Company, 1972.

Oppenheimer, Bruce I. "The Rules Committee: New Arm of Leadership in a Decentralized House." In *Congress Reconsidered,* edited by Lawrence G. Dodd and Bruce I. Oppenheimer. New York: Praeger Publishers, 1977.

Ornstein, Norman J. *Congress in Change: Evolution and Reform.* New York: Praeger, 1975.

———, and David W. Rohde. "Seniority and Future Power in Congress." In *Congress in Change: Evolution and Reform,* edited by Norman J. Ornstein. New York: Praeger, 1975.

Patterson, James T. *Congressional Conservatism and the New Deal: The Growth of the Conservative Coalition in Congress, 1933–1939.* Lexington, Kentucky: University of Kentucky Press, 1967.

Peabody, Robert L. "The Enlarged Rules Committee." In *New Perspectives on the House of Representatives,* edited by Robert L. Peabody and Nelson W. Polsby. Chicago: Rand McNally and Company, 1963.

———, and Nelson W. Polsby. *New Perspectives on the House of Representatives.* Chicago: Rand McNally and Company, 1963.

Pitkin, Hanna F. *The Concept of Representation.* Berkeley and Los Angeles: University of California Press, 1967.

Polsby, Nelson W. *Congress and the Presidency.* Englewood Cliffs, New Jersey: Prentice-Hall, 1976.

Pomper, Gerald, et al. *The Election of 1980: Reports and Interpretations.* Chatham, New Jersey: Chatham House, 1981.

Ranney, Austin. *The Doctrine of Responsible Party Government: Its Origins and Present State.* Urbana: University of Illinois Press, 1962.

Rice, Stuart A. *Quantitative Methods in Politics.* New York: Alfred A. Knopf, 1928.

Rieselbach, Leroy N. *Congressional Reform in the Seventies.* Morristown, New Jersey: General Learning Press, 1977.

Riker, William H. *The Theory of Political Coalitions.* New Haven: Yale University Press, 1962.

Scammon, Richard M., and Ben J. Wattenberg. *The Real Majority*. New York: Coward, McCann & Geogegan, 1970.

Schneider, Jerrold. *Ideological Coalitions in Congress*. Westport, Connecticut: Greenwood Press, 1979.

Schwab, Larry M. *Changing Patterns of Congressional Politics*. New York: D. Van Nostrand Company, 1980.

Shaffer, William R. *Party and Ideology in the United States Congress*. Lanham, Maryland: University Press of America, 1980.

Shull, Steven A. *Presidential Policy Making: An Analysis*. Brunswick, Ohio: King's Court Communications, 1979.

Sinclair, Barbara. "Party Realignment and the Transformation of the Political Agenda." *American Political Science Review* 71 (1977): 940–54.

Stevens, Arthur G., Jr., Arthur H. Miller, and Thomas E. Mann. "Mobilization of Liberal Strength in the House, 1955–1970: The Democratic Study Group." *American Political Science Review* 68 (1974): 667–81.

Stone, Walter J. "Measuring Constituency-Representative Linkages: Problems and Prospects." *Legislative Studies Quarterly* 4 (1979): 623–39.

Truman, David B. *The Congressional Party*. New York: John Wiley and Sons, 1959.

Turner, Julius. *Party and Constituency: Pressures on Congress*. Baltimore: Johns Hopkins Press, 1951.

United States. Bureau of the Census. *Congressional District Data Book (Districts of the 88th Congress)*. Washington, D.C.: U.S. Government Printing Office, 1963.

———. *Congressional District Data Book: 93rd Congress*. Washington, D.C.: U.S. Government Printing Office, 1973.

United States. Congress. *Congressional Directory*. Washington, D.C.: U.S. Government Printing Office, various years and editions.

———. House. *Congressional Record*. 90th Cong., 1st sess., 1967, 113, pt. 10: 12611–13.

———. Senate. *Congressional Record*. 85th Cong., 2d sess., 1958, 104, pt. 10: 12612.

Viguerie, Richard A. *The New Right: We're Ready to Lead*. Falls Church, Virginia: The Viguerie Company, 1981.

Index